JOHN KEATS

THE
NEW
ROMANS

An
American
Experience

LONDON

J. M. DENT & SONS LTD

c
C

A portion of Chapter V originally appeared in Holiday *magazine.*

SBN 0460 03854 0   6001747507

This is a book for my father, Harold Keats—athlete, singer, soldier, evangelist, salesman, newspaperman, resort manager, attorney at law, Government official, businessman; a man of as many faults and virtues as any of us—from his often-thankless child, now conscious of those debts that youth can never perceive.

That book . . . told the truth, mainly. There was things which he stretched, but mainly he told the truth. That is nothing. I never seen anybody but lied one time or another, without it was Aunt Polly, or the widow, or maybe Mary . . . [It] is mostly a true book, with some stretchers, as I said before——

HUCKLEBERRY FINN

Contents

1	Yankee at Home	13
2	First Principles	35
3	First Steps	54
4	Protest	68
5	Flight	85
6	War	101
7	Home Is the Hero	140
8	The Scapegoat and Its Kid	162
9	Second Childhood	186
10	The Hope of the Future	201
11	The Trash and the Dream	230

1

Yankee at Home

THE DEEP, CLEAN BLUE began to shade to gray, the water turning olive drab as we passed the first outbound garbage scows and toiled against the current. Then, rising out of the fecal river, there was Manhattan's preposterous clump of termite nests, and across the way, there was the familiar green corrosion of Liberty marooned on her desert island, staring emptily at nothing. As always, the first view of the city was impressive.

Everyone crowded the ship's rails, and through a mist compounded of New Jersey factory fumes and General Motors blowby, the glittering carapaces of enormous automobiles scurried over bridges toward their ultimate appointments in junkyards. Some of those cars cost more than a college education, but, considering what the curriculum could consist of these days, who is to say that the automobiles were not, in fact, more valuable?

Watching the city approach, I had a sudden vision of the American restaurant with its tired waitress mechanically asking my wife, "What's yours, dearie? You decided yet?" And I had an even clearer vision of the menu from which we would have to choose. It reminded me of the ripe fruits of Italy, and the wines and food of France. Wherefore, in my mind's ear, I heard an old, old American question asked: "If you don't like it here, why don't you go back where you came from?" It was probably the first question asked in the New World, and there has never been a satisfactory answer.

"Boy, I bet you're glad to be home again!" a fellow traveler told me. His American accent was a bandsaw keening through hardwood knots. The accent was another of those things that would complicate the problems of re-entry.

I told him something conventional, because if we had bet, he would have lost.

I was not at all glad to be returning to my native land. Nor was I particularly sorry. There are a great many American people, places and practices that I like, and a considerable number of all three that I positively detest, but I could say as much for any of half a dozen other countries in various parts of the world. I am no more at home in those countries, and no more a stranger in them, than I am in America. I was not coming home, because I am an American, and Americans do not have homes. But there seemed no point then in going into all this at a ship's rail with a chance acquaintance who was most likely merely expressing his pleasure at the prospect of going ashore again after a week at sea, and who wished to share his pleasure with me. I felt, however, he deserved a book-length answer, which I will now attempt to provide, because I think the fact that Americans have no homes is something which we, and the world we intend to rule, should quite soberly consider.

In all that follows, it must be clearly understood that I cannot speak for America. No one of us can. There is no such thing as an Average American, any more than there is such a thing as an average artist. At best, each of us can speak only for himself. Yet, I do have more in common with all Americans than I am different from others; I am more like a Mississippi savage than I am like a Sicilian bandit. More to the point, the Americans most like myself who have shared my experiences—my forty-five-year-old white contemporaries from the northeastern coastal region of the United States—exert a majority control over American educational policies, most profoundly influence the communications media, have their hands on most of the money, and principally direct the Federal Government. Wherefore, in speaking for myself, with any luck

14

in the telling I will also be reciting the story of my generation and of the social class that momentarily occupies the seat of American power. My hope is, that having met me, you will have met one who is representative of at least some Americans in their forties, and thereby will have acquired some reason to speculate why we do some of the apparently absurd things we do, and why it is that we seem so determined to establish a Pax Americana throughout the world.

To understand us, you must first of all reflect that we were born into the mindlessness of Prohibition, a time of hypocrisy; that as adolescents we experienced the Great Depression, a time of utter disillusion; that we were then marched off into the horror of Hitler's war. During these years, we lost any real interest in God; we lost faith in capitalism and to a great extent have since done away with it; the German concentration camps brought us perilously close to losing all faith in the decency of man. The atomic bomb fell as surely on us as it did upon the Japanese, and we emerged from the sorry shambles of that mad war only to find ourselves confronted by a more potent enemy brandishing nuclear weapons and led by a dictator who flatly said, "We will bury you." Grimly, we entered the era of endless tension-without-resolution in foreign affairs; the era of undeclared wars whose bugles now sound for our sons, and we did not do so because we greatly desired to expand the American empire in a physical sense, or even because of our altruistic allegiance to a dream, but because we had learned to believe dictators who express funereal intentions, and because our experience had told us it is best to shoot such people before they shoot us. We have skittered along the edge of holocaust for the past two decades now, and our policy of containment of the overt enemy has worked only in the sense that a nuclear war has not yet erupted. Meanwhile, we absorbed two body blows from domestic enemies.

One was delivered by Joseph McCarthy, a Midwestern Senator whose turn of mind was precisely that of Matthew Hopkins, Witch-

15

finder General of England in the seventeenth century. It was discouraging to us, who had killed one Hitler in Germany, and were facing another in Moscow, to find still a third in our Senate.

The second blow was delivered by a madman in one of our more improbable cities. He shot John F. Kennedy in the back of the head, firing from a building stored with schoolbooks. Such is the official version of the deed, although uglier, even more disturbing theories have been suggested as being consistent with the evidence of the crime. In any case, the murder of our President was particularly disastrous for those of us in our forties, for we are bound together into a kind of unofficial brotherhood by our common, and troubled, experience. So it was that while the world mourned John Kennedy, we felt a shock of loss that neither our fathers nor our sons could ever know. It does no good to say that Kennedy may have been more appearance than substance. The appearance and the words—those wonderful words—were enough for us. What really mattered was that he sounded and looked like the best one of us and that he never lived long enough for us to find out whether or not this was so. When he was shot, each of us felt himself to be the target of that madman. Alarmed, we feel ourselves still to be the targets of madmen, and we wonder whether Arnold's meditations on Dover Beach are not more pertinent to our time than to his.

We are very tired. We may even be a little mad, buffeted as we have been by our experiences. But we are not ready to give up. We have deployed an army and a Peace Corps around the world, and are trying to create a Great Society in America while at the same time mounting what I believe to be a defensive war in Asia. Tired and mad as we may be, we have somehow inherited that peculiar American optimism of our fathers, and we are still trying—five hundred years after the Renaissance—to create humanism in a world grown more savage than any the Florentines knew. We have a concern for who the survivors of our miserable century might be. We would like to ensure that they include Americans because of our profound conviction that the best interests of mankind would

16

be served if Americans took charge of the world until a viable world order could be established.

Here is no great flag-waving for the America that exists, but rather for the America of our textbook ideals. I find myself more committed to the America-that-ought-to-be as every passing day makes the real America more repulsive. I feel absolutely no allegiance to the America of Los Angeles, Las Vegas, Chicago, or Alabama; to the America of the inane dirty books, the febrile pursuit of far-out kicks; of fads, busywork, academic assembly lines, cretinizing jobs, snoops, nosey neighbors, fingernail-proof Cellophane packages, commercial whoop-de-do, and casual violence on streetcorners. It disgusts me to learn that our Presidential candidates have public opinion polls taken before they open their mouths, in order that they will be sure to say only what the polls tell them it will be safe for them to say, for this practice is wildly at odds with my notions of responsible leadership. Indeed, like the Lord High Executioner, I have a little list: a list of exceedingly ugly Americans and Americanisms whose existence makes me feel increasingly a stranger in my native land.

The fact that ours is a land of constant change makes me not one whit more comfortable. No small part of the American malaise may be attributed to our lack of a native culture, of traditions, of history, of a homeland to which we have been bound for centuries. Indeed, with exception of a few futile Indians who peer at us from within their reservations, we are all of us—black and white—immigrants in a strange world. We are as rootless as so many traveling salesmen living out of suitcases in cheap hotels, and are so committed to thinking that change means progress that we alter the shape of America as rapidly and as completely as a demented child, wildly shaking a kaleidoscope, changes its patterns. Thus, there is nothing in any aspect of American life that tends to develop those senses of warmth, intimacy, security, sharing, continuity and purpose that are all implied in that untranslatable word "home"—a word that attempts to describe a Vestal mystery.

For example, my mother's family arrived in America only two

17

hundred years ago, which is an insufficient time to produce a decent English lawn, but virtually nothing remains of the Colonial America that they knew, save a few scattered houses and a handful of public buildings. George Washington is now a birthday, and Molly Pitcher is the name of a Howard Johnson restaurant on the New Jersey Turnpike, and Colonial Williamsburg is a stage-set tourist trap as implausible as Disneyland. Nor is there anything much left, in either a physical or a moral sense, of the very recent America of my father's youth. He was born into an age of outhouses and horsecollars, when most right-thinking Christians believed the world had been created at 8:00 A.M. on a Wednesday in 4004 B.C., because a learned minister told them so. Between the time of my father's birth in 1890 and mine in 1920, the telephone, radio, automobile and airplane came into general use, Indian territories became states, America fought three wars and mounted sundry other minor expeditions against Moros, Haitians, Chinese, Russians and South Americans of one sort and another; locomotives lost their cowcatchers and the nation found Freud. Then, during my own lifetime, the nation fought three more wars and mounted sundry other minor expeditions against various South Americans of one sort and another (this apparently is one of our emerging American traditions), and in just the past twenty-five years we made the acquaintance of television, the electronics industry, the Organization Man, jet travel, space rocketry, dynamic obsolescence, solid-state physics, nuclear warfare, and the American Negro. In the meantime, the nation lost Freud and found *Playboy* magazine's adolescent hedonism, and seven out of every ten of us took it into our heads to live in our cities. Since I was a boy, vast stretches of both the rural and the urban landscape have been converted into industrial wastelands, moodily lit by flickering neon, swept by vapid fads, and populated with neurotic adolescents who bounce about on motorcycles.

I do not mention these changes in order to plead for a return to cottage industry and a simpler life, but rather to suggest that any one of the phenomena I have mentioned would ordinarily be sufficient to give an entire generation a great many discomforts to learn to live with and put into some rational perspective. The point is that ideas in America become accomplished facts before anyone has time to debate them; that so many different, changing things clamor for our attention that it is difficult for any one of us to sit down with himself to decide what he should do about any of them or in what order they are important to him; that the nation is so much of a vast, populous, bubbling confusion of Protean transformations that it is virtually impossible for any of us to be able to say, "I love America" or "America is my home" because the America we might have had in mind at the moment we say this may no longer exist by the time we get to the end of the sentence, or because the tiny bit of America that each of us knows has little relevance to the rest of the nation.

Worse, one characteristic of our changing scene is that the changes are not always made with a view to serving human ends, but are frequently destructive of them. For example, what was once a rather imposing (if not particularly graceful) row of town houses on New York's Park Avenue has given way to a line of shoddy glass and steel cereal boxes stood on end, and the shapes of the buildings have been determined solely by a desire to extract the greatest possible office rental at the least expense. Say what you will of the town houses, they were at least designed to accommodate human life, and offices, say what you will of them, are not. A similar devotion to the cause of money, as opposed to human welfare, was responsible for the demolition of New York's Pennsylvania Railroad station. That building, twenty-seven acres of travertine that recalled the baths of Caracalla, was pulled down just fifty-two years after its completion. It might have stood as long as the pyramids, lending some valuable difference to an otherwise depressing city, but it was destroyed so that another cereal box, capable of producing greater income for the railroad, could be erected. The same point can be made with respect to those programs of slum clearance and urban renewal that have as their purpose not so much the meeting of a human need but the creation

19

of tax- and income-producing properties. Just so, the always changing design of the American automobile has little to do with considerations of convenience, comfort, safety and the pocketbooks of people, or even of the efficiency of the machine, but almost exclusively serves the cause of making money for the manufacturer. Further examples from every aspect of American public works, commerce and industry could be cited to the point that a desire to make money, rather than a concern for human welfare, is principally responsible for much of that incessant, disruptive change we often mistake for progress, but which has so far made it progressively more difficult for any of us to feel at home in our own country.

It is not ironic, but merely inevitable, that as our efficiency increases, as our productivity increases, as our affluence increases, an increasing number of Americans are oppressed by a growing feeling of loneliness, estrangement, or downright alienation. Such a feeling particularly afflicts those of us who live in cities, and even more particularly, those college students who live there. Alienation and violence will be seen to be the last fruits of affluence. The central reason for this has to do with the fact that an industrial society's success in production is directly proportional to the degree to which human roles are diminished. Briefly, division of labor increases production, which means that production increases as each worker does a smaller fraction of the total job. This is very good in terms of corporate profits and distribution of goods, but unfortunately a human tradition says that the work a man does is what gives his life meaning, both to himself and to others. So, as our labors become more specialized, we approach the point where the work a man does tends to become the least important thing about him, and as his importance dwindles, he feels the more lonely and estranged. Until we find some other way of measuring a man, I am sure that the process of alienation will accelerate. I am equally sure that the almost frenetic search for the wild new far-out kick represents a college student's, or a stockbroker's, or a factory hand's or a housewife's sense of insignificant loneliness;

20

that this search is a human reaction to a man's learning that he has only a functional significance in a social machine already so highly organized that the very food he eats comes frozen, odorless, sterilized, wrapped in plastic, untouched by human hands, dropped into a shopping cart from a gravity-fed rack in an impersonal supermarket. In this context, if a man's reaction to lonely boredom takes a violent form, as it increasingly does, then I would say this is at least understandable, however, inexcusable.

Having said this much against America, I must also say that the more homeless I feel amid the American babble, the more I am drawn to the vision of home that the American ideal calls to mind. A more positive way of viewing the American loneliness, rootlessness, change and ceaseless work toward the perfection of an automated welfare state is to believe that we are living in the formative years of a new Renaissance, and that we are still trying to build a home in our New World. After all, two centuries is the briefest of instants, and optimism is as much an American characteristic as boredom. Every contemporary of my acquaintance is thoroughly convinced that we will one day clean up the messes we have made. Meanwhile, they and I feel that we *do* have a home in an abstract America, even though none of us feels entirely comfortable in the America of the here-and-now—in the country that one of my friends called "the land of the spree and the home of the knave."

The abstract America of our allegiance consists partly of those ideals which supposedly undergird the Republic. They are by no means original with us, but stem from many sources, including Athenian democracy, the Judeo-Christian ethic, the Roman and the English laws, and a few notions from Rousseau. These ideals, designed to create a social contract guaranteeing liberty and justice for all, are embodied in the Declaration of Independence and the United States Constitution, and both documents tacitly state that they are meant for export: that they should apply to all men everywhere. Not a few of us believe this, and our foreign policy has usually expressed such a belief, particularly in modern times. Schoolteacherish Woodrow Wilson wanted to make the

21

world safe for democracy just as much as bully-boy Theodore Roosevelt wanted to bang American sense into the world's head; John Foster Dulles, the quasi-clergyman, preached the same Gospel on the brink, and Lyndon B. Johnson surely believes that what is good for America is good for Vietnam.

I agree.

I can truthfully say that I love the America of the ideals, while simultaneously gagging at the thought of Dallas or Hoboken.

Further, there is another abstract America that claims my admiration, and curiously enough it is the one that is responsible for much that revolts me. This will be the America of the organizational genius; of the adventurous spirit that is willing to try anything once; of the blunt speech and naked desire to get ahead; of the mood of do-it-now; of the feeling that we can accomplish the difficult right away although the impossible will take a little longer. For all its gaucheries and bad choices; for all the squalid vulgarity of most of its cities; for all its success in polluting its rivers and poisoning its air and diminishing the individual's objective importance, America has nonetheless provided every man with a maximum opportunity to be himself. We have some way to go, but we have come a lot further than any other nation in this direction, and I think this is our greatest glory, even if it should prove to be our fatal flaw.

In sum, I can take pride in what we have done in the way of preserving humanism, and in providing an unparalleled material prosperity for a maximum number of people. Much of the American dream has actually come true, even for the Negro, although a large part of it remains a nightmare for him. So I have some confidence in the America that might yet be built, even if I cannot say that I feel at home in, or uncritically in love with, the America we currently have. I think the rest of the world should emulate much of our example, our ideals, our attitudes, and our systems, because I hope not only that we can turn our country into something we can call home, but that we can also be at home everywhere else in the world. I do not fear the Coca-

22

Colanization of the globe, beginning with an imposition of Pax Americana, because my faith in the abstract America is bolstered by no few of our real accomplishments, and because I have an equal faith that what is truly good for us is also beneficial to all manner of men. The problem, really, is the pursuit of the good, and despite all the outward changes in the condition of man, there is no question an industrial society can ask that was not debated in Athens.

Perhaps my attitude is somewhat that of the Christian in the arena, who, contemplating the lions, decides that an existence in Heaven seems to be a better bet than one on earth, and whose faith in a better life markedly increases as his chances for survival in this one diminish. He hoped because it was the only thing he could do, and so it may be with me. Yet, it also seems to me that as long as the dream persists, and as long as we work toward it, there is reason to hope, and it is for this reason I and my contemporaries continue to believe that the America of the here-and-now, for all its faults, is more worthy of defense than any alternative offered elsewhere in the world.

It remains to be seen whether our children will agree with us. Many of the brightest of them take one piercing look at America and decide to have nothing to do with people who are more than thirty years old. Their reaction does not always indicate their fear of being shot in Vietnam but, rather, reflects their belief that America is not worth fighting for. I must admit that every time I see a television commercial, I am inclined to agree with them.

Just as frequently, however, I can take a long look at some of our children and seriously wonder if they are worth protecting. Certain of them strike me as walking arguments for euthanasia, and I do not necessarily have in mind the boy-like girls and girl-like boys of latter-day Bohemia. More often, my eye is jaundiced by the vision of little stuffed shirts with heads full of suet who will inevitably sell insurance, and of dumb little cheer leaders from Ohio who will as inevitably become car-coated, stationwagon-driving Den Mothers in suburbia.

To be sure, each generation since the dawn of time has thought that the younger generation was going straight to Hell, and the younger generation has always thought that Hell was where it already was, and looked for ways out. And so the world has been familiar with the war between fathers and sons. But it seems to me that never have two generations been further apart than the two current American generations, and I suspect that one reason for the distance between us is that no generation has ever done more for its children than mine has. Hell hath no fury like that of a beneficiary toward his benefactor, unless it be that of the doting parent for the thankless child. I believe that one result of our child-centered society has been to deprive our children of their childhood; that another consequence of our smothering attention has been to prevent the current generations of fathers and sons from really meeting one another. The resultant situation (whatever the cause) is scarcely conducive to torch-passing. Indeed, there is a squabble over possession of the torch, with us fathers by no means ready to surrender it yet, and especially not to the likes of those who are reaching for it; with our being even more exasperated by those youth who would either ignore the gift or yawn and suggest we stick it in the sand to put it out.

I think our children should realize that they have been born citizens of an empire, whether they like it or not. Circumstances have thrust my generation into world affairs as no American generation has been thrust into them before. Either despite or (more likely) because of our two hundred years of incessant warfare, our nation has grown so commercially and technically successful that we have moved, willy-nilly, to the forefront of affairs, possessed of the world's greatest military power. After Hitler's war, we inherited the late British empire's role of international policeman largely by default, but we were then so strong that it did not really matter whether there was a British empire or not. It seems to me that we are in many ways the new Romans: pragmatic, eclectic, mercantile, selfish, aggressive; confident that ours is the best of all possible systems and that everyone else in the world should aspire to American citizenship; superb soldiers, lawgivers and road builders. I would say that we are now much in the position of the Romans whose accretion of wealth and power inevitably brought them into conflict with Carthage despite the fact that the Punic Wars were really of no one's seeking and were, like all wars, theoretically avoidable. Then, emerging from these wars, Rome was inevitably engaged in others. Such may be our fate. In any case, one effect of success was to give the citizen of the Roman empire a feeling that the world was somehow his, and such is the effect of the success of the American empire upon us or, at least, upon me.

For example, I cannot escape a feeling of smug satisfaction on reflecting that I am a member of the ruling white race of the most powerful nation on earth. Intellectually, I know that having been born white and American was more of an accident than an achievement, but there it is. Although I am very well aware of the foolishness of pride, it is also a fact that deep in my heart (as Barry Goldwater would say) I cannot take seriously the emergent African and Asian nations, or imagine that in the United Nations any squalid little country of huts and witch doctors should have a vote equal to our own. Nor, for that matter, can I take seriously the presumption of Charles de Gaulle that France has anything to say in world affairs. I know—intellectually—that America has contributed almost nothing to the basic scientific inquiry that has given her power. I realize that for the most part our highly technical civilization may be attributed to our talent for adapting foreign inventions and engineering them into artifacts, then mass-producing, packaging and marketing them. The telephone, a European invention, is one example. Radio, television, the automobile, aircraft, rockets and nuclear weapons are others. Yet while I know this to be the fact, I cannot really convince myself that a Frenchman can learn to drive an automobile, or that an Italian can navigate, or that the Russians have actually sent a rocket to the moon. For all that I know—intellectually and through personal military experience—that the Japanese can fly, I am nonetheless more comfortable in an American airliner than in a Japanese one, because I was brought up to believe that we invented flight and that Japanese manufactured goods are poor copies of our own and that all Japanese have defective vision because their eyes slant. Granted, none of these notions will bear examination, but even though I know they will not, it is nevertheless true that I am still emotionally committed to them. I suggest that a great many of my contemporaries feel exactly the same way. I know it is not fashionable to say these things: No one is more appalling than the bounding, backslapping, grinning booster from the small town in the American heartland. Yet I think that we who murmur and send our children to the Ivy League colleges and read the Sunday *New York Times* should understand that a chief difference between the bounding booster and ourselves may simply be that he is more open and honest.

So, no doubt, was the Roman of the latter empire as inconsistently and emotionally committed to the superiority of Rome as we are to America. It will be recalled that the Romans, like ourselves, chiefly borrowed their glories, although there is no question that they were the best soldiers, merchants, engineers and lawgivers in their world. For all their many faults, and much as they may have lagged behind any particular people in any particular respect, the Romans were—*on balance*—actually superior to the peoples they conquered, including the sophisticated Greeks. For, like ourselves, the Romans were somewhat in the position of a track and field team that wins no first places, but which piles up so many points in second and third places that its aggregate score is higher than that of any of the other teams in the meet. Again like ourselves, the Romans were victorious warriors not so much because they had superior causes, physiques and weapons, but because they had a genius at organization and a profound simplicity of thought.

Not long ago, like a Roman citizen of the early Republic, the archetypical American felt himself to be something of a bumpkin when he ventured abroad. Characteristically, he felt apologetic about being an American and was flattered to be mistaken for an

26

Englishman. Today, however, he is no more apologetic than the Roman of the empire. For instance, I simply assume that Paris, London and Rome are as much my cities as New York and Philadelphia are. I am willing to regard any man as my equal until he proves himself to be otherwise. The fact that the fellow may be the president of his nation, while I am an obscure citizen of my own, means absolutely nothing to me. It remains to be seen what sort of fellow he is. Then I will decide whether he deserves my interest, and if so, to what extent. I would suppose that my attitude, which is not so much arrogant as it is confident, stems from the fact that America is supposed never to have lost a war, and that I feel the American power is somehow at my back because I am an American citizen who once marched in one of our conquering armies. I am sure my derisive view of France as a political entity stems from my belief that we Americans on two occasions had to save France from its German neighbor. I would suppose that what gives a nation its place in the world, and its citizens confidence in themselves, is—in the end—nothing more glorious than vulgar strength. In their time, the British moved about as if *Rule Britannia* sounded always in their ears, even when they strode through the streets of civilizations older, subtler, and in some ways finer than their own. Now a good many of the British seem to be a little bit bitchy in our presence, perhaps because they have spent their money, relinquished their empire and abandoned the seas to the United States Navy.

A second source of confidence, and a consequence of empire, is relative wealth and opportunity for travel for the ordinary citizen. Compared with the peoples of other civilized lands, class by class, we Americans are veritable millionaires, and compared with those of primitive nations, we are gods. In our earlier days, this was not always the case, but today I, who am by no means a wealthy American, can live in a style that a man like myself in my father's generation, simply could not have imagined. As recently as my father's school days, ordinary Americans lived out their lives in comfort, but not in opulence, within a few miles of the farmhouses where they were born. This mode of life was conducive to an American provincialism and insularity. But I have a town house in an American city, and an island in Canada, and spent the last year in an Italian villa beside the Tyrrehnian Sea. I have traveled sufficiently to be able to give traffic directions in cities on three continents and two major archipelagoes. Going their separate ways, my three children, two of them not yet in their twenties, are even more widely traveled, not only having crossed and recrossed our own continent from east to west but also from Mexico to Alaska; having hied themselves to Europe and Asia and, in this age of jets, having looked down upon the North Pole. None of this will sound impressive to my contemporaries, much less to my children's generation, but it would startle my father, and it would dumfound our first agrarian progenitor in the New World. That worthy, if he could hear this, would no doubt halt his mule, scratch his head and spit on the ground. Then he would hitch up his pants and resume his plowing of his Pennsylvania hillside, thinking that no good would ever come of messing around with foreigners. After all, he came to Pennsylvania to escape the Europe of his time.

Frankly, I do not know what will come of messing around with foreigners either. I know only that we Americans now stride confidently through foreign streets, quite probably toward a meeting with the equally confident Asiatics. Indeed, it seems to me that we stand on the verge of another Punic War, the first episode of which is taking place in Asia. In this regard, it is interesting to reflect that the world thinks no two peoples are more alike than ourselves and the Russians, who are the most dangerous of our potential enemies. The same judgment could have been made of the Romans and the Carthaginians, with one important difference. As Polybius remarked, "At Carthage, nothing is regarded as disgraceful if it brings a profit; at Rome, nothing is more disgraceful than to receive bribes and make a profit by immoral means." There are those who say that the Russians are stern moralists, and that we are venal hedonists, and so it might be that my comparison of the

Romans and ourselves is not so accurate as a comparison of the Carthaginians and ourselves would be. One would hope that we are not the new Carthage. One would like to believe that it was the morality of Rome, and not a superior general, that defeated Carthage.

To be sure, the slightest knowledge of history leads one to speculate on the fatuity of imperial hopes and of national pride. It is tempting to agree with my Quaker friends and with the ardent young pacifists of my son's generation, and to say that such notions are footless, and that the only thing that matters is human survival. The view from my writing desk last year was a seductive argument for their cause. I could sit in the early morning sunshine on the terrace of my villa and reflect that there were ancient watch towers on every headland of that Tyrrhenian coast, and that every single one of them had fallen to some enemy.

At the elevation of the terrace, there was always a light wind stirring among the almonds, the olives and the figs in the early morning, although the sea was tranquil. It would be hot in the narrow stone streets of the tile-roofed town below, but there, high above town and sea, the light wind was cool. In the fall the almonds and the figs were ripe. I remember thinking that I could not write if I did not have faith that, in time, the olives, the lemons and the oranges in my garden would also ripen and that there would be people to eat them. Of course, hydrogen bombs seem to make a mockery of faith, but faith need not be founded on reason, and it is generally impervious to mockery.

I could look from the terrace and see, just below and to the right, a monument to the ruin of the hopes of Spain. It was a small sixteenth-century fortress pocked here and there by twentieth-century machine-gun fire. Across the harbor there was a boatyard that had been a torpedo factory in Mussolini's time. The Spanish fortress which had been captured by the French in an almost forgotten campaign, was a schoolhouse when the bombers came for the torpedo factory. The bombers obliterated the factory and in the process inadvertently flattened the town as well, all except the fortress, which was built more solidly than the houses, as fortresses always are.

Looking past the shoulder of the mountain and across the bay, I could see a gray patch on a farther hillside. That was an Etruscan city the Romans captured and enlarged. The city was deserted more than fifteen hundred years ago when the barbarians moved on Rome. Now it is only great, gray-white, beauty-eyed and long-horned oxen that move slowly along the city's silent streets, cropping the new grass that grows between the paving stones and thrusts up through the broken floors of roofless houses. The oxen wander across the portico of a temple where they were once brought garlanded to be sacrificed.

I know there is an olive grove within the tumbled walls of that deserted city, and that someone harvests those olives and keeps the cattle that graze beneath the trees and along the ruined streets, and I know, too, that a school is once again kept in the Spanish tower, and that the town the bombers flattened has been rebuilt. Indeed, you would not know that a war had come to the town except for the evidence the bomb fragments engraved in the thick walls of the fortress. Wherefore, I know that if one lives among the ruins of the hopes of dead princes, one also lives among the hopes of the present. Knowing this, I am urged to agree that it really makes no difference which way the wars of this day go, so long as we can believe that when they end, the olives will ripen and that there will be someone to eat them. Perhaps the survivors will build another empire that will also fall.

Well, perhaps so. The world is full of evidence to the point. But I am too much committed to my rearing and to my experience to view matters from the aspect of eternity. Perhaps a reason for my obstinate imperialism, shared by many of my contemporaries, is our great desire to build a home we never had—a home we have been trying so hard to create. So far our efforts have been subverted by enemies both foreign and domestic—and by domestic enemies I not only mean Communists, Birchites, Klansmen and lunatics, but also such crooks and chiselers as the conspiring vice presidents of electrical-goods manufacturing concerns. We have a great many enemies of divers sorts. One is the traffic engineer who thinks in terms of moving traffic instead of in terms of moving people, and who puts a superhighway through a residential zone. He is almost as much our enemy as Hitler was in the sense that both men will be seen as enemies of mankind. So is the schoolteacher who says we must educate our children to their functional significance in an industrial society, when the abstract America of my allegiance is predicated on the notion that society should be a function of individuals. It is increasingly difficult to speak for humanism in a technological age, and no doubt the difficulty of the task helps to increase my obstinacy. In any case, I do not believe that my contemporaries and I will easily abandon the almost hopeless task we have been working for so many years to advance: the simultaneous translation of the American reality into a reasonable semblance of the American dream, and the extension of that dream throughout the world, *pro bono publico*.

I do not know whether this concept of home, or need for home, weighed in upon prior American generations, but I do know that it concerns me and my generation, who have all our lives been wandering in a wilderness. I am sure that our attitude is more international than it is Chauvinistic; that we would prefer to live in the world, rather than in a country. It is as if we believe we have first to make the world peaceful, before we can get on with the job of living in it, and that we believe the pioneer virtues and the ideals of the eighteenth century can be applied to a world that contains societies ranging from Stone Age primitives to space walkers.

In all this, we are wonderfully inconsistent. In candor, I cannot hold up the reality of American daily life to English or Italian friends and suggest they imitate it, particularly when much of that American reality disappoints me, and when I find their daily patterns of life so much better in so many ways than our own. I can in

31

good conscience suggest to them the majesty of our law and the grand concept of our political dream, but then I would have difficulty in explaining why, if such is our law and our dream, we do not practice what we preach. Further, I can hardly urge the imposition of a Pax Americana on the world unless I am willing to say we should be strong enough to enforce it, but being that strong requires the elaboration of a technological society which in so many ways is inimical to humanity—breeding, as it does, alienation and violence. We Americans would seem to be in much the position of the cowboy who, advised that the gambling wheel was crooked, said he knew dern well that it was, but it was the only wheel in town.

Another way to see ourselves is to imagine that we are engaged in a holding action, trying to keep the front from caving in by counterattacking. Surely, we are the world's most reluctant imperialists. The very word "empire" is anathema to us. We covet no one's territory. We do not want to keep our soldiers spread around the world. We do not glory in military adventure. We are, we like to think, pacifists. On the other hand, we are hardly unwarlike. In the 190 years of the Republic, we have fought—sometimes more than once—against the Russians, sundry nations of American Indians, the French, Germans, Italians, English, Spanish, Algerians, Mexicans, Cubans, Haitians, Nicaraguans, Filipinos, Moros, Igorots, Chinese, Indochinese, Japanese, Koreans, Santo Domingans, and once, for lack of anyone else at the time, ourselves. We like to believe that all these wars were thrust upon us; that they were in defense of our way of life; that in any event, they were concluded by a settlement beneficial to the conquered. I know of no other nation that has fought so many different peoples in so short a time. And yet we believe that we love peace. And more than anything else, we want to be loved. When we are not loved, we think this is because people do not understand us. Today, in order to ensure a more perfect understanding, we send food, guns, propaganda, Peace Corps workers and military advisers to the undecided. If they still do not love us after all that, then we escalate (as the

Pentagon would say), believing that those who do not love us would be better dead than Red. We call this the battle for men's minds. Oddly enough, I think it really is.

It is also curious, if you will grant that we believe ourselves to be defending an ideal, that we are so long in making up our minds as to the courses we should take. I would attribute our hesitation to our wealth (which we do not wish to jeopardize) and to our intellectual belief that there are usually at least two sides to any question. For the purposes of this discussion, I would say that choice is often a greater burden than simple obedience, and that the more intellectual the man, the more heavily the burden of choice sits on him because the more sides he sees to any question. A by no means unfamiliar figure is the intellectual whose arguments within himself are of such duration that he fails to act at times when any action would have been better than none. Equally familiar is the intellectual who avoids choice by being tolerant or permissive—thus allowing events, which he might otherwise have controlled, to overwhelm him. I believe that, as the members of my embattled generation grow increasingly wealthy, better educated, and more tired, we tend to suffer agonies of choice in the torture chamber of leisure, and thereby often become the uncertain masters of ourselves, and the confused, babbling captains on the bridge of our ship of state. One thinks of Eliot's Prufrock descending a stairs, wondering whether he dare eat a peach. An empire should not dither or stutter, and it will be interesting to see whether these, the first days of the American empire, may not prove to be analogous to the last days of the Roman; whether we have arrived at the end of our empire at the moment of inheriting it, because wealth can be subversive of purpose, leading the irresponsible to hedonism and, as I have indicated, betraying the thoughtful into cataleptic casuistry. No such problems beset either the private citizens or the governors of Spartan states on their way up, although they do seem to be characteristic of empires that are about to be overthrown.

What no one can doubt is that we Americans now stand at stage center in the world, a confused, contradictory, potent nation, the guardian (by default) of what is called Western civilization. I take it that the phrase refers to a set of principles rather than to a physical description, and I am bemused by the thought that the physical facts of our civilization increasingly suggest that the principles cannot be applied to them. For example, it is surely a Western concept that citizens should vote in free elections, but as the civilization grows increasingly technical and specialized, the more difficult it becomes for anyone to vote intelligently upon the issues of the day, or even to learn what the issues might be. Still, those of us who are now in our middle forties are trying, like the cowboy, to win against the wheel, because it is the only one we have and because we cannot believe that all we have done is pointless, and because we continue to hope that our system for all its faults nevertheless promises a way toward the New Jerusalem. These may be very foolish hopes, but nonetheless they are ours, the property of the generation and social class that has the governance of America in hand, and therefore I think it would be profitable for us, and all the world, to take a close look at ourselves to see (if we can) who we really are, and how (as we say) we got that way. The life I offer for examination is my own, believing it to be typical of the lives of many of my contemporaries in its general outlines. I know that I can really speak for no one but myself, but I am equally sure that no one is more full of contradictions, confusions and certainties than I am.

2

First Principles

PSYCHIATRY TENDS to the view that our first experiences are of crucial importance in determining what sort of people we will become, and so with respect for that theory, let us begin with childhood. I would not have you think mine was an unhappy one. Rather, it seems to have been quite a normal one for the America of my time and social class, filled as it was, from the first moments on, with loneliness, a sense of estrangement, and visions of violence. Its culminating episode occurred late one night, when I heard a man shout.

That is, at first it sounded like a shout.

Then there was a desperate breathing.

"No!" he shouted. "Don't!"

Then he screamed.

There was the sound of an automobile starting up below my window, and the sound of it racing away. I did not look out the window.

In the morning, no one said anything. I was afraid to ask if anyone had heard anything, and I suppose they did not want to ask me if I had. Later, I learned that a man had been murdered not a hundred yards from my bedroom, which looked across a street to a strip of woodland.

We then lived in an almost-but-not-quite-fashionable section of Baltimore, a not-quite-fashionable city. We never lived in a fashionable neighborhood because we were never rich, and at the time we lived in this fine, almost fashionable one, everyone was becoming poor.

The man who had been killed was a criminal. The nature of his criminality was that he sold alcoholic beverages to people who were thirsty, at a time when it was then against the law to make, own, sell or drink such beverages. His specific crime was that he had been selling whisky in an area which other illegal salesmen of whisky regarded as their own. So his business rivals gutted him like a hog, and left him in the bushes at the edge of the little wooded park that was one of the amenities of our excellent neighborhood. They left him there for the police to find and explain.

Now, this occurred when I was twelve years old, and so it is not the first memory of childhood, but as I have suggested, it may have been the last. Perhaps it is rationalization, but I regard my memory of a man screaming as a kind of commencement exercise; as a sort of welcome to the world. At all events, there had been a certain body of evidence accumulating during the first twelve years that confirmed the idea of which the scream seemed to be the last necessary proof: America was dangerous.

My *first* memory is that of a Kiddie Koop—a baby's bed. It consisted of a mattress set in a box made of fine-meshed wire painted yellow. When they put you down in it, they closed the lid.

And fastened it from the outside.

Perhaps I remember my Kiddie Koop so distinctly, from so obviously a very tender age, because of the bat. My mother and my aunt were shouting and waving brooms, and my father was flailing around with a tennis racquet and some one of them closed the lid and fastened it so the bat would not get at me. I can only presume, on the basis of later hearsay, that this was the reason for doing what they did. All I can really remember is their doing it. They raced about waving those brooms and that tennis racquet and someone closed the lid on me. No one opened it. I think I stayed

36

awake all night waiting for them to do so; most probably I waked to find the lid still closed in the morning. I know I cried.

At the time of the bat we lived in a not-quite-fashionable neighborhood in Washington, near the Austrian embassy. My memories of this time include being pushed along 18th Street in a baby carriage to Kornhauser's toy store where they sold little wooden animals carved in Germany. I remember lying on an upstairs bed with my aunt holding a broken umbrella over us, and our laughing because the rain and the sun came in through the holes. I have only the dimmest memory of the deaths of my grandparents. I am not sure they ever died. I think the explanation was that they went away. It was all right with me; I seldom saw my grandfather and I do not know to this day what he did, and my grandmother's odor was unpleasant to me. Everyone called her The Lamb, not because of the way she smelled, but because of her gentle nature.

Everyone had animal nicknames except my parents and me, their only child. My boisterous aunt was called The Bear; my great-uncle, a professor of history, was called Reynard because his intelligence was supposedly that of a fox. I called him Bough, because he used to rock me on his knee and sing "The Mistletoe Bough," a sad ballad about a lovely young lady who, while playing hide-and-go-seek with party guests, hides in a great chest whose lid fastened on the outside. When they found her, she was dead. This may have had something to do with my aversion to my Kiddie Koop, and so, perhaps masochistically, I kept begging my great uncle to sing by saying to him, "Bough."

My mother and father were called Mother and Father by me, and Harold and Helen by everyone else. My name was John. My mammy had no name but Rose, and because we were not rich, Rose was not only my mammy but also the cook and the maid.

Properly speaking, a mammy was a Negress who was the servant, companion, and governess of a white child, and in tradition— and so far as I am concerned, in fact as well—there was genuine love between mammy and child. It was Rose who sat me on the pot; Rose who dressed me; she who served me at the little table in my upstairs room where I ate what were otherwise my lonely meals. It was not until Christmas day of my seventh year that I came to eat with the family and saw my father standing to carve at the head of the table, the high-backed, three-crowned chair tall behind him. It was Rose who let me follow her about downstairs; she who let me play in the kitchen and taught me to eat onions like apples, and she must have also been my first object of heterosexual love. For, now that I look back on it, I remember showing myself to Rose one day in the kitchen. I suppose if Oedipus had been raised in the American South, his problems would have been more complicated than they were.

Rose had a son my age, and I played with him until I went to school. Then he disappeared. I wanted him to come back. I was lonely without him. He was my friend. The girl with the yellow curls next door was not a friend, and the shoemaker's son stole our milk. Rose's boy was my friend.

But Rose . . .

I can remember exactly how she looked when I asked where he was. She looked as if her face were coming apart and as if she were trying to hold it together. She looked also as if she had swallowed something bitter and was trying to get it down and conceal the bitterness because I was, after all, not its author but its victim.

"You got your life, Mister John, and he got his," she said.

For the rest of it, Washington was where the lamplighter came down Kalorama Road just before dusk, climbing his little ladder and lighting each gas lamp in turn, and your mother read you Stevenson's poem when you complained about going to bed while it was still light. It was where the roof of a motion picture theater fell in during a snowstorm and, though it was some blocks away, you heard and remembered the dreadful soft whump of it that shook the house, and your father, who was then a newspaperman, stayed up all that night and worked all the next day helping to dig the bodies out of the wreckage.

The architect shot himself.

I remember that, too, not from having heard it subsequently but from hearing them talk about it at the time. An only child is fair game. Everyone is anxious for his great success, particularly when, for medical reasons, it has become clear that he is to be the only child. Everyone says, hopefully, that he is exceedingly intelligent, and everyone tries to develop his mental powers. When I was growing up, memory was regarded as a criterion of intelligence. Wherefore, I was read to, and was rewarded for memorizing what I had heard. As a child who knew his alphabet long before entering kindergarten, and whose first book was not a primer but *A Child's History of England in Words of One Syllable,* I can make a fair claim to having a contemporary memory of the theater disaster and of their talking about the death of the architect. The lesson was, if it is your fault, you must kill yourself.

There were other lessons, and the first of these was that our family had few equals and no superiors. It seemed that we were English, although we were Americans. For this reason we were superior to both the Italian organ-grinder and his monkey. I was given to understand that I was somehow related to John Keats. It was explained that he was a great poet. No one seemed to know just what the relationship was, and reliable scholarship indicates that no relationship exists; but it was a family conceit that a superior poet was one of us. What was not in doubt was that my great uncle had been presented to Victoria at the Court of St. James's by Disraeli, and he was always invited to social affairs at the British embassy. This was the most important embassy of all. It was much more worthwhile to be invited there than to the White House. I would not know, never having been to either place for dinner. I do remember eating cinnamon toast and tea on the Presidential yacht, *Mayflower,* because a woman friend of my mother's was the friend of one of the sailors. Perhaps the food at the embassy would have been better. My preference was for the ice cream at Avignon Frères, which The Bear called The Frères Brothers to show that she knew better. The French were not our equals. Only the British were, and some of the old Washington families.

39

Much was made of the fact that President Wilson had admired me in my baby carriage one day at Lafayette Park, but while everyone talked about this, it seemed that President Wilson was not our social equal. For one thing, he was a politician; for another, a politician of the wrong party; for a third, he had married a jeweler's wife.

People who were in trade were not our social equals. The closest approach to a non-English, non-Washington social equal was someone from the German or the Austrian embassy, or an Army officer. Mother used to love to watch the polo matches at Fort Myers; it later turned out that she admired the skill of handsome George Patton at polo and the striking appearance of Douglas MacArthur. I think her honest musical preference was a Sousa march. The other music she enjoyed was that of Victor Herbert. She put an end to my learning to play the piano as soon as, returning from a stay in hospital, she discovered The Bear was teaching me. Her explanation was that she did not want her son to be a sissy.

I must make clear that my parents always did what they thought best for me. Medical opinion then inclined to a great belief in roughage in the diet, thorough mastication, and the ingestion of at least six glasses of water each day. The objective was a regularity of bowel movements. Various unimaginable but catastrophic illnesses were the certain consequence of irregularity. It is literally true that I have not drunk a single glass of water since leaving my parents' roof.

Also for reasons of health, it was thought best that I should not associate with the common children. It was a theory based on some fact: The Bear, who taught music in the public schools, reported lice in the students' hair, and one day I contracted impetigo after exposure to the commonality in a public park. Yet, when it came time to enter school, I was thrown in among the lousy rabble. I was confirmed in my relative superiority, however, by being skipped into second grade. I remember sitting with those older children, wondering what on earth was going on, and at recess periods, when the whole school was turned out into the cinder yard, my vision was chiefly of a hurtling-past of long legs—my eyes being approximately on a level with the kneecaps of the multitude. I made no friends at that school, and learned nothing that I can remember. This, in large measure, could be said of all my subsequent schooling. An only and very lonely child, I lived chiefly inside myself, reading widely but not in schoolbooks, nourishing myself on a relatively fact-free diet and wondering from time to time who my social equals might be. I would have very much liked to meet one. But a precocious reader is likely to meet them only in his fantasies.

The following year we lived in a country club near Annapolis. My father was its manager. He had been a lawyer and a newspaperman and now he was an agent of real estate. The country club offered bathing, tennis and golf, and no one who was not our social equal was allowed to join it or to come as a guest. The only foreigners granted admission were the diplomats of northern European nations. I suppose it was a fine enough country club, although the golf course had only nine holes instead of eighteen, and then, it was on the wrong side of Chesapeake Bay. The fashionable side was the Eastern Shore, and we were on the western.

During the first year, before other families bought houses there, my only near-contemporary was the fourteen-year-old son of the chef. His being a German named Moltke was in his favor, however, and Father hopefully asked the chef whether the family was not related to von Moltke, a Prussian general. The chef doubted this, but Father was sure that some relationship must exist, and so young Moltke and I played at being soldiers.

At this time, my life had a strongly military cast. I had quantities of lead soldiers, ranging from Roman legionaries to British Guards, all brightly colored and heavy to hold in the hand. I had a castle that the Romans defended; I had knights with lances in rest, charging the Black Watch. I knew a great deal about war from all of my books. There had been war in the *Child's History of England,* and in the monosyllabic histories of France and Germany

41

that followed it; there was fighting all through the novels of Mr. G. A. Henty that Father had read as a boy and had saved for a son; there was war in Robin Hood and in King Arthur and in *Ivanhoe*. I read Sir Walter's book too early for a perfect comprehension, but not too soon to enjoy the fighting.

I was fascinated by all this bloodshed. The first motion picture I saw, at age five, was quite as satisfying. When I walked into the darkened theater with The Bear, a man was being machine-gunned to death and bullet holes were appearing on the plaster wall behind him. The next film I saw showed airmen shooting at one another over France, and men burning in the wrecks. In another film, sinister Chinese killed people with hatchets, and then, of course, there were the cowboy pictures. There were two kinds of natives in the pictures that had natives in them. There were good natives and bad, and the good ones were those who helped us kill the bad ones. These entertainments formed a perfect counterpart to all the books about war; to the stories in the pulp magazines that Father read aloud to Mother. In all the books, stories and films, we, the good Americans or the honorable knights, always triumphed over the treacherous, cowardly, evil enemy. In every case, good triumphed over evil, and the form of that triumph was always violent.

Carrying these visions over into the real world was no problem at all. For example, in Washington there had been the clatter of cavalry in the streets and the rhythmic crash of marching boots and the blare of bugles and tubas. Everyone removed his hat as the flag went by. If I had then heard an American philosopher say, "War is the health of the state," I would have understood him. Clearly visible from our country club were the great warships in the Annapolis roadstead. The *Pennsylvania* was my favorite because it was the flagship and because Mother said our family came from Pennsylvania. My parents had many friends at the Naval Academy, all of them officers, of course. One was a flier who swooped over our house almost every afternoon, leaning out of the cockpit of his warplane to wave to me, and I would wave back, and he would rock his wings and soar over a stand of trees and out across

42

Chesapeake Bay. At the Academy, you could see men fight with swords on Saturday. I was told that I might one day be a West Point cadet or a Naval midshipman. Mother said the cadets were the finest, bravest young men in all the world.

But young Moltke told me the Germans were the best soldiers of all. Mother said No, we were: we had beaten the Germans. We had never lost a war, she said. There was a picture of my father in an Army uniform. He had been in the victorious war against the Germans. Father had not gone overseas, however, because the Government would not let him. He had been too valuable to the Government in Washington, where he had been a sergeant in charge of community singing. But he had wanted to go to France. My Uncle Louis, who was not really my uncle but a man who had married The Bear, had been an artillery officer in France and he had an Army pistol. One of my grandfathers had been a cavalry officer and we had his sabre. I carried this weapon when I played war with lead soldiers with Moltke, but I always lost because I was six years younger. Moltke, however, said I lost because the Germans were better. There was one true thing I did learn from Moltke. It was the meaning of the word "complicated." It was the first long word I learned.

When not playing soldiers, I was learning to swim, and finding out how to catch the Maryland blue crabs that came flittering across a little sandbar to enter a shallow cove where they grew soft shells. The lifeguards liked me because I was the son of the manager.

The attention of the lifeguards confirmed that I was the privileged son of a privileged family. Another confirmation lay in the apparent fact that our family did not have to obey the law. For example, despite the law against drinking, there was always beer and whisky at our house. Father got the whisky from the Navy and the beer from the sheriff, who called him "Sir." Mother said the policemen were our friends, and it was only criminals who feared them. She also said policemen were our servants, and for this reason she was enraged when a Washington policeman, seeking to

43

explain my Father's automobile accident, said that Father had been drunk. To be sure, Mother was quite upset by the accident—it seemed that Father had gone off a hillside at night, and had been thrown through the windshield of his motorcar, and had very nearly been killed. He spent some weeks in hospital. At any rate, Mother was angry as well as upset. She said our good friends and servants the police had no right to say things like that about Father, who was a lawyer and who would have them fired for saying he was drunk. She asked me, as we left the hospital where Father was unconscious, to be brave in case my Father should die. I immediately agreed. In fact, I rather looked forward to the opportunity. Meanwhile, I shared Mother's cold view of servants who would lie about my Father, and understood that policemen were supposed to do what you told them.

I was also given to understand that, no matter what, I must never, never be a sissy. Father was very clear on this point, and so was Mother, although neither explained what a sissy was. I took this to mean that I must never be a girl, for all the children I had ever met had told me that girls were sissies. While I knew in an unexamined way that the world was composed of males and females, I wondered if boys who failed at being boys turned into girls. Judging from the somewhat cryptic answers I received for my questions, I gathered that this was more or less the case. But what, apart from being brave and becoming a soldier, was required of a boy in order not to be a sissy and so turn into a girl? For some days, I was haunted by a fear that I really was a girl, after all, dressed in a boy's clothes. My doubts were partially resolved when a family with several children moved into a new country club house near our own. Investigation disclosed that the two brothers and I were identically constructed, while the younger sisters were built exactly like one another, but differently from ourselves. That settled one question: For the time being, I was a boy. But if I was ever a sissy, would it fall off and become a fold of flesh? My companions did not know. It was not a question I could take to my parents, because to do so would have meant that I had seen a girl,

44

and the reason why there were separate locker rooms at the country club's beach house was so that you would never, never see a girl. Everyone was strict about never going into the girls' locker room because you were absolutely not to see girls. Thinking about this one night, subsequent to having seen the sisters, I experienced the first erection that I can remember as having occurred at a definite time and place, and I remember wondering what a girl would think if she could see that. At the time, I didn't know what to make of it myself.

During the school terms, I was driven to and from Annapolis each day. I remember almost nothing about that school except for having my lunch box taken away as punishment for my having used the polished undersurface of it to shine a lightbird against the schoolhouse wall and then into my teacher's eyes. Mother said the teacher had no right to take away my personal property. She demanded it back, and the teacher apologized. Personal property, Mother said, was something that no one had any right to take away from you.

The other memorable event of my Annapolis education was being struck and knocked sprawling by a truck. I remember the sudden loom of the truck, and people bending over me, and waking up in hospital. The doctor who X-rayed my head informed Mother that my skull was not broken, but that I would never grow to be more than five feet tall because growth stopped when the brain filled the skull, and my brain was almost touching the cranial walls now. This learned opinion was perhaps as sound as any medical advice of the day, and Mother believed every word of it, and I suppose—poor soul!—she continued to believe it until the passage of time proved the doctor mistaken. When Father found out what the doctor had told the distraught mother whose only possible child had been struck by a truck, he promptly sued the doctor. But nothing came of the suit, even though it should have been perfectly clear to the court that doctors have no right to say such things to people like ourselves.

The two years that the country club lasted were marvelous ones for me, for so much seemed to hover just a little distance away, while what lay round about was exciting in itself. There was the bay to swim in and boat on; the club's property included a woods where I could play at Robin Hood and explore alone for chinquapins, persimmons and English walnuts. In winter, young Moltke made a sled with wooden runners, and we would start atop a little hill, slide down this and rumble across a small, frozen bay. Moltke had a hatchet and he chopped frozen perch out of the ice of the bay. In spring, the grass was a brilliant green on the golf course, and the gatekeeper always touched his hat to Father, who drove a Reo Flying Cloud sedan. The gatekeeper wore a pistol to keep southern Europeans and other undesirables away, and I discovered he had sons my age. In the summer I played with these country boys and their friends. We pulled up big-rooted weeds and threw them at each other, warring with spears.

My only appointed occasions were school hours, mealtimes and bedtime. For the rest of it, I was turned loose to play at whatever I found amusing, and it was understood that it was up to me to amuse myself. Yet, there were ground rules which obtained at all times, not only in the house but out of it. They had to do with being a Gentleman, and a Gentleman, it seemed, was divided into two parts: Manliness and Manners. Manliness involved always telling the truth; never snitching or carrying tales; fighting your own battles; not being a bully; never crying when it hurt but gritting your teeth and bearing it, above all, never crying to Mother when someone hurt you; standing up straight, and getting that whiney tone out of your voice. On somewhat more exalted levels, it meant always playing fair and remembering that your word was your bond. Manners meant doing what you were told without complaint; saying "Sir" to your father and all older men; standing up when ladies entered the room; holding doors and chairs for ladies; not speaking until spoken to; never saying, "Yeah"; and never saying, "What?" when someone called you, but replying, "Yes, Mother" and then immediately going to where she was so that she did not have to shout to you.

It will be seen that both Manliness and Manners begin with the word "Man," and in the further interest of making a man of me, Father packed me off to McDonogh School, a military academy near Baltimore, when I was nine and a half. I was to enter the sixth grade. It was the fifth school I entered, the others having been in Washington and Annapolis.

"You will learn to take care of yourself," Father assured me, and in a way he did not suspect, he was right. For the principal lesson I learned was not that of responsible individuality, but of the necessity for self-preservation. The headmaster, Major Robert Lamborn, made the point quite clear to us New Fools, as the new boys were called as soon as our parents and guardians were out of earshot. We all stood in a line outside a stone buiding while he, a bald, burly man, stood on the stone steps, glaring at us like Mussolini, putting matters straight.

"When you fight, I want you to fight fair," he said. "If somebody bigger than you are picks on you, though, then I don't care if you pick up a rock, or a stick, or kick him or what you do—as long as you fight back. But don't come whining to me about it. . ,.."

There was more in this militant line, and we heard it all again at sundry times from our teachers, nearly all of them National Guard officers who wore boots and spurs and sabres.

It is easy to say that a sick sexuality brooded over that military monastery: a homosexual sadism perpetrated by grown men upon little boys. I do not mean that this was overt. Rather, that such is the subconscious rationale of any military boarding school. Mc-Donogh was probably no worse than any other. The faculty had their favorites and their toadies and their victims, and their refusal to listen to whiners surely permitted the cruelties the students visited upon one another—cruelties of which the faculty could not have been totally ignorant. Wholly apart from the routine viciousness of sadistic punishments inflicted by cadet officers on children who failed to keep their shoes shined (standing them under cold showers; beating their bellies with hairbrushes), and wholly apart from the way the badgered group would turn on someone singled out for minor reprimand and join in the jeering, McDonogh's students were capable of inflicting sophisticated tortures on one another. For example, late one afternoon, another nine-year-old and I came late from the playing fields to the locker room, and there we saw a group of older boys intent around a rubbing table.

They had a boy spread out naked on it, and while several of them held him down, another boy manipulated him. The boy was crying and trying to get free, but he was erect just the same, and when he spurted at last they all laughed at him and his terror. Then one of them caught sight of us standing there horrified and fascinated, and he grabbed us by the arms. "If you tell anybody, we'll get you," he said, and he meant it.

The boy they had been manipulating believed that masturbation caused insanity. His father had assured him of this, referring to a book popular in my parents' time, written by a medical doctor. The boy believed it, and had made the mistake of saying so. With that, the others had taken him to the locker room. They told him they were going to drive him crazy. They would catch him whenever they could and go to work on him.

Perhaps they did drive him crazy. I do not know what became of him, but some of his torturers bore famous names and went on to become prominent in the affairs of Maryland. After all, many of the students at McDonogh came of wealthy families. For the first time in my life, I had been placed among my social equals, and by the end of that school year, I had at least become man enough to be very sure that I wanted nothing further to do with any of them. I think there is a point beyond "being man enough to take it." I think the next step is "being man enough to refuse to have anything to do with it," and McDonogh at least set me on the way to taking that next step.

There was no question of my returning to McDonogh the following year, for the banks had closed, and we could not get our money out. Next, the banks failed, and there was nothing to get out. The country club was finished. We now lived in Baltimore, where Father was trying to make a living in real estate, and for the next two years I attended Baltimore public schools; one in a wretched part of the city where we first lived; the second in that excellent neighborhood for successes to which we moved as soon as Father was sufficiently successful, and where a man screamed as he was being stabbed to death beneath my window.

These experiences are by no means all that I remember from the earliest years to those of puberty. I have merely tried to illustrate my practical experience of certain concepts widely shared in the 1920s in the homes of affluent, college-educated white urban Americans of the Eastern seaboard. Granted that mine was doubtless different in detail from everyone else's childhood, I think it safe to say that most children of my class had some practical experience of the same concepts. These would include pride in race, pride in family, pride in manhood, pride in nation, an insistence on self-reliance and individual responsibility, a view of the soldier as a hero, a vision of sex as black magic, and treatment of the child as a separate, subordinate sort of human being. I am equally sure that we children all had an early acquaintance with violence in literature and in the motion pictures, if not personal experience of it through schoolyard fights, football games, being hit by trucks and finding corpses under bedroom windows.

A rather Roman catalogue. It would be easy to extrapolate from this catalogue a group of purposeful, self-righteous, militant imperialists, and so explain our posture in Asia today, were it not for the fact that most of us subsequently rejected almost every one of these concepts. Our divorcement from them today is by no means complete, and the fact that we still cling emotionally to many of the concepts we have rejected intellectually is a source of my generation's apparent schizophrenia, and contributes not only to a stuttering domestic program and foreign policy, but also to the wide separation that exists between our children and ourselves. A preliminary way to discuss these somewhat esoteric matters is to consider, first, a curious change in popular legend.

49

The legend is that of the hero. The hero we were taught to emulate no longer exists in the popular mind, save as a figure of fun.

He was someone on the order of the Henty boy. He was good at rough games; a plucky and honorable lad who was a universal favorite among the villagers, and he would have been a leader among the village boys even had his dead father not been the lord of the manor. What though a stripling of sixteen, he had nearly a man's growth and strength. He had a frank, open countenance and a sunny smile, a warm and generous heart, and he was as courteous to his inferiors as he was to his superiors. He had a strong determination to be as worthy a man as his saintly father had been, and to support and protect his widowed mother and innocent young sister. It was up to him to recoup the family fortunes, brought to low estate by the evil machinations of a dastardly, cowardly fop who had wormed his way into the good graces of the misguided king, and who had designs on the boy's sister and would stop at nothing to gain his ends. Two hundred pages later, honesty, grit and pluck had won the day, the cad was dead, and the villagers tossed their hats and cheered as the kindly king confirmed the youth in possession of his reconquered barony. All this was thoroughly consistent with the concepts held up to us as ideals. The Henty hero embodied them. It would have been absolutely impossible for the Henty boy to cheat his way into the sixth form. Not only would he have not known how, but he would have been scandalized by the suggestion. Applauding him, I remember that we reserved for the classroom cheat exactly the same scorn we held for that dastardly fop, the Henty villain.

Today's children, however, would write off the Henty hero as a rather simpleminded square; they would dismiss the happy peasantry as a clutter of chuckleheaded yo-yos and, having read *Candy* in the seventh grade, would find the Henty hero's sister hopelessly out of it. To them, none of these people is cool. Their idea of the really cool hero, as is evidenced not only by their choice of reading matter but also by no few of their actions, is someone like this:

50

He is a violent sneak, a conspicuous consumer of gadgets, modish costumes and resort accommodations, utterly amoral, at once the object of torture and the practitioner thereof; a casual murderer with a license to kill, whose view of sexual congress is purely exploitive, who is provided with limitless funds by a spurious corporation that assigns him a cipher for a name and a dead-end job. Cheat in school? Of course he would. He would never give the matter a thought, as long as it seemed an effective way to beat the system. It is as if Mordred had become the hero of the modern Arthurian legend.

But the legend, too, has changed, as a typical motion picture about the new hero makes clear. The elements of the film *Goldfinger* include expensive alcohols, luxury products, dangerous speeds, deceit, casual heterosexual contact, sadism, Lesbianism, vandalism, rape, mass slaughter, and electrocution—all superbly enacted and wonderfully photographed in glorious color. The film begins with an explosion and a murder that have nothing whatsoever to do with the subsequent story (such as it is), but serve to introduce the hero, who is a hired assassin. The heroine is not the naked soubrette first encountered. That unfortunate waif is murdered by being painted with gold leaf by a maniac. The heroine turns out to be a Lesbian gangster first in league with the maniac, but who is converted to the assassin's side, and to more normal (if equally amoral) sexual behavior by being raped by him. This development should not be unsuspected by the audience, for her very name gives promise of uncommon lubricity. It is Pussy Galore. In the course of the film, two expensive automobiles are smashed— one of them crushed into a lump of metal with a drugged man inside. A public treasure house containing most of the world's gold is extensively damaged. A jet airliner is destroyed. Sundry other damage to real and personal property occurs during the course of the tortures and the killings. In the end, one vandal kills the other and parachutes to a desert island to explore at leisure the charms of Miss Galore. The only point made is that one man is more murderous, deceitful and clever than another, and if there is any catharsis for the audience to experience, it is on the order of that which a wet dream might provide.

Now, what interests me about legends is that they are accurate indicators of public mood. For a legend or a work of fiction to be popular, it must be grounded in some reality which the general public recognizes, and with which it is ready to identify itself. What specifically should interest us for the purposes of this discussion is the fact that my father's generation produced the hero we worshiped as boys, while we have produced the anti-hero that our children regard as cool. The difference between the two legendary heroes therefore must represent an exact measurement of the change that has occurred in the American outlook between the time of my father's youth and my son's. Since all of us are what our experiences make us, the change in legend must therefore be descriptive of what happened to my generation. And for our children to be able to identify with a sneaking, promiscuous, destructive spy, there must be something in the contemporary American reality that makes his actions seem not only plausible but heroic.

The new hero did not arrive as suddenly and as unexpectedly as a changeling in our house. He evolved, inevitably, as first one and then another of our Hentyish beliefs were abandoned either as being foolishly pretentious or as being inapplicable to contemporary reality. He is, in a sense, the vicious little brother of the Hemingway hero—the hero who emerged from the Kaiser's war. The Hemingway hero was still something of a Roland at the pass, or Henty's plucky lad, but stripped of all illusions, conscious of a terrible loneliness, expecting attack and expecting to be killed in the end, but determined to preserve his integrity until (as Hemingway would say) his position was overrun. He was tough, cool, alert, leery of abstracts, suspicious of all systems, appreciative of the good things of life which, to him, were largely the pleasures of the senses; committed to no ethics but his own. Still, his ethics generally fell within the area that our father's generation would call manly and honorable: the Hemingway hero fought under tattered flags, and he was a conservative in the sense that he was someone who tried to preserve things which seemed to him to be valuable. He was fated to lose, and after Hitler's war we apparently decided the Hemingway hero had lost, for we brought forth the new champion, who neither creates nor even conserves, but who simply consumes and destroys within a legend that has no point and no future.

To me, an overwhelming question is: How in the world did we ever arrive at the frame of mind that enabled us to conjure up the anti-hero? What was there in our experience that led us to abandon certain beliefs, and what changed in our world from the time the Henty hero could be related to actual reality to the time when the anti-hero could be related to reality?

I can only continue to recite the facts of my American experience in order to show what happened to me, and by extension, to us, but the account should be suggestive of some answers. It should also, incidentally, suggest reasons why many of today's honor students hold cheating to be no crime but a practical necessity we have thrust upon them; why the most intelligent generation of Americans yet to appear is also largely a generation of emotional cripples. But we will get to the new generation when it appears in due course of chronology. At this time, it is important to consider some aspects of a fundamental change in the family and in the national fortunes, and the effect of this change upon the growing consciousness of an adolescent boy.

3

First Steps

EVERYBODY SAID Prosperity was Just Around the Corner. But no-body knew how to get to it or even where the corner was. Father thought he had a glimpse of it in Baltimore, but then it seemed to him the corner might after all be in Chicago, and so we moved to that city in 1933, when I was twelve years old.

I remember the countryside growing flatter and more depressing with every mile west out of the Alleghenies, and then the gray squalor of the manufacturing cities, the first I had seen, with the lines of gray men outside the factory fences staring at us as we drove by. I had never seen anything so dismal, nor even imagined such a thing, as Gary, Indiana, but Gary was a place of lilting joy compared to Chicago. We entered that city down a wide, straight street where we saw policemen with drawn revolvers crouching behind parked automobiles, peering up at the blank windows of a gray row house. I was anxious to see what would happen, but Mother was not, and Father drove quickly on.

Father said the Chicago police were sending pickpockets into the Loop, as the central shopping area was called. They would strip the pickpockets before sending them into the crowds, follow them as they worked, and strip them again back at the station house to be sure they missed nothing of the pickpockets' gleanings. The pickpockets were allowed to keep a share of their gains and the police divided the rest, and in such manner was the police force paid. Should a prominent citizen report a loss, the police would find the missing wallet with miraculous speed in the hope of

54

encouraging the prominent to think well of them, and also in hope of reward. There was a sign on a city prison reading CRIME DOES NOT PAY and the public was invited to pay admission to wander though this jail as if it were a zoo. There were small stores whose plate-glass windows had been shattered and whose storefronts were now boarded over, and signs tacked to the boards said the storekeepers refused to pay protection. Father explained that if the storekeepers did not pay gangsters sums of money to be protected from people throwing bombs through the store windows, then the gangsters would throw bombs through the windows.

He also said the schoolteachers were being paid in scrip, rather than in money. The scrip could be exchanged for food at designated grocery shops. Everyone had to watch carefully lest the grocer slip stones in among the potatoes as he filled the sacks.

As in Gary, gray, pinch-faced men in cloth caps and drab tatters stood in hopeless lines outside locked factory gates. Similar lines formed along trash-strewn streets, waiting to be given hot soup. Elsewhere in the city, grown men rented jigsaw puzzles to one another for fifteen cents a week as a means of livelihood, and played miniature golf at each other's miniature golf courses built in vacant lots, and motion picture theater owners gave crockery away to anyone who would please buy a ticket. Men sold one another apples on streetcorners, or drifted about a despairing city looking for any kind of work at all, and some, finding none, stepped off the window ledges of the shining skyscrapers of the downtown financial area, hoping that their widows and children would be able to collect the insurance.

Along the lake front, however, there was an endless carnival of bright lights. Here were buildings of fantastic shapes and colors, and a sound of music, for Chicago was holding a World's Fair to celebrate what the city called its Century of Progress. The principal attraction at this Fair was an almost naked woman who pranced about waving fans. Another display was a demonstration by a motion picture company of the way it had filmed a fantasy about an ape so enormous that it climbed the tallest building in the world as if it were a tree, and from its summit swatted and caught warplanes in its hands as if they were flies. You could ride an elevated train from where we lived in suburban Oak Park into the city and down to its waterfront of marvels, where sound amplifiers continuously broadcast "Who's Afraid of the Big, Bad Wolf?"—an optimistic song that said no one was afraid of the wolf at everyone's door. Refreshed, you could ride back to Oak Park, looking down, as the train clacked along, into the filthy streets through which men shuffled in broken shoes.

Each morning in the Oak Park Junior High School we saluted the flag and pledged allegiance to the country for which it stands with liberty and justice for all. Then we sang about America the beautiful where the majesty of purple mountains overlooked the fruited plains from sea to shining sea. Every time I sang this I crossed my fingers to let God know, privately, that I did not mean it. God knew, and I knew, that America in 1933 was not beautiful. It was a very shabby place filled with crooked cops and gang battles and dirty streets and amoebic dysentery and lines of idle men.

Mother said the men who waited for work were desperate men. She was very much afraid of them. To her, any man who did not have a job was a sort of criminal. Yes, she would admit, there was a depression, but if a man really wanted to work he could find something to do, look at your Father. And I would have to admit that Father not only had found work, but that he worked eighteen hours a day, and even if we seemed to have fallen from the Paradise that had been the country club on Chesapeake Bay, Father had saved us from the Hell that was Chicago. We lived simply, but not uncomfortably, in the Oak Park Arms Hotel, insulated by Father's efforts from personal experience of the disasters that had befallen the desperate men in the dirty cloth caps who shuffled in soup lines in the trash-blown streets. Yet, I could not wholly accept Mother's argument that if Father could find work, anyone else who really wanted work could also find it, because it seemed to me that Father was an exceptional man. Mother herself agreed that he

56

was, but she still seemed to feel that the Depression was largely the fault of the depressed. It turned out, however, that Father did not find in Chicago the corner around which Prosperity allegedly lurked. He felt there was reason to believe the corner might be discovered in New Jersey, and so at Christmastime we three were traveling east in Father's free-wheeling Auburn touring car. En route, we stopped at an inn to keep the holiday.

Because it was Christmas, Father had found and set up in our room a tiny, bedraggled evergreen. When we had lived in Kalorama Road with The Bear, the Bough, The Lamb and Rose, the Christmas tree had always touched the high ceiling of the drawing room, and round it ran an electric train loaded with clear sugar candies, and in my stocking were shining five-dollar gold pieces, and there was a whole toy store's worth of presents waiting to be unwrapped, and mistletoe, and the children from the Austrian Embassy would come at Christmas eve, and I would visit them on Christmas day, and there was song and eggnog. But on Christmas day, 1933, en route from nothing in particular to nowhere in general, there was a pint bottle of cheap whisky, a pathetic shrub on a bureau top, three presents done up in a red ribbon that held more light than the winter sun, and a gray world outside the window. There was not even any snow. My present was a basketball. It was not a basketball of the first quality, although it must have cost more than a man could earn in three weeks in a Chicago slaughterhouse. Knowing what it must have cost Father, in terms relative to our resources, it was difficult to smile as I said my thanks. It would have been far easier to cry.

I remember thinking at the time that we three were drifting like a chip on a flood, and it is easy for me to see that we were closer to one another then than we ever were at any time before or since. But even so, I was drawing naturally apart from them as I grew older while we drifted together, and I remember being vaguely conscious of that, too, at the time.

It was in New Jersey that I drew both figuratively and literally away from my parents, even as Father discovered the corner, and

57

Prosperity, in that state. There, his real estate business began to burgeon at the lowest point in the nation's fortunes, and when it did, we moved once again to one of those neighborhoods for successes, a place called East Orange.

I was not particularly impressed. Taken as a whole, New Jersey was then very nearly as much of a frightful stench in the senses as it is today—a dog's breakfast of lumpish clutter inhabited in its northern counties by a population that spoke the most unpleasant of all American accents. Estornch, as the natives called it, like a Roland Park in Baltimore, an Oak Park near Chicago, or a Scarsdale near New York, was one of those flaccid communities that are so distinguished by their total lack of character. I can best describe East Orange by saying that Duncan Hines would have enjoyed the food at the Hotel Suburban. Life there was like a placid dream you cannot recall. The bad dreams all occurred in nearby Newark, Elizabeth, Paterson, Jersey City and Hoboken—stark, sour little Chicagos sick with breadlines and gunmen.

These judgments may sound most uncharitable in light of the fact that Father worked incredible hours to provide for us as best he could, and inasmuch as East Orange was certainly a far, far better place for us to be than the dreary Chicago to which we had sunk; but it was also a fact that I was beginning to see things otherwise than my parents did. Until my thirteenth year, my tastes had been theirs. At least, I rather shared their enthusiasm for Victor Herbert and accepted Father's dismissal of symphony music as being long-haired pretense, and jazz as being a discordant noise. I read the *Reader's Digest* to increase my word power without seeing anything specious in the sunny outlook of that popular journal, and laughed with my parents at the inanities of radio comedians. I did not contest my parents' idea that Broadway musical comedies were very fine things, although the shows bored me beyond belief, and I could not honestly see whatever it was that my parents found so amusing about them. Today, I would say that musical comedy is a failure because it is a bastard art form of minimal information content, wherein acting and music are as indigestibly combined as are dining and dancing in the same room at the same hour. But when I was thirteen, I had not yet formulated reasons for my tastes. So I read the Hearst press along with my parents, not yet able to say why I found its lurid pages so improbable, and we three went to the prize fights and wrestling matches where I pretended to enjoy the spectacles to a far greater degree than I actually did. Still, at the same time, I was beginning to absorb the data that would become the basis for future judgments. The first real shock that jarred me loose from my parents' gravitational pull occurred one day in 1934 when I brought a school friend home for lunch.

I thought Mother had liked Bob, and that we had had a good time. But Mother was furious.

"John," she said, "I never want you to bring another Jew into my house."

I was absolutely appalled. I was not so shocked by my Mother's attitude as I was by the distance between us. Of course I knew that my parents shared the Teutonic derision of Latins, Africans, Slavs, Jews, and Celts, although in our house we did not refer to them as wops, niggers, hunkies, kikes and micks. Only the lower classes did that. The upper classes merely refrained from having anything to do with them socially. But I had never heard either of my parents express racial prejudice so personally, vehemently, or—as in the case at hand—so utterly without the slightest provocation. Now, what was shocking was the fact that *I knew I was right and Mother was wrong*. This was not abstract intellectual knowledge derived by a process of reasoning, but something I knew quite positively from personal experience of classmates in schools in five different cities. I had for some time thought that people were wrong to make judgments of other people on national or racial grounds alone, but Mother's words suddenly brought this knowledge to the forefront of my mind to the point that I perceived what different people my parents and I really were.

When a child knows something to be true, and discovers that his parents are mistaken in the matter, his human response is to beat

59

his parents over the head with the truth he has found, avenging himself for all those past occasions when they had been right and he wrong. I was not yet quite at the stage of clubbing my parents, but now that I was conscious that an abyss yawned between us, I began to inspect all other matters more closely.

There was, for example, my parents' circle of acquaintance. The owner of one of the real estate properties that my Father managed had made his money as a bootlegger. Our chauffeur had been one of his musclemen: a man who rode armed on the beer trucks, guarding against rival gangsters who might try to hijack the load. The chauffeur had a careful, studied flatness about him and he carried a Colt .45-calibre Army automatic pistol in a shoulder holster. He said he wore it because he had bad friends. The chauffeur was an indication of our gathering prosperity (we had never had one before), and his being armed was somewhat exciting, but I did not like Father's being associated with an allegedly retired gangster millionaire, nor could I understand how he could go into a certain restaurant when all the world knew that its proprietors had been criminals during Prohibition. Everything about the New Jersey where we lived, and the New York City where we went for entertainment, had a gamey smell about it—an odor that could not be equated with manners, manliness or honor.

"Stand up straight," Father would say. "Get your shoulders back. Get your third vest button out. Smile! If you stand straight and smile you can't help feeling better and you can't help doing better. Clench your fists as you walk; you can't help feeling more determined! A man who slouches around and frowns all the time will never get anywhere. Nobody likes him. Take your hands out of your pockets! And shine your shoes. You can always tell a gentleman by whether he keeps his shoes shined."

Father's shoes glistened. He also associated with gangsters.

"Straighten your tie," Mother would say. "Take your elbows off the table and put your napkin in your lap. You know better than that! I don't know what's got into you. What did you say? I can't understand when you mumble. Harold, we will have to send John to someone for speech lessons. I can't hear anything he says."

But I had heard what she said.

And I was beginning to see the shape of their lives. What did they *do?* So far as I could determine, Mother's principal activity was shopping. Her only friends seemed to be the wives of Father's salesmen, or the kind of shopkeepers who send you Christmas cards in return for your patronage. She said Hello to headwaiters. These were the people she wished to impress with my manners and our position. She went nowhere without Father, and Father's principal activity was work, which he carried late into most evenings. When Mother hired an interior decorator from a department store to decide what colors, fabrics and furnishings our lives should have, this seemed to her to be an enormous adventure. I wondered why it should. I wondered what Father was getting out of life except money, and for that matter, what good was the money? He was putting it into insurance policies, whisky, large new cars, furs and jewels and interior decoration for Mother, and into parties with the most stupid people I had ever met (I was meeting adults for the first time), and none of this meant much to me other than that my parents' lives seemed empty. From reading Richard Halliburton, I gathered that other adults went romantically around the world on tramp steamers; from the newspapers I gathered that people did all sorts of things other than sit home and listen to "Amos and Andy," read the papers, and go to restaurants on the maid's night off. I daresay the trouble was, I was judging my parents by that relentless standard, "False in one thing, false in all." It was one of the maxims Father himself had taught me.

Today I would say that there was insufficient communication between us—a fault which tended to make our actions and attitudes mutually inexplicable as we looked at one another across the widening abyss, wanting to love and not knowing how. They had as little insight into my world as I had into theirs. There was, for instance, the matter of the suit.

I tried to explain. I said I did not want to wear coat, vest and tie to school because I was the only boy in the class who did. I was told my argument was irrelevant. I was supposed to wear a dress appropriate to my station, even if everyone else slouched around in sweaters, open collars, slacks and saddle shoes. We had a position to maintain, Mother explained. So far as I could see, the position was ludicrous, and I was the only one who was maintaining it. This led to duplicity. I would take off coat and vest on reaching school, and sit in class in shirtsleeves.

There was also the matter of the dancing class, which I could not even have begun to explain. All I could do was blurt out that I hated it, and Father laughed and said all boys say they hate girls, when really they like them. But what Father did not know, and what I could not tell him, because we had never discussed sexual matters in any greater detail than Father's once telling me that all the acts of Nature are beautiful, was that I had already some experience with intercourse. The event had taken place in a club-house we boys had built of boards and tarpaper in a vacant lot in Baltimore, when I was between ten and eleven, and the demonstrators had been a sixteen-year-old who shaved and had a news-paper route, and a fourteen-year-old girl who was the friend of sailors. Upon conclusion of their performance, the young lady invited the rest of us to try. And in Oak Park, and here in East Orange, there had been the books of photographs passed from one nervous hand to another under desks in school. The trouble with the dancing class was that the style of the day called for you to hold the girl close. "No daylight between the partners, please," the dancing master would primly (and, perhaps pruriently) say. And I, knowing what I had in my arms, would experience the male response, which meant that at the end of the dance, flushing scarlet and walking back across the ballroom floor in a kind of necessary crouch, I would be sure that everyone was staring at me. I made a tongue-tied refusal to attend another dancing lesson. Thinking to compromise, Father then arranged for the mistress of another dancing school to give me private lessons alone in her home, and he was angry when he learned that I told the good woman I absolutely refused to dance.

Then there were the summer trips and winter holidays which were not the complete successes they might have been. For example, in my fourteenth winter we went to Quebec to keep the Christmas holiday at the Château Frontenac, and while I have only happy memories of the dining hall with the suckling pigs with the apples in their mouths, and the view from my tower room of that fine hotel, I still have a horrid memory of the ice skating. I should have been delighted to learn to skate by myself. But my parents hired the figure-skating champion of Quebec to teach me, and she turned out to be sixteen years old and French. Nothing can be so devastating to a fourteen-year-old boy who fancies himself as being rather good at games, as to be propped up and hauled around a rink in public view by a beautiful girl who assures *M'sieu* that he is in very truth doing formidably although his ankles are scraping the ice, while an orchestra sarcastically plays "The Skaters' Waltz." The reality of that scene was at considerable odds with my imaginative view of myself as one of Henty's young heroes.

Looking back, it would seem that I had been for some time discovering the inapplicability of the Henty *Weltanschauung* to the facts of life in more serious ways than this. Consider for a moment the matter of pride in race and family. Long before Mother told me never to bring another Jew into her house, I had begun to wonder just what, after all, was so special about the Keats family. My memories of the earliest years in Washington and Maryland surely indicate a basic suspicion of such pretense; there was much talk of social equals, but we never seemed to meet any. It is always the special province of the child to sense parental inconsistencies, even if he may not be able to formulate them. I came quite soon to such sticky points as these: How can you say you must always be polite to everyone and considerate of the other fellow and then turn around and bar all southern Europeans from the club? Such an action was not Hentyish, but instead of taxing Mr. Henty with

63

failure as a realist, I taxed my parents with failure to practice what they, and Mr. Henty, preached.

It would have been perfectly all right to believe in, and act out, the part of the noble son of a noble house, justifiably proud of his family's high honors, estates and impeccable morality, had the family indeed been so noble and had I felt myself to be one who acted always in an honorable way. But all during my childhood, I was living to some extent in the world as well as under my parental roof. I went to school and met other children and their parents and I read the newspapers. To the extent that I lived in the world, I was naturally affected by it. In this regard, I do not think it possible to overestimate the effect that Prohibition had on every man, woman and child in the land. For example, it was impossible not to know that your parents, and everyone else's parents, were consistently breaking the law. I knew this at age seven when, coming to my first family meal at holiday, and receiving a few drops of claret in a glass otherwise filled with water, I gathered from the cryptic remarks and general ambiance of the occasion that we were all doing something that in some way was not supposed to be done. It was also impossible to grow up during Prohibition and not realize that the gangster was a hero to adults, and the policeman a villain. There had been a similar view in the stories of Robin Hood, but there was in America a real difference, apparent even to a child, between Robin Hood and a simple hood like Scarface Al Capone; between the Sheriff of Nottingham and the cop you saw each day at the intersection of Main and Elm, on your way to school. Your parents said that policemen were your friends, or your servants, and that everyone must obey the law, but you heard parents boast to one another of gangsters they had met, and of how if you got a traffic ticket, they had a friend in Police Court who could fix it. The fact that the whole country was breaking the law was considered to be a joke. Will Rogers, a comedian of the time, said, "If you think this country ain't dry, just watch 'em vote. If you think this country ain't wet, just watch 'em drink. You see, when they vote, it's counted, but when they drink, it ain't." I cannot pretend to have remembered this jape from my youth, but I do remember that the adult community thought that both Will Rogers and Prohibition were funny and that gangsters were important people, and I think it fair to agree, now, with those who say that after the gunfire quieted down and repeal had come, the net effect of Prohibition was that it had contributed to America's aspect as a moral swamp. As a Federal prosecutor in Philadelphia remarked, "It wasn't only the law that was broken; it was every rule of ordinary decency among men."

It was also impossible to grow up during Prohibition years and not be affected by the concurrent phenomonon of the Great Depression, even if you lived on Park Avenue in East Orange. Indeed, if you drove around in a Buick Limited behind an armed chauffeur at a time when practically everyone you knew was walking to school in frayed, outgrown clothes, you were a rather special victim of the Depression—the prey of doubt and guilt, and the object of a certain amount of suspicion in the eyes of your classmates. Inasmuch as early adolescence is a time when it seems important to be just like everyone else, an awareness of privileged difference can be most uncomfortable to the growing boy, and in my case it helped to deepen and widen the chasm between myself and my parents.

For practically everyone else, the Depression had more immediate, bleaker meaning. It was not just the value of money that was depressed, it was the middle-class morale. The kind of people who lived in places like East Orange had hitherto believed their good fortune could be attributed to their prudent intelligence and hard work. Then, for some reason beyond their imagination, no one wanted them any more. They were willing to work hard, but there was no work to be had. There was no more market for what they had to offer. They tried to temporize; to work at the same jobs for less money. But as time went on—as 1930 deepened into 1931, worsened into 1932, and stagnated in 1933—a man's pay would be cut again and again, if he were lucky enough to be able to hold his job, and he would have left his comfortable house for a small, drab apartment; his wife would have learned to buy stale bread at the bakery, wet it, and rebake it; he would have learned to fit cardboard into his shoes because it cost seventy-five cents to have a pair of shoes resoled and heeled. What made such a condition demoralizing was not so much the business of contending with adversity, but the apparent fact that prudence, intelligence and hard work did not guarantee success. There were some successes —Father was one of them; but for the most part the middle classes were faced with the fact (whether they understood it or not) that the national economic structure operated by laws that were not subject to control by exercise of the middle-class virtues. Faced with the inexplicable, some men just gave up. Such is an appraisal I would make today, although at the time I lacked the information necessary to form appraisals. All I knew then about men giving up was the fact that the father of one of my classmates did. There came a day when he decided to stay at home rather than go to the small office where he conducted a real estate business that did no business. He spent most of the rest of his life smoking in bed in a room separate from the one he had shared with his wife. She went to work as a door-to-door saleswoman of hosiery. The job was created for her by a relative in the hosiery business. The situation was shocking because the middle class cannot imagine a man who does not work, and for a wife and mother to have to go to work was then considered a middle-class tragedy. It certainly was tragic enough for the boy, whose respect for his father turned to active hatred.

To me, the principal fact about the Depression was that there was something very badly wrong with the nation that my parents believed to be so great. This thought had not escaped Franklin D. Roosevelt, whose administration was involved in a frantic proliferation of expedients, very nearly all of which Father thought were crazy. Father's view (which history may very well confirm) was that the administration was wasting tax money on boondoggles, and that the men who accepted the busywork offered by the Works Progress Administration were a bunch of loafers. The fact that

66

some WPA workers *did* loaf on some jobs was apparent enough even to a thirteen-year-old, but the reason *why* they loafed was equally clear. It was because (*a*) they needed to stretch the job out as long as they could in order to achieve some sort of security and (*b*) they did not believe in the job in the first place.

A feeling of disbelief in every sort of value was surely in the air of the 1930s, and I think it profoundly important that my generation wandered through adolescence in such an atmosphere. A historian might say that the seeds of skeptical disillusion were sown among the corpses in the French mud during the Kaiser's war. He might trace the growth of doubt through the flapper and the hip flask hi-de-ho of the pointless 1920s. I can only say that the atmosphere of the 1930s was such as to encourage the adolescent's natural growth away from his parents, and that for a good many of us, this growth took the form of questioning practically every value that our parents endorsed. The rather obvious economic and moral collapse of the nation was everywhere evident, and this was brought to our attention at precisely the time of our dawning awareness. We were about to inherit a mess from our parents who had made it. Understandably enough, many of us were ready to listen to those who suggested that the world should be remade quite differently, and the time of the campus radical was now at hand. In high school and college there were those who argued that everything our parents believed in was wrong, and I, for one, was ready to listen to the new voices who sought to explain to me the reasons for my doubts.

4

Protest

THE PRINCIPAL LESSONS any school offers are those the students teach each other in the surreptitious forum of the adolescent underground. The value of any school may therefore be said to depend upon the qualities of those who attend it. In this regard, I was extremely fortunate, for my friends in high shool and college included homosexuals, Communists, nymphomaniacs, one full-blown Nazi who openly worshiped Hitler, a poet, various athletes, a Sicilian who carried a knife, a painter, a ballerina, a young scientist who went to college at age fourteen, three people who became professional writers, and a number of straightforward youngsters who had been Life or Eagle Scouts and who later were medical doctors, lawyers and engineers. What my friends had in common was the fact that they were all better informed and more intelligent than I was.

In addition to these souls, there were also cliques that led a social life, and a vast procession of ordinary spear-carriers. I drifted among the various groups, neither popular nor entirely unwelcome, playing games with the athletes, carrying a spear at times, looking in on one or another of the social sets, but being drawn more and more to the odd and the purposeful although I had no marked oddity or particular purpose of my own. Their developing differences, talents, ambitions and incessant arguments were attractive. They seemed willing enough to tolerate me as an audience and they gave me views of the world that I had not seen before. One of them—a girl who later became a writer—gave me a copy of Hemingway's *A Farewell to Arms.* The startling moral I drew from this was that if you did not like the system, you could always desert from it and strike out for yourself, although you would have to pay for whatever you did. I felt that Hemingway was a more certain guide than anyone else I had read, for the Hemingway hero was disillusioned, and so was I. So, I thought, were we all.

The disillusionment stemmed from the fact that nothing worked as it should. In school, for example, we learned one thing about the glories of democracy, while in New Jersey the practice of democracy was as malodorous as the sour industrial wasteland of the marshes beneath the Pulaski Skyway, wherefore the dirty little mayor of dirty little Jersey City could truthfully and openly say, "I am the law." It did nothing for us to reflect that Mayor Hague and President Franklin D. Roosevelt supported one another. It was disappointing to learn how great a distance there was between this American dream and the American fact.

Meanwhile, everything else one read in the newspapers every day bore out the cardinal impressions of my childhood: that the world was filled with vicious people, capricious disasters, stupid systems and wars. Within our own country there were bloody labor wars; the Ford Company security police force sent to hospital many of those workmen who tried to organize a union of Ford workers. Only slightly more subtle means characterized industry's conduct of labor relations in general. It was an age of company spies, agents provocateurs, company unions, blacklists and lock-outs. In the due course of events, a Bonus Army of veterans of the Kaiser's war had gone to Washington to ask for payment of a veterans' bonus, only to be thrown out of the city by Federal troops who burned the veterans' pitiful camp of huts and tents. As the 1930s wore on, and the Depression continued to deepen despite the Roosevelt administration's resort to make-work projects, doles, huge Federal construction programs, and practical grants to businesses and industries, so too did an economic and moral depression continue to deepen throughout the world overseas. In that foreign world, too, it seemed that there was a distance between dream and fact, and nothing worked as it should. One dream was that a League of Nations would guarantee peace, and the fact was that the world was full of marching warlords. We who were in school saw no one stop Mussolini's invasion of Ethiopia, the Japanese invasion of Manchuria, or Hitler's remilitarization of the Rhineland. We read of a disillusioned Russia's withdrawal from the League of Nations upon the Russians' discovery that no nation was willing to take the concept of collective security seriously and we were to watch major European nations use the Spanish Civil War as a testing ground for their weapons and tactics. There seemed to be no one to trust, and it was easy enough for me to generalize my observations about my parents, and the state of the nation, and the state of the world into a kind of adolescent suspicion of everything. So I began my own retreat from Caporetto, but mounted little counter-attacks along the way whenever I could. The first of these took the form of my refusal to read from the Bible or salute the flag during the morning opening exercises in high school. This infuriated one teacher and appalled some of my classmates, and both wanted to know why. I was delighted to explain.

I said I thought all religions were superstitious nonsense, but in any event the United States Constitution guaranteed separation of church and state, so that when the state made children read from the Bible, the state was illegally supporting religion. Next, since use of the Protestant Bible was insulting to both Catholics and Jews, the state was supporting one religion as opposed to others, which was far from the intent of any American law. Third, a public mumbling of some cryptic mumbo-jumbo out of context was scarcely religious in the first place, so that the whole affair failed both in its religious and in its legal aspects. Finally, I said, if this was a free country, I was exercising my freedom not to babble gibberish.

As for saluting the flag, I argued that a man was either patriotic or he was not, and if he was not, his saying that he was would not make him so, and his pledge would be a lie; that if he was patriotic, pledging to be so was insulting to his honor. In any case, 1 said, patriotism was not something that could be forced on anyone, and organized flag-saluting impressed me as being the kind of thing that went on in Hitler's Germany, not as the kind of thing that ought to happen in a nation of free men.

"You would be a capitalist in Russia, or a Communist in Germany, just to be different," a horrified classmate said, and at the time he was largely right. It was not only that I was finding it difficult to say Yes to things, but my dissent was darkening into a general contrariness. Like any adolescent Narcissus, I was dramatizing myself and falling more in love with myself, arguing to hear myself talk and taking a mordant joy in being the one who said No.

To be sure, there were many inviting targets. Apart from public affairs in the nation and abroad, which were a perpetual source of gallows humor, there were the everyday contradictions to be observed in school. If the school really believed in free speech, then why did the principal censor the school paper? How can you believe that the school insists that varsity athletes keep up their grade averages when it permits our All-State end to earn *his* academic credits in physical education and glee club—subjects for which no one else receives the same credit? How can you say that college football is played by students when the whole world knows it is played by hired ringers? And if you don't know this, then let me introduce you to boys on the team who have been offered money by college coaches. . . .

Obviously, no one can fight all the battles of the world all by himself with any hope of success. Nor can anyone but a Quixote or a martyr rationalize his lunacy into the guise of revealed truth, or consider his incessant defeats to be a series of victories. Unless the rebel is to lose his wits entirely, he needs to win a point now and again, and to have at least some people willing to listen to him. In this regard, it was lucky for me that some of my high school friends were as much out of step as I was. They provided the company beloved of misery.

I carried my contrariness off with me to college. I really did not much want to go. During the 1930s, the average American had no more than an eighth-grade education. There was no great pressure on youth to finish high school, much less go to college—except perhaps in homes like mine. Father made it clear that college attendence was like going to dancing class: it was simply one of the things that a gentleman had to do. "It is not what you learn, it is the friendships you make," he said.

What he meant was that in college you met people who would later give you their money in one way or another, such as by hiring you, or buying your goods, because you were such good friends. Inasmuch as I did not notice Father associating with any former college friends, or anyone giving him money as result of a collegiate friendship, I was not enormously impressed by his argument. Besides, what I wanted to do was to run away to sea and seek my fortune in what my friends and I called the real world. We were convinced that the worlds of East Orange and the campus were not real. But, lacking the courage to act out my fantasies, I went meekly off to college because there really was nothing else for me to do, and just as I had suspected, the University of Michigan was, for me, nothing more than a continuation of high school. The students were required to take a great many courses of study solely because someone thought these courses would in some way be good for them. After four years of this, the students would be given degrees. Like all systems, it was an insensate one. But, like all schools, Michigan contained students, and those I met were all drunk. They were drunk on words, on music, on form and color, and virtually all of them were political radicals.

The radicals were so much more alive than everyone else! They dressed in a fascinating assortment of incongruities that I now recognize to be the immemorial uniform of Bohemia. They wore their emotions as earnestly as they wore their sandals, workmen's shoes, peasant dirndls and corduroy trousers. Their essential temperament was that of the artist who must necessarily stand outside society in order to possess his different view. They somewhat

72

loudly paraded their differences. One of them, a small, dark-complexioned graduate student, was brilliant, profane, and claimed to be a whore's bastard, raised in a brothel. We all regarded him with proper awe. One local poet (well regarded then and today by literary critics) was a forthright homosexual who generously said he saw nothing wrong with other people having heterosexual relationships, but that he did not choose to engage in them himself. His point of view seemed sensible enough to me, for did he not have a right to try to live his own life in his own way? Did not we all? The girls said they believed in free love, although it turned out that none of them practiced it—at least, not with me. Still, such a profession of faith was encouraging; one could always hope that on the next date matters would proceed a bit further. As it was, matters on those dates proceeded much, much further than they did with the majority of girls, who wore sensible sweaters and skirts and joined sororities.

The rooms of the radical students were brightly different. The walls were filled with artistic productions of their own devising; there were books of unquestionable excellence, nearly all of which were to be found on the Catholic Index; the music was folk music or Stravinsky rather than Tommy Dorsey and Benny Goodman. They all looked down on the then popular music, although they danced to it. The swing of the 1930s was possibly the best dance music ever written, but the radicals made it quite clear that swing was merely a corruption of Negro jazz. They were knowledgeable in Negro slang, thought of themselves as hip, called the solid citizenry square, and wondered how many radio-network executives realized that the English translation of a popular song, "The Flat Foot Floogie with the Floy Floy" was "the broken-down whore with syphilis." They read Henry Miller at a time when his books had to be smuggled into the country, admired Picasso when most Americans had never heard of him (even though Picasso was then middle-aged), experimented with marijuana, and called themselves *avant-garde* to indicate they spoke French. I found marijuana disappointing (it would seem that I was either one of those on whom it has no effect, or that the cigarettes in fact contained no marijuana and everyone else had hypnotized himself into believing that they did), but I found everything else about Bohemia exciting. The evenings were always furious with argument; I agreed with the majority that age eighteen should be given both the bottle and the ballot, and that a university has no business trying to regulate the private lives of students in any way, nor should it dictate what studies they wished to pursue. Evenings in the rooms of other students were quite different. The rooms of the other students contained their college textbooks, college pennants, and boys who talked about girls and automobiles without knowing much about either.

Most of my new friends came from New York City and some of them were members of the Young Communist League. To a man, they were contemptuous of fraternity and sorority members, dismissing the lot of them as "fraternity morons"—a description that was only partly accurate. In turn, the fraternity boys wrote off the radicals as "a bunch of New York Jews," which again was only a partially correct description. In a time that seethed with political debate, I managed to exasperate both factions by writing a letter to the university newspaper, urging that every voice be heard. My Communist friends were particularly furious. They said they had thought I was intelligent, but now they saw me for what I really was: a politically naïve little rich boy; a good fellow, perhaps, but a fool. I had better come to their meetings, they said, to get politically straight.

During those years, the Communist Party claimed a membership of one hundred thousand Americans, and I see no reason to quarrel with that estimate inasmuch as the nation was deep in an economic swamp, and ready to listen to anyone who could point to a possible way out of it. It was a time of native fascists like the Silver Shirts; of a genuine Nazi Party that claimed some twenty thousand adherents in and around New York City; of Townsendites and Technocrats; Socialists and Trotskyites; of political parties of practically every description except Republican. The

74

Republicans were a bad joke. The Communists of the era were then cooperating with Roosevelt's New Deal and were urging all left-wing organizations to do likewise in order to create what they called a popular front. Their basic point was something that no one could deny: capitalism had failed. Their claim was that only the Communist Party could explain, scientifically, how this failure had come about, and that only their program was capable of building, scientifically, the one society that could create an equitable Golden Age in which there would never again be want or war. Their public program sounded plausible enough: they apparently endorsed the right of labor to organize, opposed racial discrimination, urged that production be planned and controlled, and said they believed in democracy. Not a few intellectuals agreed with all this. In fact, some of the brightest people I knew in college were proud of their membership in the Young Communist League, and out of respect for their brilliance, I began to go to their meetings.

It was the private face of Communism that was so lugubriously implausible. I discovered the adult leaders of the discussion groups to be sad, middle-aged men in shabby clothes who would laboriously try to explain what Marx had even more laboriously written. They said the Communist Party was the one party capable of leading the working class, and looking at these men, I could feel sorry for the working class if this was the leadership they were to enjoy. They spoke of leading the revolution of the proletariat, seriously imagining that there would be an armed uprising, and they explained that this revolution would be forced upon the working class by the capitalist bosses, because the bosses would not relinquish power if voted out of it, but would use the military and police forces to nullify the results of an unfavorable election. I was amazed that my bright friends could believe this, but I was absolutely stupefied when I heard them call one another "comrade" with all the solemn awkwardness of so many village bumpkins calling one another "brother" at a meeting of Odd Fellows. This was nothing, however, compared to my emotions when I heard them sing "The Red Army Machine Gunner's Song" at the end

75

of an educational meeting. They sang as earnestly as any group of Methodists baying a hymn, and I, who detested displays of patriotism toward my own country, was certainly not about to appreciate a display of patriotism for someone else's country. Nor was I drawn to the notion that the workers of the world had only to strike off their chains to inherit the world and make a universal soviet of the human race. First, I doubted that the workers of America had chains, and next, I was not willing to join the human race myself, and said so. My friends told me that I was simply ignorant, and that they could explain everything. They led me to a table piled high with books and pamphlets. These, they said, told the whole story: *Das Kapital, The Communist Manifesto, Ten Days That Shook the World,* the *Constitution of the USSR,* Engels on scientific versus Utopian socialism—these, and many more, were available at prices ranging from ten to fifty cents inasmuch as they had all been printed in the Soviet Union, where the book publishers did not make a profit out of the labor of helpless workers. The only profit would be made by the Communist Party in selling to me books the Communists had received as a gift from Russia.

The educational-meetings ended in a social hour to which everyone contributed his twenty-five cents for beer. All the girls made a point of dancing with the Negro boys. Oddly, there never seemed to be any Negro girls. The depressing dowdiness of the meeting places—dirty rooms in a cheap part of Ann Arbor assiduously chosen to create a proletarian atmosphere—and the utter seriousness of the instruction and the festivity, created the impression that the young people were an amateur theatrical troupe attempting to portray the reaction of a Central European village to the news of a cabbage blight.

Then there were the trips, so determinedly undertaken, to the Negro section of Detroit in order to demonstrate our solidarity with that unfortunate race. We would sit shrouded in smoke, drinking raw gin, listening to jazz, trying to convince ourselves that we were the Negroes' friends, that gin was a palatable drink, and that jazz was a responsible art form. We had only to enter a Negro drinking place and the happy noise would die down, and people would begin to leave. The only Negroes who spoke to us were what I believed to be beautiful dancing girls until they came to our table and proved to be male whores in drag.

In general, the Communist position with respect to racial discrimination was impeccable. They opposed it. More important, they did not practice it. But still, they forced themselves on people who did not want them and at the same time they advocated segregation, for it was—and is—Communist policy to create a Negro soviet in the American South when the revolution of the working class takes place.

There were many other inconsistencies. The appeal of the Young Communist League was not, therefore, particularly attractive either to the aesthetic or to the logical mind. Rather, its appeal was emotional, for the League was a kind of fraternity house for the estranged, complete with its own arcane passwords, special language, rituals, and religion. Like any other fraternity, its members held themselves to be better than anyone else. The very fact that the university faculty and the House Committee on Un-American Activities found Communists repulsive was a powerful inducement for the rebellious student to want to join the League.

Certainly this was true in my own case. For all that I was a dissident among the comrades, arguing with them in their meetings, I felt that the outside world's view of them was most unfair. At that time, the Communist Party was officially considered to be a political party like any other, which anyone had a right to join if he wished. But, having made this concession to political freedom, the adult world, in the form of the university authorities and the House committee and the Federal Bureau of Investigation then treated the Communists as if they were not just another political party, but a conspiracy traitorous to the United States. Indeed, the party was exactly such a conspiracy, although no one I knew in the Young Communist League conceived of himself as a conspiring traitor. The enemy of youth was not the United States of America, per se, but racial discrimination, nationalism, and capitalism. Radical youth did not believe there should be nations, or that there should be any race but the human one. The Communist Party was the only party that endorsed this point of view, and thereby it won the support of many idealists who might disagree with it on other grounds. Meantime, the young Communist league supported all the liberal causes on campus. They endorsed the nationwide students' strike for peace in 1937; they carried the signs that read THE YANKS AREN'T COMING, and, later, when Hitler invaded Poland and England went to war, the signs that said LET GOD SAVE THE KING. The League backed the formation of interracial cooperative boardinghouses for students, championed academic freedom, and contributed pickets to the embattled union lines at the nearby Ford factories. None of these actions was traitorous. League members also circulated petitions to have Communists' names put on the Michigan ballot forms, which was hardly either a clandestine or an illegal activity. My view of the comrades was that much they did was right; that many of their ideas were mine as well (such as my conviction that religion was nonsense); that they were a much brighter and more interesting group of people than any other group of students on campus; that if much of their love of Russia was as synthetic as it was uninformed, this was an innocuous absurdity; that inasmuch as their most vehement enemies were as grotesque as Chairman Martin Dies of the House committee, the Young Communists merited my support. I therefore applied for membership in the Young Communist League as a matter of principle.

The result was that I was shunned by both right and left.

The Communists turned me down on grounds that I was politically unreliable, and the university expelled me for precisely the same reason.

There was an amusing sequel: some two score of radical students were thrown out of school at the end of the academic year, although so far as I know, none of us had broken any laws, nor even any university regulations, and we were all in good academic standing. The school gave no reason for the dismissals; the form letter merely said, "It is the decision of the authorities that you not be readmitted." The university president was pressed for an explanation.

"Well," he began uncomfortably, "we don't want this school to be known as radical."

He paused, judiciously.

"Nor do we want it to be known as conservative," he broadmindedly said.

"Then I suppose you are also throwing the conservatives out?" one of us asked.

I laughed derisively with the rest, and the president was angry— angry at himself, I should now say, although at the time I thought he was angry with us for having exposed him as a traitor to academic freedom.

It would have been perfectly possible for me to be reinstated in Michigan on the promise not to associate with radicals, or to transfer to another university. I believe I was the only one of the expelled students who did not follow one course or the other. But so far as I was concerned, I did not care whether I ever saw the inside of another school. I had seen enough of them to believe they were all alike, and since I was not attracted by any of the learned professions, I saw little reason to spend three more years learning lessons in a glorified high school. At the same time, I was rather glad to have been expelled. It was as if someone had touched me on the shoulder and dubbed me knight. At last I was someone different. I had always thought this to be the case, and now here the world had agreed with me, attesting to my difference with a document bearing the arms of a university.

My parents seemed not to understand what a cuckoo had been hatched in their nest. Mother agreed with Father's belief that it had all been the university's fault: if Michigan had been doing its job, it would have never admitted radicals in the first place, so there would have been none on campus to seduce me. They believed this had been a lesson to me, and that I would know better than to let this sort of thing happen at the next college I attended. They had no knowledge of my intentions, which I confided to the girl who had given me Hemingway to read, and to certain other former high school classmates.

I told my friends I felt it was high time for me to stop maundering about in the Rotarian world of East Orange, and in the hypocritical world of the professor. I argued it was time to experience the real world that real people lived in. Therefore, I intended to work my way across the Pacific as a wiper in the engine room of a ship, and join that little band of international soldiers of fortune who then flew fighter aircraft against the Japanese in the pay of China. I would become a soldier of fortune and, like Hemingway, live a real life, the kind everyone wanted to lead but never did, and earn my living by writing of my adventures for the edification of those who were afraid to have adventures of their own.

One of my friends saw nothing wrong with this idea. Ralph and I decided to run away together to the war in China. As a first step, we stole a railroad map from the Newark Public Library. We did not feel like thieves. We reasoned that we were the only people in New Jersey who had a real need for a railroad map, because no one else would want to make his way across the country by riding freight trains.

Ah, well. We might have been wrong about that, because in the 1930s, running away from home by catching a freight was almost the conventional thing for the unconventional boy to do. Moreover, it was almost a socially acceptable thing for a boy to do. Our parents called this sort of thing "sowing wild oats," and said that boys needed to find themselves. They were confident that the fugitives would do so very shortly, and promptly return home.

And, echoing the conventional wisdom of his time, Father hopefully said that if a boy was not a Socialist at eighteen there was something wrong with his heart, but if he was still one at age twenty-five, there was something wrong with his head. Father's saying this indicated to me that his generation did not understand

80

the sweep and depth of radical youth's protest, which began with an almost total rejection of our parents' world—the world that was so demonstrably a failure.

Another point that escaped my parents was that the young radicals were serious. Indeed, my contemporaries are still seriously trying to build the Great Society that their then radical points of view began to suggest. For example, despite the current agony of the Negro people, there is nothing today like the thoroughgoing racial discrimination that my parents' generation practiced, and the reason there is not is that my generation of blacks and whites has been working for its abolition, whereas my parents' generation never did. If I may consider my generation to include all persons five years younger and five years older than myself, then I can say it was we, and not our parents, who pressed for an end to segregation in the public schools and set in train what has become the civil rights movement. It was our internationalism, and suspicion of nationalism, that helped to create the United Nations: it was our parents' generation who refused to enter the League of Nations. It was my generation, rather than our parents', who chiefly manned the New Deal offices and borrowed from Marx what seemed applicable to the American circumstance. Evidence that my youthful protest was not always uniquely my own may be seen in the case of the public school prayer. One of my exact contemporaries argued before the Surpreme Court for the abolition of such prayers, and his argument, and the Court's ruling adopted very much the same view that I had expressed as a high school freshman. I doubt that the issue would have been heard by the Court thirty years ago. I think it significant that the matter was raised by one of my contemporaries and argued by another.

In retrospect, I can easily see how far we have come in the past thirty years. Labor's battles are largely won. No one seriously opposes the concept of social security today, just as no one will seriously oppose the possession of civil rights by every citizen tomorrow. Today, anyone can buy Henry Miller's not particularly improving books in most major American cities, and the censors continue to lose one headquarters after another, as they inevitably must as more people agree with what we as college children said a long time ago: Freedom of press and speech cannot be limited. As with politics, so too the musical and artistic tastes of the *avant-garde* of the 1930s are the conventional, if not old-fashioned, tastes of the moment. Our youthful advocacy of free love is now quite commonly practiced by our own children who, by the way, pursue their amours much more openly than we. Looking ahead, I can see a time when our universities will no longer act *in loco parentis* to students any more than European universities do; to a time when the use of hallucigens will be standard procedure in psychoanalysis, and when the draft-card burner will be remembered not as a traitor but as having been instrumental in initiating a necessary revision in the Constitutional process for waging wars. The shape of the immediate future should be easy enough to extrapolate from the issues of the moment, for the facts of life seem to indicate that we spend our adult lives doing that which we were formed to do, or decided to do, in our youth.

In this connection, I would say that the movers and shakers of any tomorrow are always drawn from the *avant-garde* of any today. While it is generally true that nearly all American adolescents part company with their parents at some time in one way or another, most do so reluctantly, uncomfortably, and never venture far. While certain college youth today may seem most peculiar, the majority of contemporaneous youth are not spectacularly rebellious for the same good reason that the majority of youth of any generation have never been wildly far out. The reason is, most people are lumps. Huge numbers of college students are (as they have always been) the "conforming little time-servers" that one educator called them; a great many more will be those students who tacitly agree with the positions of their radical colleagues while not acting out a radical role themselves. In any case, revolutions are always instigated by minorities, and all revolutions are essentially protests that a canyon yawns between the way things are and the way things should be. The purpose of a revolution is to

82

close that gap. A revolution may hope to re-establish a prior state of things or move on to a new condition, but in either event it is an attempt to attain an ideal, and by definition, such attempts are never undertaken by those who are content with, or willing to put up with, the way things are. All changes in the human condition result from some protest; all progress stems from dissidence.

Nothing said here should indicate that there is always something good about the protestant or his ideas, or that the ideas that my generation's *avant-garde* espoused were in any way original with us. Our actions were merely the sum of our reactions to the world we entered; they represented the uses we chose to make of lumber that was lying around the premises when we arrived. In this sense, we did no more than any generation does, although it may be said that the ideas our *avant-garde* seized upon were indeed momentous (including, as they did, the ideas of Freud, Darwin and Marx), and that a high percentage of us were protestants (for the time clamored for departures), and that the changes we effected spread swiftly (thanks, in no small measure, to a concurrent and dramatic improvement in the means of communication), for ours was the first generation to be given the radio, the motion picture and the truly mass-circulation magazines.

I should say, too, that although my being dismissed from college may seem to indicate that I was one of the most wildly radical of our *avant-garde,* this was very far from the truth. I was, rather, one of the majority who agreed with the dissidents to a greater extent than I was willing to actively participate in all their crusades. A Communist friend of mine put the matter exactly (if not in a very flattering way) when, in a short story, he cast me as a character who put on and took off radical causes as if trying on new coats.

I suppose if I had been truly moved by man's fate in the 1930s I should have worked to become a labor leader, or gone to Washington to join the New Deal, or set up shop as a proletarian writer. But I did none of these things. My reaction was simply to run away from the whole mess, just as Hemingway's Frederic Henry did when he deserted the Italian army. I suppose that, had I such a boy today, my reaction now would be to pack him off to a psychiatrist for readjustment to society. In the 1930s, however, a confused boy could always catch a freight to spend a little time in self-analysis. As I have said, it was almost the conventional thing for the unconventional boy to do, and I was nothing if not conventionally unconventional.

5

Flight

RALPH AND I considered the possibility of police pursuit. We
briefly debated the advisability of disguises. We decided that the
wisest course was to try to postpone pursuit. To that end, we
would tell our parents that each had been invited by the other
boy's family to spend the summer in Michigan. We made our
secret plans, and one afternoon we uttered our little lies and
headed for the railroad yards. That evening, while our families
were no doubt discovering that neither owned a summer camp in
Michigan, we were already far from East Orange, clattering west
across America, bound for war in Chinese skies.

Two weeks later, America was still clacking past, but now there
was not a tree or house in sight. We slid the boxcar door wide
open at dawn to see a vast prairie, pale gold in the east, dark in the
west. Mountaintops shone above the shadows as they caught the
first light. We were lonely, stiff from sleeping on a jittering wooden
floor, cold, and tired of eating canned dog food. I have a clear
memory of that morning in the morning of my life, now more than
a quarter-century ago. I can see in mind's eye those empty distances, and feel again that emptiness inside me. I am certain that
Ralph was as fearful as I that day, but we did not admit our
misgivings to each other. That would have been almost as much an
admission of failure as returning home.

As we sat in the open doorway, watching the day brighten and
the Rockies draw slowly nearer, I reflected on the recent past. No
small part of the charm of running away from home lay in the

presumption that the world was full of dangers. Naturally, we were eager to encounter them. Nothing was more pleasant than to imagine returning home as bronzed soldiers of fortune, bearing interesting scars, and laden with the gifts of a grateful Chinese Government. En route to the wars we would, of course, slay the usual number of local dragons. We were not running away from life, but into it. We were sure that what we had left behind was lifeless. The New Jersey suburbs were pudgy with Buicks and Packards; with clean linen, toothbrushes, electric razors, the once-a-week sound of the maid running the vaccum cleaner, and the empty conversations of soft-bellied people who worked in offices and played bridge and went to Bermuda in the spring.

Our view of ourselves, now that we rode boxcars and rolled our own cigarettes, was that we were tough. We wore blue denims, and soot from the coal-burning trains was ground into our clothing and our skin. Our adolescent stubble was always three days old. The men we now met were, for the most part, illiterates. The only woman we had seen on the trains was a moron who was the chattel of a man who offered her to us for a dime each. One of the boys we had met was a male prostitute bound for Los Angeles. Two of the men in the gondola ahead of us looked to be thieves. There was no question about it: we were seeing Life. Unfortunately, it only too closely resembled the one we had left.

I could not help thinking, as we clacked along, that we knew two thieves at home. One was a member of Rotary; the other, a son of a respectable family who stole from the Woolworth counters. How was the man with the moron different from the parents who haunted summer hotels like Poland Springs in perpetual hope of selling their unattractive daughters into matrimony? In fact, was not even the best of marriages a form of prostitution? One of our high school classmates had been established in a New York apartment by a successful businessman. The difference between that boy and the one headed for Los Angeles was that one moved in wealthier—I almost said better—circles. I have said that Ralph and I were inwardly fearful, but I should make clear that what we most secretly feared was that life would prove to be not challenging but merely dull. In fact, we were finding it not only dull but dirty.

There were perils, but they were largely mechanical. For instance, one of our fellow passengers, an elderly nondescript, made the mistake of dozing in the sunlight near the forward edge of a boxcar roof. When the cars banged together as the fast freight began to brake, clattering down the long hill into Cheyenne, the first, sudden lurch tossed him forward, off the roof, and under the wheels, which rapidly and accurately bisected him. One night when Ralph and I sheltered from the rain in a sort of cave formed by overhanging boards piled on a flatcar, we narrowly escaped a similar fate when the load shifted as we rounded a curve. Stupidity, we realized, was lethal. But where were the vicious dangers with which the world was supposedly replete, and which the newspapers so faithfully reported? Specifically, where were the toughs and murderers who, in the public mind, so thickly populated the hobo jungles and the Hoovervilles?

We met none. The well-fed burghers of our parents' acquaintance, to whom the Depression was more of a nuisance than a catastrophe, regarded the scarecrows as dubiously as a French marquis might have looked on a Parisian mob in 1790, but they were wrong. My Communist friends regarded the defeated as the potential heroes of a glorious revolution of the proletariat, but they were wrong, too. At least in the West, the hobo jungles were unofficial public campsites tenanted by a slowly changing population of migrants down on their luck, but who, far from revolutionary, shared the American optimism that things would soon get better, and that in America, each man was free to make what he could of himself. Feeling a need for government, these men formed their own. Many were veterans of the Kaiser's war, and in camp after camp former sergeants were elected or appointed leaders. They greeted new arrivals, assigned them huts or sleeping spaces, and

87

explained the rules: *No fighting, thieves get beat up, you keep your place clean. And remember, try to bring back something for chow. Everybody brings something for chow.*

In the America of that time and place, everyone understood everyone else's problem, because it was his own. If a man could not find work in one town, he tried another. Having no money to spend for transportation, he thumbed rides (which those who had automobiles were glad to offer), or he hopped a freight (while the brakemen looked the other way). The people on the road were not derelicts. The derelicts, then as now, lived in the Skid Rows of our cities, animals as urban as pigeons. All the men and boys on the road, however modest their abilities and backgrounds, were looking for work. Some were bindlestiffs who had known nothing all their lives except stoop labor, moving forever from harvest to harvest. Others were genuine hobos—men who could work at nearly any trade, but whose free choice it was to hold no job long. All hobos said they intended to settle down someday, but not just yet. There was still a lot of country they wanted to see first. With rare exceptions, we met none but friends. Perhaps it is true that in good times no one takes to the road but the bad, but in our bad times we met virtually none but the good.

Ralph and I looked for jobs whenever the trains stopped on our way through the Midwest, and while we found none, there were always housewives who would put their cares aside to consider ours. In small towns everyone knew the train schedules, and we would be told, "Gracious, there *is* some work I do want done, but you boys won't have time for it before the train leaves, so why don't you just sit down and I'll try to find something in the icebox." Often as not, they would also give us a package of food to take to the train.

It was disappointing to be welcomed everywhere, when it was so important to us to learn whether or not we could make our unaided way through a violent world. Of course, we heard that the railroad detectives were the sadistic enemies of the tramp. We heard they loved nothing more than to beat a defenseless man insensible and toss his body on an outbound freight. The most famous of these detectives was one Green River Slim. Alas, we never saw a yard detective, and Green River Slim turned out to be just as imaginary, and as ubiquitous, as that other great American whose name was found chalked upon a thousand boxcars (and who would later go to Hitler's war)—Kilroy.

In retrospect it is clear to me that Ralph and I were the only people of our acquaintance on the road who were dangerous. We were looking for trouble; everyone else was looking for work. Our ambition was to prove to the world how tough we were. Nobody seemed to view us in just this light except, perhaps, a toothless old wreck with a breath like a vulture's, who accosted us outside a Skid Row bar.

"Want to see how hard you can hit?" he asked us. "Gimmie a quarter, I'll let you hit me. See can you knock me out."

He followed us for nearly a block, pleading, promising not to hit back, flattering us, and finally, when he saw it was no use, cursing. Looking back on it, I think we fled from him.

Novelty, rather than true discovery, entertained us to the foot-hills of the Rockies. It would be years before I learned the truth of Montaigne's remark that the traveler must take himself wherever he goes. Yet I do remember that our first sight of those mountains seemed a mockery; I remember the feeling of emptiness they created inside me. In themselves they were an enormous fact, and consideration of one fact led to a consideration of others. One was that no one wanted us to do anything for him except leave town; people were glad to help us on our way. Another was that we had nothing to offer anyone except manual labor, which was not in demand, or our money, which was. We had left home with two hundred dollars between us, all saved from the unearned money our parents had allowed us. It had cost us twenty dollars to purchase blankets, denims, work shoes and sufficient dog food to carry us to South Dakota. Canned dog food recommended itself to us as the cheapest comestible to be had. It constituted a balanced diet, and was rather tasty—at first. The meals donated by housewives were occasional banquets, but as the trains rolled farther west and the towns thinned out, dog food became our staple, and it seemed that we might have to consume another one hundred eighty dollars' worth of it if we could not immediately find a ship for China. I now suspect that what caused my feeling of emptiness was a premonition that one could not live without money, but that no one could earn money save at the loss of one's freedom. The world seemed a jail.

In the high Rockies, two boys our age boarded the train. One was a Chinese-American from Fresno; the other, a Russian-American from Los Angeles. They had gone adventuring to the East Coast and now were returning to California; the Russian to join the United States Army and the Chinese to rejoin his family's gambling house where he would run a dice table. We told them of our plans, and they decided to come along with us instead. In that moment we became an army, and the world brightened considerably. By the alchemy of a dream, the mountains' vast sterility was transformed into magnificence. We would sort the facts of life to suit ourselves. Crossing the Pacific would be no problem. Everyone knew that boys could get jobs as wipers in engine rooms to work a passage. Boys had been running away to sea for centuries. We had only to find a ship that needed four wipers.

Before it was over, we must have walked the docks of every port on the West Coast—including those of minor fishing towns. *Were we members of the union?* No. *Let me see your identification papers.* We had none. *Do you have passports?* Passports?

We went to the union offices. *Buddy, we got three thousand guys on the beach, and every single one of them is an Able Seaman.*

Ralph and I, blue-eyed and blond, went to Scandinavian shipping companies, saying, "Ay bane Swade. Ay yust want ship home." And they laughed and said they were sorry.

We persisted until it was clear to us that the only way we could cross the Pacific would be to stow away, or to steal a boat, and then someone told us the truth about the volunteer fliers in

China. It seemed that the volunteers were not just anyone, but were carefully selected pilots from the ranks of the United States Army, Navy, and Marine Corps. When we heard that, we went to the recruiting offices, only to be told that we would need at least two years of college credits to qualify for the aviation-cadet programs. At this point, we all went down to Fresno to think things over.

College was out of the question for our Chinese and Russian friends, but Ralph and I had only to ask to go, and our parents would gladly send us. In Fresno, I began to see the fallacy of our position: our confidence in ourselves had all along been based on the assumption that we were different from all other men; not on the slightest feeling of identity with mankind. This could not be helped; we were what our first eighteen years had made us. At any moment we could have walked out of the shacks of the hobo jungle to the nearest telegraph office, and hours later been dressed in decent clothes, sitting down to the best dinner in the best hotel of whatever town it was, while a hotel clerk booked reservations for us on the next Pullman headed for New Jersey. A principal difference between us and all others was, as Smollett would say, wholly matter-money. I suppose in the back of our minds we had always known this, and it was the source of our strength and the source of our great weakness: it helped us to hold something back in our relationships with others; helped to keep us from identifying with them; thus a barrier, built of dollars, helped to shut us off from the kindness of Midwestern housewives, from the radicals I had known at Michigan, and from our Chinese and Russian traveling companions.

I do not mean to say that I worked all this out in so many words at eighteen, sitting at the bar of a tacky, one-story gambling house in Fresno, watching Chinese playing poker and Americans shooting craps. I simply mean that I was then dimly but uneasily aware of what I am now saying. Today, I would add that the America of the moment is very much like the boy I was then—sealed off from the world by its romantic dream of itself, by its strength, by its desire to be violent, and by its dollars. But at age eighteen, sitting at a bar in a gambling hall, full of doubts and disappointments imperfectly understood, and of abilities as yet unperceived, my first need was for rationalizations.

Ralph and I wondered aloud whether going back home to college would not be an admission of defeat, but we managed to convince ourselves that the *only* path to war in Chinese skies led through two years of college followed by an aviation-cadet program. This decided, we broke what had been a summer-long silence and wrote our first letters home.

The immediate answer was a large check, which we expected, and the utterly demoralizing news—which we had not expected at all—that our parents, confident that we would get over our silliness, had already entered us in colleges for the fall term. It seemed that my Father had gone to Michigan, extracted from them a transcript of my grades that did not mention my expulsion, and had arranged for me to enter the University of Pennsylvania.

Our parents' casual certainty about us was infuriating. We therefore determined upon one final gesture that would restore to us something of our romantic view of ourselves as hard, tough men. Our Chinese friend had a motorcycle. If he would let us borrow it, we would ride it east and send it back to him. Ralph's father owned a manufacturing concern (Ralph showed our friend the company letterhead) and Ralph would have the shipping department crate the motorcycle and send it back.

Oddly enough, the Chinese boy agreed. Perhaps he was intrigued by our idea of trying to drive across the continent without stopping except for gasoline. We all wondered if anyone had done this before; if it really could be done; if so, in how little time. So we were taught how to start and stop the thing, and we bought a pillow in a five-and-ten-cent store to wire onto the back fender to form a seat for the one who would not be driving. With that, we shook hands and went blasting out of Fresno forever, learning how to ride a motorcycle as we went.

We raced furiously to Sacramento; scuttered over the mountains and into Reno with our backsides beginning to turn black and blue. We sped across the salt flats; paused for gasoline, coffee and a bottle of whisky at a Wyoming town where all three were sold at the town's one store. Our headlights, at ninety miles an hour, suddenly illuminated white-faced Herefords wandering across an open range in Montana and we went off the road to avoid them, shouting and scattering gravel and cattle; somehow wobbled back onto the road again and out of the herd. We gradually drew closer to what we believed to be the lights of a town, shining far ahead in the clear Western distances, only to realize at last that, in our grogginess, we were creeping nearer and nearer to the tailgate of an enormous, brightly lighted trailer truck. We drank black coffee at the next gas pump; black coffee laced with whisky. We fell asleep rounding a curve in Iowa. I remember seeing a shower of sparks, and eventually realizing they were caused by the foot peg grinding along the pavement while centrifugal force and a banked curve were keeping us alive. I shouted to Ralph to stop trying to show off, and he woke up suddenly, caught himself, and swerved back to our own side of the road.

Eighty hours after leaving Fresno we were streaking along the new Pennsylvania Turnpike at night, with a police car moaning after us. They did not arrest us. They merely wanted us to know that the road was not yet open; that a thousand yards ahead was a place where a bridge would be, when it was built. When we reached New Jersey we slept for two days, and it was some days later before the swelling left our hands and arms and the bruises faded from our buttocks.

Then, having nothing better to do, we went to our different colleges, and I never saw Ralph again.

I should say that the venture was about par for youth's course. We seem to have gone through the motorcycle phase about on schedule. Girls of twelve like horses, and boys of eighteen ride motorcycles. At about the time it is customary to do so, we had been cruel to our parents. As is customary for parents, ours had waited patiently for us to need them again. And, being children, we had not got far on our first lurch out of the nest. All that we had really done was spend an aimless summer—or so it might seem from an adult point of view.

I prefer, however, to regard that summer's flight as one central event of my life, and when I obediently trudged back to school I looked upon the collegiate experience with different eyes. For one thing, I had lost all appetite for causes that were not truly my own. For another, there may have been some interesting students at the University of Pennsylvania, but I did not seek them out. This time, I felt more estranged than ever. All I saw about me were the tame children who would unquestionably and unquestioningly evolve into the lawyers, doctors, engineers and insurance salesmen who would play bridge and make no-conversation in suburbia. I made friends with none of them. They joined fraternities, cheered Penn's professional football team, did their homework, earned their grades, went to the dances and swung and swayed with Sammy Kaye while I, in my arrogant innocence, looked derisively on all this from an outside world. I was six thousand miles by boxcar and motorcycle apart from them even while sitting in Franklin Field with them or attending classes. I knew that we were different, and they did, too. Just to be sure they knew, I roiled my own cigarettes and dressed in sooty denim pants.

Looking back on it now, it seems odd to say that I felt such a difference between myself and the college children, particularly when I have indicated that, in a formless way, I had begun to suspect that the artificial differences between one man and another are inconsequential when compared with the similarities that unite them. Moreover, I was now back among what presumably was my own kind. Why then the studied insolence of the Bull Durham and the dirty Levis?

I suppose, now, that the pose and the costume was my way of saying to the other collegians, "You know nothing about it." I would audit an economics class, and the others would brightly chatter with the young doctoral student who was their instructor, not mine, and I would slump back in my chair with my hands in

94

my pockets, angry and silent, hearing nothing of this footless patter of cyclical depressions. Instead, I would again see in my memory's eye a Colorado filling-station door open, and a woman in a man's coat and hat emerge, a scarf wrapped around her nose and mouth to keep out the driving dust. She would wad another protective rag around the nozzle of the hose and the opening of the gas tank to put two dollars' worth of gasoline into a wretched jalopy crowded with an empty-faced family of spindly children and bearing on its roof rug-wrapped bundles and the flat steel web of a cheap double bed, and I would hear (again) the man ask whether, instead of paying the money, he could stay and work for two days. Marx could no more explain this tableau than the young doctoral student could.

An *ad hominem* approach to Economics 201A was not a certain path to success in the subject, but it had been a long time, now, since I had stopped believing that acquiring an education and earning grades were even remotely related. The collegiate world of parents, teachers and students still thought they were. The feeling grew on me that no one in college, including the smug young instructors with the Phi Beta Kappa keys, knew what the devil he was talking about; that they were all playing at an intellectual game that insulted the dignity of experience—just as the Michigan radicals had been doing in their own way.

At the time I sat moody, angry and bored in college, feeling trapped by moths, I could not have put all these thoughts into so many words. At nineteen, I had only the unexpressed knowledge, sitting silent inside me, that there was no place for me then, or perhaps ever, in any world I did not make for myself. Indeed, in retrospect, this seems to have been the cardinal lesson of the summer's trip. It has been seen that Ralph and I had failed to make our dream come true; that our first young search for the stuff of life proved only that we were not at home in either the suburban or the proletarian worlds. Nor was I at home in either the political or the academic world. In fact, I would never be at home in any patterned world. No one ever is. No matter how much we may outwardly share with all mankind, our true distance from our neighbor becomes apparent when we at length discover the unexplored darkness within ourselves, and begin to understand that he who travels furthest and fastest into this darkness must travel alone; that no one can really help him; that the ultimate destination of every traveler is always himself, and that not until he has discovered something of himself can he offer anything to others.

An intimation of this void within me was the one great thing the summer trip had given me. It was my first, urgent warning to get to work to try to fill it; my first inkling that any claim to identity would be entirely determined by my experience of myself and what use I should make of what I discovered. The thought began to bear in upon me during that second year in college. Going back to school was not so much a return to society as it was retirement to a neutral corner wherein I could mull over the meanings of my first experiences. As far as school was concerned, I took no interest at all in what happened when you applied electricity to a dead frog's nervous system, nor did I care to speculate as to the effect on the nation of the Federalist papers. I attended two English courses I liked, skipped two required courses that were boring beyond belief, and wandered about the university auditing various courses in which I was not registered, to see if by chance anything might be going on in them. I was not in college for a purpose. I was not really spending the year there in order to qualify for military pilot training. Flying in China's skies had been a pipe dream all along, said more to impress a girl than for any other reason, but, once announced as an ambition, it had served as an excuse for running away. I could see this now, for if I had really wished to be a military pilot, I had only to go to Canada, where the Royal Canadian Air Force was welcoming volunteers for Hitler's war. I really did not think often about the war in Europe, nor can I remember it as being in the forefront of anyone's mind except the pacifists'.

It was odd how people thought less and less about the war as it came closer to us. In earlier school years there had been a great to-do about the Japanese invasion of China, and in 1940 there was a great period of mourning for fallen France and a great gathering of Bundles for Britain on the Eastern seaboard, while an isolationist movement called America First swept the Midwest. But, despite these different public enthusiasms and the daily war headlines, I distinctly remember that a kind of national apathy deepened as our own time drew near. It was as if we did not wish to think about going to the dentist. Certainly we in college knew that we would enter the war, and that we would have to do the fighting. For the first time in our history, the nation had a military conscription without being in a state of war, and no one really believed Franklin Roosevelt's promise that not one American boy would fight overseas. But we did not think about what we did believe. We read the newspapers as if they were reporting on events in another world. It was very strange. We all assumed there would be war, and we all trusted that there never would. We also assumed that when we did get into it, we would win, because America always wins all her wars. One newspaper printed an article proving how we could defeat Japan in sixty days.

But I felt as detached from all this as I felt detached from the college. To me, reality was not an approaching war but the whistle of a freight train at night, and I wondered what it meant. As I sat in class I could hear the deep tones of foghorns in the mists of the northwestern coast and some part of me was still sweating at unloading watermelons from a truck in Portland; I was still shivering atop a cattle car in the winds driving through the snow-covered high passes of the Rockies. There was and is still, in whoever I am, the wink of campfires in hobo jungles and the sight of a drunken man jumping across a fire and someone hitting him with a railroad spike and him falling into the fire. I can still see the lights of San Francisco and of Alcatraz from Coit Tower, and the delicate faces of the Chinese girls that our young gambler had found for us. I had a memory of walking the docks in the rain in Seattle, and of sleepless nights in fumigated blankets in flophouses run by the Gospel Mission; of the Western badlands creeping past and a hawk stooping on a gopher. Most clearly, I

97

saw and can still see the faces of hopeful men who would never know anything other than disappointment, and the burst of spray against the rocks and among the tidal pools of Monterey. I remembered lying on rattling floorboards at night, wondering whether I would wind up in jail, or whether any girl would ever want to marry me, and if I would ever see my family again. I have many memories, as acute today as they were in that college year, although they are not now so clamorous for explanation. I was not sure what my experiences meant when I was sitting in college, but I was at least certain that I was whoever my experiences made me, and that I would become whatever I could find within myself.

As one might suppose—given a student who followed a curriculum all his own—the dean of the college had two words to say to me at the end of the academic year. He said I would have to go to summer school to make up the required work I had not done in the courses I had not attended. I told him that my going to college was really my parents' idea, not mine. I told him I was sorry to have wasted the college's time, and my own, but that I had no intention of ever returning to a school.

The dean was a large, tough, rather kindly man. Rumor had it that he had been an Army chaplain in the Kaiser's war, and he looked as if he might have been one. He began to speak in terms of waste, loss and opportunities being thrown rashly away by uninformed boys. I felt sorry for him: he had to say these things. He said he was thinking of my good. I told him our interests were identical: I was thinking of nothing else, myself. I had no more *reason* to leave college than I had to attend it. But what I did have was a profound *feeling* that I had to leave. It was quite inexplicable, this feeling, but nonetheless quite real. Today I should say that a great problem with colleges is that they are each operated for the greatest good of their greatest number of scholars, but at that time I was not inclined to be so charitable. The greatest number of scholars did not include me, nor for that matter, most college students, for very few who go to college are seriously interested in scholarship as defined by the system. Most students go to college

98

because there is no other socially acceptable place for intelligent adolescents in America.

I went to work at night as a copyboy on a Philadelphia newspaper. The job was fetching coffee in paper cups from an all-night cheap restaurant on a dark asphalt street, and carrying it back into a large room where men in shirtsleeves sat smoking cigarettes under overhead lights; a clickety of typewriters, ding, zip, clickety-clickety; an endless rattle of teletype machines; the cigar of the city editor wet, chewed and unsmoked in the wastebasket; high principle brought to the resale of gossip and hearsay; a constant demonstration of the utter formlessness of life. Less space in the newspaper was devoted to the war than to advertisements for underwear. The column devoted to astrology (today, Sagittarius, you should take advantage of your opportunities as you sweep the factory floor) was longer and more widely read than any editorial. I handed coffee to men and ripped yellow strips from the rattling teletypes and handed these to desks that variously concerned themselves with motion picture actresses, race horses, and slaughtered armies. For these services I received sixteen dollars a week (the times having vastly improved) and much of these funds financed conversations I cannot remember with people whose faces I cannot recall in taverns I cannot describe other than to say that they were all dark rooms and that in some of them girls undressed as they danced on the tops of the bars.

This was experience, but was it Life? This was what it meant to have a job and so pay one's way in the world? Where *was* the world? Where were all the worlds of Eliot, Joyce, Conrad and Hemingway? Those worlds were all in their heads, of course, but at twenty I thought such worlds actually existed and that the writers had been describing them, and that it was the world that *I* inhabited that was unreal.

Three weeks passed on the job and no one asked me to become the editor of the newspaper.

I left a brief note on the editor's desk, to the effect that I would send him some articles from Asia some day, and went back to my apartment, wrote a note to my parents, stuffed some clothes into a haversack, and walked back to the freight yards, once again bound west across America, but this time truly alone at last. It is impossible to say what a prolonged wandering might have made of me, because the following winter the war arrived to put an end to everything but its own demands. Together with thirteen million other young Americans, I spent the remainder of my most formative years in uniform.

6

War

THE LINE of helmeted men entered a pier shed, where it doubled back and forth upon itself like an anchor chain flaked out on a deck, and it disappeared, finally, into a canvas-covered gangway that presumably led to the ship we could not see. Each of us carried two blue barracks bags that contained all our worldly goods, including the winter uniforms that would be so useful to us in the tropics. The bags were marked A and B. The A bag contained what we might need, and the B bag contained everything the Army had given us that we had never needed, and never would. We pushed these bags ahead of us, or dragged them over the concrete pier as the line inched toward the gangway, hour after hour, each man in the line moving from one end of the shed to the other and back and forth again and again before he could say Yo to his name and, shouldering one bag and dragging the other, move up the gangway into the steel dusk of the ship. We stood in line down an infinity of ladders, arriving at last somewhere deep below the water line and well into the bow, beside our appointed cots. The cots were suspended from tubular steel pipes in double stacks. Each stack was three cots high, with fourteen inches vertical clearance, two inches horizontal clearance, and each double stack was separated from the other by eighteen-inch corridors. Someone said the converted passenger liner carried fifteen thousand men, and I could believe it. There was absolutely nothing to do but lie on the cots or stand in the narrow corridors between them. There was nothing to see except the steel hull and the cots and the men, and the only illumination was provided by low-wattage overhead electric lamps. We had each been provided with emergency rations for six days, and for lack of anything else to do, we ate them.

Hours later, we felt the ship move. We learned that we would pass under San Francisco's Golden Gate bridge. It would have been good to see it. We knew we must have passed under it, and out of the harbor, when in our close, sweat-smelling and dull-lit bow hold, we felt the steel deck press up against our feet and then drop down away from underneath us, and we braced ourselves for the heavy-sounding crash of the bow falling into and shearing the sea. Then we began to roll as well as pitch. There is always a confused sea off the San Francisco harbor and the excellent advertisements of the Matson Line, showing happy, suntanned, well-fed prosperous people in bathing suits and bright sports clothing having drinks served by smiling white-jacked mess attendants about a sunny deck swimming pool never quite prepare the traveler for the facts of that first day and a half out of San Francisco. I am a fairly good sailor, but it was a relief to me when the order came to form a line to move to the mess hall amidships. There, the motion would be less pronounced.

The fare was chili con carne, an apple, and a bar of vanilla ice cream encased in chocolate. There was a clear yellow grease that sloshed back and forth across the surface of the chili, and we hung onto the edges of the mess tables with one hand as we stood up to our meals. There were neither benches nor chairs. Not everyone got the food down, and I appropriated the apples of diners who hurriedly left. By the time I returned from this feast, there was a heavy odor in our hold. Its source was the adjacent bow latrine, or head as the Navy called it—a womb-dark room vaguely lit by small blood-red lamps, its steel deck not quite two inches awash in surging urine and vomit. We were told that we would be twenty-eight days at sea, and that twice a day we would be fed, and that twice a day we would be permitted on deck for fifteen minutes at a time. I lay on my cot breathing the odors of our hold and considered the fact that this day of departure was my second wedding

102

anniversary. I shall presently discuss the circumstances of my marriage; at this point, I wish to say that it felt odd to be married, because a troop ship and marriage have nothing in common. At the time, I merely reflected upon my accommodations and decided to make a small change in the Army's plans for my Pacific cruise.

The following morning, when we were first allowed our fifteen-minute turn on deck, I did not rejoin my unit when it formed a line to climb down the ladders back to our quarters. Instead, I stepped into a line that was coming up from the holds for its first turn on deck. Every quarter hour I kept rejoining the lines of arrivals, and with the exception of two occasions each day, when I would join those lines descending for food, I managed to pass each entire day on deck, depending upon the fact that the Army always presumes that everyone is where he is because someone has ordered him to be there. Sure enough, no one ever questioned me. On fine nights I rolled into a blanket beneath a lifeboat, and the Navy deck crews never bothered me. The Navy knew how the men lived in the holds.

For four weeks I traveled with the Army, but somewhat apart from it, across the slow-heaving and uncaring Pacific. We saw nothing of the war on that long passage. In fact, we never saw another ship. Ours did not travel in a convoy, but plowed back and forth alone across the ocean, depending upon its speed for security against Japanese submarines. I felt as lonely as the ship. I was not traveling with a self-contained combat unit, but was a part of something called a "casual unit"—a phrase that was exactly descriptive. We were a random collection of reinforcements destined, after arrival in New Guinea, to be distributed among Air Force and ground forces organizations in scattered parts of the Southwest Pacific Area theater of operations. We had never seen one another before being collected to board the ship, and we would never see one another after we left it. It seemed to me that life itself was nothing more than a trip undertaken by a casual unit, and that the Army was a small, precise mirror of life. In the Army you were moved about by forces you could neither control nor particularly affect, and wherever you went you met a number of people and made friends, and then your friends were moved away or you were, and you never saw them again, but made new friends with the next people you met, knowing these friendships would all be ephemeral. In this sense, it was not much different from moving from school to school, always being the new boy. It was interesting to consider that, once you left a place, whatever went on at that place continued to go on without you as if you had never been there, just as it had been going on without you before you had gone there, and that wherever you went, you had only to do whatever the thing was that everyone else was doing there.

For example, while I drifted across an ocean on one side of the world, people in Philadelphia were standing at the Chelten Avenue station of the Chestnut Hill local, waiting for the train that would take them to their offices. Had I been one of the commuters, and had one of them taken my place aboard the ship, the world would not have noticed the difference. We were each members of casual units, and so were the Stone Age primitives who knew not what to make of the fantastic events taking place in their New Guinea jungle; so were the executioners and the men and women shuffling in their lines toward the gas ovens in German extermination camps; so were the workers in the munitions factories in England and the old gentlemen in New York's Union League Club and Mr. and Mrs. North and South America and all the people on all the ships at sea and everyone else who was going to press in a flash.

Whatever anyone did no doubt seemed terribly important to him at the moment: the British machine gunner firing at Rommel's troops; the next Jew in line outside the fatal door; Rosie the Riveter opening her lunch box; the Parisian gamin chalking a V on a wall; the stockbroker boarding the commuter train and the men playing poker on a tarpaulin hatch cover—all these people were prisoners of their immediate moment and circumstance and any of them could have changed places with any other, Rosie included, and it would have made no difference to the world, or to the conduct of the war which, once begun, obeyed abstract rules of its own as if it were not waged by men.

The impressive thing was, each human life was objectively unimportant; in the Army's word, expendable. The only things that were of objective importance—and only then in terms of the intricate social games the world played—were the arbitrary demands of the various tasks. But who did the job was never important: if you did not do it, or were killed trying to do it, the world would not care. Another expendable casual would take your place, for in society people are interchangeable parts. In sum, it began to be clear to me as I spent otherwise empty hours at a ship's rail, watching flying fish scutter across the slow sea hills, that it did not really matter what anyone did in life, and that the present moment is the only one any of us can ever know. If you wished to shoot a storm trooper and so save some grandmother from incineration, or if you were a storm trooper and wished to stuff someone's grandmother into an oven, or if you were the grandmother involved, your actions and emotions were all inconsequential when seen from the aspect of eternity. Who the devil will care when the sun explodes and our galaxy winks out? The only things that are important are whatever values you wish to ascribe to whatever tasks you set for yourself in the ephemeral moment. Such, I would say, is the liberating philosophy of our time, to which we have been lifted, or reduced, by our science and the circumstances of our technological society. The circumstances of our society in this century have been, of course, those of constant war, which our science has served marvelously well.

There was time, there was nothing else but time, to reflect on such matters during the four weeks of our seafaring to the island where we were having the war. Time is the greatest gift the Army gives the soldier, for even when he is not simply sitting on a ship for a month, the soldier has very little to do. For example, the Army told me what to eat and when to eat it, what to wear and when to wear it, when to go to bed, when to get up, how to act upon every sort of occasion, what to do at any moment, and whom to shoot. It cared for all my bodily needs, gave me a little money to spend on beer, cloaked me in perfect anonymity, and set me tasks that were so well defined and simple that I had a luxury of time in which to reflect upon my recent experiences and speculate about whatever sort of man I might be capable of becoming.

In fact, I had found a home in the Army. There is an old Army joke about how a recruit will find a home in the Army, where every day is like Sunday on the farm, but it is one of those jokes that are more true than funny. I recommend the Army for all alienated boys who are in search of themselves. Perhaps it is possible for a confused young man to come to terms with the world in some other situation, but the Army makes the process easier because it takes care of all his essential needs while he does so. For me, enlisting was something like being born again. The Army took all my clothes away and sheared my scalp. I joined a line of naked men to be examined and measured and fingerprinted, and inoculated against all manner of diseases. In the course of this stripping and shearing, the Army destroyed all barriers between one man and another; wiped away all pasts and former conditions; did away with thoughts of college, jobs, aimless drifting, girls, worries, doubts, fears, ambitions. Next, the Army thrust all of us recruits beneath the level of manhood by dressing us like clowns. I sometimes think that the Army general staff deliberately designed the fatigue uniform to destroy anyone's pride in his personal appearance. A fatigue uniform is a sloppy two-piece suit of work clothes, and when I entered the Army it meant a pair of blue denim pants and a blue denim jacket, and a blue denim hat with a wide floppy brim. It was a uniform for a scarecrow, and the supply sergeants, no doubt reflecting the wishes of the genius on the general staff who had designed this thing, issued it in two sizes: too small or too large. Clad in an outrage, a man could only aspire to something better. Meanwhile he could see himself and his fellows with different eyes. The rule that so soon became apparent was, if a man looked well in fatigue clothes, it was because he belonged in clothing like that, and therefore had something badly wrong with him.

The Army's next contribution was delivered by my infantry drill sergeant who set matters right on first acquaintance:

"I want to tell you men this one thing: If you play ball with the Army, I guarantee you that the Army—[he paused]—will break the bat off in your ass!"

We all laughed, as he expected us to, at this switch on the cliché, but he was seriously expressing a profound truth: it is the Army, and not whatever nation the Army happens to be fighting when you enter it, that is the first enemy of the soldier. The Army is, after all, an authoritarian society insistent on its own peculiar needs, wherein all the members of the society have a functional significance, and in this it resembles an absolute monarchy, a fascism, a Communist dictatorship of the proletariat, or a huge business corporation. The last vestiges of any Marxist enthusiam I may have felt for planned societies disappeared in the Army. The rule I discovered in training camp was that *all* organizations of men are potentially the enemies of man, and that the larger they are, and the more highly organized and efficient they are, the more terrorized, limited, and less consequential are the men in them. In all the years since my first Army days I have never had reason to believe otherwise but, rather, have found additional evidence to support this opinion as administration increasingly becomes the mode of human existence.

But, I found a home. Our home was a two-story barracks; it was our shared experience; it was something more. No one has ever satisfactorily explained what the word "home" means. It seems to stand for a kind of magic composed of familiarity, security, a sense of well-being, and other difficult-to-describe concepts. I can only say that home, to the soldier, is first of all his cot. It is somehow different from all other cots: it is his; it has his odor; it is the place where he sleeps; the place where he is alone. On it, hung from it and at the foot of it are all his possessions. Next, home to the soldier is the barracks floor on which his cot stands—particularly the area immediately adjacent to his cot, and his closest

107

relatives are the two soldiers to either side of him. The other men in his platoon, who also have their cots on the same barracks floor, are his second next of kin. Family cousins are the men of the other platoon on the other floor of the two-story barracks. It would seem that all men need to create the special, indefinable magic that is the ethos of a home, and you could see the home-building process at work on those occasions when we would meet one another off duty in the soldier-swarming, squalid little Georgia town at the edge of camp. Recognizing members of our platoon or company in the crowded bars, we would make our way through the press toward each other to drink together, not necessarily meeting as friends, but as members of the same family or tribe. In fact, much as we might sometimes dislike one another, we felt more comfortable drinking together than drinking with the strangers from other families. Within the family, the rule was that two soldiers would be particularly good friends, or as the Army said, buddies.

The Army encouraged the buddy system. The friendship was not particularly deep, but it was something more than a tolerant acquaintance. It was essentially an alliance. You and another soldier would establish an offensive and defensive alliance of two men, a kind of mutual nonaggression pact, that was first of all directed against your common oppressor, the impersonal Army of the insect regulations and arbitrary stupidities. You would, for example, do such things as take turns answering the roll call in the predawn blackness of a freezing Georgia reveille. One of you would answer to both names while the other slept late. It seemed to require two men to defeat the Army; to understand that if you were to survive in the system you had to find some way to use the system; to give the Army obedience up to a point, and complete obedience only when there was nothing else to do but comply. I am not sure that my last sentence describes storybook patriots, but I am quite sure that it describes soldiers. In any case, a buddy came with the home. When you moved to another post, you acquired a new buddy. The concept of home that the Army was helping me to arrive at was that it must be a place where, together with people you could trust, you lived and worked with them at some common task.

I am aware that the criteria I have been setting forth would qualify a prison as a home, but the remarkable thing to me is that privacy, familiarity, security, a sense of well-being and a shared experience with trustworthy friends to some common end does not characterize the American civilian household. It does not describe, exactly, the relationship enjoyed by Mom, Pop and the kids in Levittown. I can only repeat that in the Army I found something that seemed more nearly home than anything we ordinarily call home—even though the Army, being a system, was debasing of manhood.

I neither loathed, loved, nor feared the olive-drab beehive—an odd statement to be made by one who has heretofore said how little use he had for systems, and whose *beau ideal* had grown from the Henty boy into Hemingway's deserter, Frederic Henry. Yet the curious thing was, I had enlisted gladly enough. The Japanese attack on Pearl Harbor put an end to both national vacillation and my own. I would say that most Americans went to their inevitable war with something like a sigh of relief after ten years of depression at home and unresolved tensions abroad. Now, perhaps, all the tensions would be relieved through violence. At least, the war provided us all with some immediate purpose. Unlike peace, a war has a definite beginning, middle and end. In this, it is like a game, and Americans most usually approach anything they do as if it were a contest which can be won. Our salesmen speak of penetrating the market, as if they were about to conquer an unwilling woman, or as if they were a spearhead of tanks smashing through an enemy line or so many fullbacks driving off tackle for a touchdown. The image is always of male thrust toward pleasure, and whatever else I was—disbeliever in systems and admirer of deserters—I was also sufficiently male, and American enough, to want to get in the game and win it. Acceptance of the war was made all the easier for me because we had been attacked. I was no Christian, willing to turn the other cheek. Instead, I agreed with

Hemingway when, in another context, he said that if you ever get into a fight, the only thing to do is win it.

It never occurred to me for a moment that America might lose the war. Americans always win because we are bigger and stronger than anyone else. Mother and the history books said so. The only member of my family that I can recall as being on the losing side was a British commander during the Revolution, but then, he was fighting against other members of my family. True, I had not enjoyed military school, but stories of battle always fascinated me and my favorite game had always been football, which is a little war waged in armor. I looked forward to the big game. I was curious to test myself. If they were giving a war in my time, I did not want to be left out of it. I suppose I could look at this now with Viennese eyes and say, "Aha, the young man was doubtful of his virility, or he would not have had this need to test himself," but this explanation might not completely account for the fact that war has always been the principal activity of mankind, and that enlistment in the war band has always been a kind of compulsory initiatory examination for all youth. In any case, I presented myself as a candidate for scrutiny, and the prospect of the test ahead enabled me to put up with the first unpleasant aspects of becoming a number that jumped at a shout.

While I think my attitude was a quite general one, certainly true of the majority of fighter pilots, for example, I discovered that other men had acquired serial numbers for different reasons and entertained quite different opinions about the Army and battle. In my first infantry training camp I had met two completely different tribes. Our company was almost evenly divided between young men from the Deep South and youths of Polish or Balkan extraction who came from the grim industrial wilderness around Pittsburgh. The Southerners tended to be tall and spare, soft-spoken, good rifle shots, slow to make friends, but thereafter loyal as hounds. They had come down out of the pine hills, or out of the river brakes, used to looking after themselves in open country since childhood. They had come running to the Army; they had enlisted to a man. They had come to the Army to hunt. The war aim of the Southerner was to see how many men he could kill before he was either killed himself or victorious. The Pennsylvanians, on the other hand, had all been drafted. They generally had the barrel builds of Central European peasants, were loud, contentious, somewhat thick-headed, docile and sullen when confronted by authority, lost, confused, and given to self-pity. They were city boys who did not quite know what to do without their familiar streets, bars, drugstores, automobiles, motion picture houses, and girls. Their war aim was to get home alive as soon as possible. While the Southerner was loftily contemptuous of the Army, the Northern city boy detested it in a hopeless sort of way. I would suppose that the difference between them was not only that of country hawk and city pigeon, but also that of a race descended from hunter-warriors as contrasted with a race descended from peasants harried century after century by invading conquerors.

At first, the two different tribes did not get along at all well together. To the Southerner, the northern city male lacked dignity. Listening to the hubbub of a group of Pennsylvanians arguing as they played football on an idle Sunday afternoon, one of my thin-lipped southern friends gravely remarked:

"Now, they sound just like a bunch of Nigras, don't they?"

To the city boys, the country boys were so many primitives.

"I bet you never wore shoes before you was in the Army, huh?" one of my Polish friends asked a Southerner.

"No, I never did," the Southerner replied. He paused, considering. "Except on Sunday, of course."

Puzzled by the laughter that followed, the Southerner asked with dangerous politeness, "Now, just what the hell do you all think is so Goddamn funny? My folks was poor, sure enough. But they ain't none of us so stupid as to laugh at a man because his folks was poor."

As the training weeks wore on, with the Southerners learning their military lessons because they wanted to and the Northerners learning theirs because they had to, we settled into something like

111

a family until, one night, an event took place that sorely tried our nascent unity.

It seems that a Negro soldier, returning to camp from leave, stepped down from the bus at the town bus depot with his tie askew and his collar unbuttoned. A Military Policeman approached to tell him to fasten his collar and straighten his tie. The Negro who, as it turned out, was a day late in returning from his leave, evidently thought the white-helmeted MP was about to arrest him. He started to run. The MP caught him by the arm. The Negro swung around and struck the MP.

At that point, the MP either reached for his service pistol, or the Negro grabbed it—no one was sure how it happened—but what is quite certain is that the pistol was discharged. The MP fell. The pistol clattered to the floor. The Negro stared with numb terror at the scene, then shot off through the crowd that made way for him.

"He has a gun!" people said.

The news flickered through that small Southern town like heat lightning.

"Nigger soldiers are shooting the MPs!"

There was a howl of sirens and a whirling of red lights as military and civilian police squad cars moaned through the streets. There was not a Negro to be seen. As if reacting to instantaneous telepathy, they melted away: soldiers, men, women and children. Even the streets in the wretched adjacent slum called Niggertown were empty; its bars closed and dark. White civilian and military police ranged through the streets, banging on the doors of Niggertown and kicking them open, riot guns in their hands.

During the scuffle at the bus station, it would seem that the Negro soldier's cap had fallen off. Bloodhounds sniffed at it.

The trail led, not to Niggertown, but to a swamp. Some people said a gun battle ensued. Others said the Negro was unarmed. There were certainly a great many shots fired, after which the Negro's body was dragged out of the swamp.

"What a brave bunch of guys," one of the Polish boys in our

112

barracks said. "Thirty-eight cops, shooting holes in one poor, un-armed jig."

He spoke to two of the Southerners. He was absolutely dis-gusted.

"You really understand the colored people, huh?" he said.

"Yes, I reckon we do," one of the Southerners tightly said. "And I reckon they understand us right well, too."

"That boy was one of your northern Niggers," the other South-erner seriously explained. "None of our Nigras would have done a damn-fool thing like that."

Seeking to be helpful, rather than to argue, he went on:

"If you want to love Niggers up North, why, I reckon that's all right for you to do up there, if you want to. But one thing is Goddamn sure: you ain't going to do anything like that down here. We're just not going to let you. These here are our Nigras, and we know them, and they know us, and we get along just fine. But if somebody from up North wants to come down here and start messing around with our Nigras, why damn if we wouldn't shoot him just like we would any Nigger. I would myself, and that's a fact."

We were still a family of sorts, but a badly divided one. We tried to reach toward one another, discussing the racial problem as carefully as we could, making an effort to withhold our anger, but we really did not listen to what the other said. Northerner and Southerner each told the other what he believed, and each was absolutely convinced that he was right. This certainly was appall-ing. It was very clear to me that the basic causes of the Civil War still existed, and when we called one another Yank and Rebel now, there was an old, deep sting in those words. White superiority was an article of Southern faith, and I had known the Southern point of view since my earliest years; Washington, for instance, was then essentially a Southern town. But what I had never truly known was the depth of that belief, and it was heartbreaking to learn that one Southerner, otherwise as fine a man as anyone could ever hope to know, could actually believe that he had a right to shoot a

113

Negro for insolence, and what was more, that he would actually do so, with no more remorse than he would feel over stunning a fish.

It was profoundly discouraging, all the more because I was far more drawn to the Southerners than I was to the Pennsylvanians with the foreign names. The Southerners of my own British stock and Revolutionary antecedents were in almost every way much more my kind of people than the first-generation Americans from the Balkans. But in the one matter most important then, and now, in the world, it was the first-generation Americans who were right, and the Southerners who were wrong, and in the United States Army in my twenty-first year I knew that the Civil War would one day be resumed and that I would have to side with those with whom I had very little in common except philosophical agreement on a fundamental issue, against those whom I admired in almost everything else.

I am sure we all knew that the racial problem would have to be dealt with after the war, but we put the matter aside as best we could in order to deal with the immediate problem of getting along with each other. The matter was made the easier to ignore because the Negro soldiers were segregated from us and we seldom met them. They lived in a distant part of the camp, and were destined to be used principally as labor troops. The Army felt that Negroes would not make good combat soldiers, and the Army was right about this—up to a point. Some commanding generals, like Patton, believed Negroes lacked the intelligence to fight well in armor, and Patton frankly told them so. But I preferred to believe that a Negro soldier I talked with had a better explanation.

"What we want in a white folks' war?" he asked me. "Man, they ain't nothin' in a white folks war for us. I go die for you. Okay. You going die for *me?* Die for yo' country! Man, it ain't *my* country, it *yo'* country, so I say, Man, *you* go die for it and let me be."

So I learned that three tribes lived apart from each other together in that training camp, and the Army furnished me with a world of time to reflect upon this, and other matters relative to the American experience, in the two years it took the Army to get me to its Southwest Pacific theater, and in the two more years the Army took to finish the war and send me home again. But it was in New Guinea and the Philippines that matters came into sharper focus, perhaps because Americans in America are not so clearly visible as they are overseas—particularly in primitive areas overseas. It was in New Guinea for instance, that I encountered the Negroes' agony once again, stated in the clearest possible terms.

On the predicted twenty-eighth day, the island where the war was came toward us out of the sea. There was no more indication of a war than there had been on those empty endless days on the ocean. After all, New Guinea is one of the largest islands in the world, and we arrived off Milne Bay at the very foot of it, nearly two years after the fighting ended there.

Coming into the bay, the bow slitting a calm sea in a long, curving line, we could see mountains to either side rising blue above a low wreath of clouds. The mountains turned green with black shadows as the ship moved deeper into the bay, and we could see the hills were covered by a thick vegetation that grew down to the water line. We were looking at a tropical rain forest, and steam from this forest rose to form the low clouds, and when we were well into the narrowing bay, we were under the cloud, and it was raining, and we could no longer see the tops of the mountains.

Not until noon the following day did amphibious trucks swim out to the ship's side to take us off, and we dropped our barracks bags down into their wet, muddy beds, scrambling down the cargo nets after them like so many maladroit spiders in a strange web. When the trucks were filled, they wallowed away from the ship that now seemed safe, familiar and enormous, to chug slowly across the harbor in the rain. As we drew closer to the land the air grew increasingly hot and we soaked one side of our clothing with sweat while rain soaked the other. The trucks climbed ashore and splashed along a deeply rutted mud road that was the consistency of gruel, into a jungle that held out the light but not the rain. We drove for miles along areas of tents under dripping trees, past an infantry regiment that was sleeping in pup tents on the squelchy jungle floor, and past a Negro engineer battalion that had built tent platforms raised on oil drums, and that had made a company street bordered with whitewashed stones.

It seemed that the Negroes had been among the first Allied troops to arrive in Milne Bay. Japanese attacked, and the Negroes ambushed them and buried the Japanese with a bulldozer when the fighting was done, and they had been there ever since in the heat and the mildew and the rot and the rain, without furlough to Australia. The Australians had been glad to have them help keep the Japanese out of Australia, but not to the point of allowing the Negroes to see the nation they had helped to save. Only white men were permitted to enter Australia. No one asked the Negroes to go anywhere else, either, because of the feeling that Negroes were not very dependable troops and because the mission of that battalion was to maintain and expand the facilities of Milne Bay. Some officers explained that this was no hardship on the Negroes, because, they said, Negroes did not like to fight anyway, and because they were naturally comfortable in the jungle because the Negro people had so recently come from the Congo that they were still acclimated to a dank, arboreal life. Two years later in the Philippines I heard that those Negroes had mutinied, and when I heard the news, or rumor, I wondered what had taken them so long. It seemed a wonderful testimony to the patience of their race, for I was tired enough of Milne Bay after an hour ashore, and I was sick of it by the time my orders to leave that particular swamp arrived six weeks later.

My orders were to report to ADVON, or Advanced Echelon of the Fifth Air Force, and I looked forward to something rough and primitive, full of bomb holes, harried men and a sense of urgency. What I found was a large, placidly busy airfield over which transports circled in their landing patterns, and from which there came a never-ending low thunder of engines. The airfield, Nadzab, was a

116

wide kunai-grass-covered level area of the Markham River plain. It was for some months the busiest airport in the world, and the Japanese had raided it at night, but by the time I arrived the Japanese were no longer raiding. I reported to the Fifteenth Weather Squadron, which I found to be living in a range of hills that looked down upon the airport on the valley floor and across the plain to the Owen Stanley mountains beyond. My colleagues were growing watermelons in the volcanic soil. The corn, they said, had not done well.

It was cool and pleasant on our hillside, and each day we drove in a weapons carrier down the curving dirt road to the valley, and on a road through the man-high kunai grass to the operations building where we enjoyed the facilities of a large, clean office equipped with teletype machines and radios. The building was made of woven nipa, roofed with galvanized iron, but it was not uncomfortably hot despite the steady 90-degree heat of the valley floor. Except that the returning fighters came whining in to their landings, the wind whistling in their gunbarrels and indicating that the guns had fired, shooting out the tape that had covered the muzzles on takeoff, there was nothing to suggest that Nadzab was a fighting airfield; no particular reason to imagine that it was an Air Force Headquarters. It seemed to be just another military backwater, not unlike others to which I had been condemned ever since I had been transferred from the Infantry to the Air Force nearly two years earlier.

But Nadzab was something more than that. Bombing strikes and fighter sweeps were mounted from it every day; Nadzab was a fighting airfield, but one where air crews were given a final polish before being sent to grimmer battles farther north. Each day, bombers were sent out to smash at Rabaul, once a Japanese bastion on New Britain island, but now a pock-marked mudhole. Intelligence officers believed 50,000 Japanese to be starving in the jungles in and around Rabaul, and the Japanese would fire a few antiaircraft shells at the students from Nadzab each morning, just to let it be known that they were still there, and still unconquered.

117

In short, Rabul was now what the Air Force called a milk run, meaning a mission no more hazardous than a milkman's daily delivery route in the suburbs. Flying a milk run to Rabaul did not seem to comprise much of a war, but it was the only war around, and to my intense satisfaction, I discovered that weathermen could take part in it.

The reason weathermen were asked to do so was that weather forecasts are made on the basis of measuring temperatures, humidities and wind directions, these measurements being simultaneously made in hundreds of scattered locations. The more such reports, the more accurate the forecast—and since the Japanese did not tell us what the weather was over the areas they held, it was important for someone to go there and find out. So weathermen flew from shore stations with Navy air crews on search-and-destroy missions, ranging out over the seas, and here at Nadzab there was a dawn flight every morning. A single light bomber, a B-25, would set out carrying a load of bombs, a student crew, and a weatherman who, when the aircraft was over Rabaul, would then radio back to Nadzab a description of the weather for the edification of the other students who later that day would come trundling out to Rabaul in the heavy bombers, the B-24s. Because flight was officially believed to be hazardous, the Air Force asked for volunteers and paid them half again their regular military salaries. If, instead, the Air Force had sold tickets for those flights, I am sure just as many men would have volunteered for them. As it was, so many weathermen asked for flight duty that we had to take turns.

I flew in the bombardier's greenhouse, or plexiglass nose of the B-25, and when the sun was up, stripped down to a pair of shorts to sunbathe while the shadow of our aircraft fled over the blue wrinkled paint of the sea. We made landfall at Tawui Point, and when I first saw blots of black smoke appearing below us and to the left, and heard the splitting cracks, I did not immediately know what was going on. The pilot heaved the B-25 around the sky, and then I realized we were under fire; that this was the war I had been

118

so anxious to see; that this was the initiation into the fraternity. I watched it as if it were a newsreel.

Then we were sinking fast and straight through the air. The aircraft's bomb-bay doors whined open, and the B-25 leaped lightly as the yellow five hundred-pound general-purpose bombs slid smoothly out. We curved steeply away, and I saw the yellow-orange winks of fire appear in a neat row in the jungle considerably to one side of the ruined Japanese airfield. When we came sweeping around to inspect our work, the jungle looked as dense as ever. There was no sign that bombs had fallen in it. Hanging in the sky behind us were black smudges fraying in the wind. I made my radio report.

There was the long flight back to Nadzab in the sunshine over the sea. I found myself sweating coldly in the sun-warmth, and realized I stank of fear and sweat. I was, or had been, very badly frightened once the danger was over. The shooting had taken me so much by surprise that I had not had time to be frightened then, and watching the bombs fall had been interesting, but the fact was I was thoroughly scared, and thinking this through, I decided that I was not frightened by what had just happened, but by the prospect of taking future trips to places where people actually shot at you. This would never do. Therefore, when we landed at Nadzab, I hurried off to where the B-24s of the morning strike were warming up, and rode immediately back with them to Rabaul, acting on the theory that if you fall off a horse while learning to ride, you must remount immediately or you will never become a horseman.

On all ensuing flights I was careful to dress in exactly the same clothes I had worn on the first trip, being a true believer in Bona Dea. It is only the organized aspect of religion that I oppose; otherwise, I am as superstitious as the Pope. Included in my clothing was a little folder of Leica photographs of my son, shown playing in a heap of fall leaves with his mother. I would look at the two of them, Margaret and Christopher, playing and laughing together in the leaves as the bombers above, below and alongside bobbed

119

gently in the tropical air while the shadows of our power fled silently over the Bismarck Sea. I would not look at the pictures on the way back to Nadzab.

Margaret was a girl I had met while hitch-hiking through the West during the summer before the war when I had run away from the University of Pennsylvania, from home, and from my first job. I can best describe her by saying that she seemed a sufficient reason for me not to go on to Asia. I returned East with her to Philadelphia, and we had a few dates together before I joined the Army, and thereafter asked her to come to Georgia to marry me. She wrote back saying she would not come to Georgia to marry me, and this gave me great hope, for I took her answer to mean that it might be only the location, and not me, that she found so objectionable. With Georgia off the list, that still left forty-seven other states, the District of Columbia, and sundry United States possessions and territories to suggest as possible wedding sites. At about this time, the Army gave me one of its glorious gifts of freedom. I had applied from the Infantry for the aviation-cadet program, and had been accepted. But since many more applicants had been accepted than there was space for them in the hurriedly expanding Air Force schools, the Army gave me a ninety-day furlough so that I could wait at home until there was a classroom seat.

We were married in Philadelphia in April, 1942.

It may be fairly said that we were as ready to be married as any two people can be who have no future. In our time, there was no future. No one knew how long the war would last, much less who would be alive at the end of it. Everyone was conscious that time was hurtling past, but into an unimaginable emptiness. There was certainly a conscious, if not always verbally expressed, determination to grasp at life in what time there might be. Then, too, Nature may have had a part to play, fearful for the survival of the species. For during times of war, or of such disasters as the medieval plagues, mankind almost compulsively mates, and it is a statistical fact that a disproportionate number of male births ensue, just as close-pruned trees devote their growth essentially to bearing fruit. There is no question but that during wars, people marry at far earlier ages than they might have married in times of peace, and it is conventionally said that such marriages represent a frightful gamble on the part of heedless youngsters who do not really know much about one another. But I am inclined to think that, in time of war, the process of choice is often merely quickened. The engagement period may be sometimes telescoped into hours, but who is to say that in those intense hours, the lovers do not reveal themselves as fully to one another's heightened consciousness as they might otherwise have done slowly during the footless months of peace?

Nothing that happened on my furlough, other than the wedding itself, was planned. We went to New York City to see *Porgy and Bess,* and then at a hotel desk asked where people went for honeymoons. We were sent to a small country hotel in the Adirondacks where we rowed on the lake and walked through the forested hills, wearing sweaters around our heads to keep off the black flies. In the fashion of honeymooners, we were not unduly disturbed by the black flies, being much too preoccupied with one another. We might have stayed there the entire ninety days, but the war drove us out of the Adirondacks. Gasoline rationing had come to America, and the remote country hotel had to close for lack of guests. We wandered south to the Skyline Drive of the Blue Ridge Mountains to enjoy the early-morning mists, and, when the sun was well up, the stupendous view of the flowering apple orchards of the Shenandoah valley. We were wonderfully content in the lonely hills, beginning the process of endless discovery, living in a cabin adjacent to the Skyline Lodge hotel. But the war came there, too: the Lodge closed. We drifted north to live in a house belonging to one of Margaret's brothers in the country outside New Hope, Pennsylvania. It was a brown-and-blue house near a millpond and because of its color, her brother called it The Bruise. The war came there, too, this time in the form of orders for me to return to the Army.

It all had the quality of a dream. In 1942 the honeymoons of

121

others were often compressed into the seventy-two hours of a three-day pass, spent in overpriced rooms in the tacky plasterboard motels and boardinghouses adjacent to the training camps. But the Army had given me wealth of time incredible in a war, and simultaneously made it impossible for us to do anything other than enjoy it. We could do nothing but live day by day. Fortunately, I had inherited the means to do so. My great-uncle had died, leaving me his library and some four thousand dollars in cash. In something under three months, Margaret and I spent all but seven hundred dollars of it—a feat that takes on meaning only when you consider that thirty-three hundred dollars was considerably more than the average annual American family income. But what was the point of our saving money? What was the point of making plans when the Army was making the decisions? If I returned from the war, then no doubt I could find some sort of job. After all, most men eventually do. There would be time, after the war, to hunt out the young couple's first, inexpensive apartment, and to furnish it with the customary first things: the cheap studio couch that also served as bed; the card table that would also be the dining table; the five-and-ten-cent-store kitchenware. But now there was the war, and wars are dangerous, and I had volunteered to fly about in airplanes. We had no future that bore close inspection. We did not talk about it. Instead, we lived in the present, and we spent what we had, our money, our emotions and our bodies, as well as we could.

I remember how odd it seemed to return to the Army, and how strangely glad I was to return to it. Of course I was bitterly lonely for my new bride, but apart from that, I was delighted not to be a civilian. It was not entirely a matter of glorying in a uniform and looking down on those who would never know combat. There was that in it, but I found civilian life relatively messy and aimless, whereas the Army life was clean and purposeful. I have said that I had lost interest in planned societies, but there is this to be said for them: they do have a plan and they work at it and everyone in such a society knows what he is supposed to do. Herein, I think, is

122

the appeal of a totalitarian state: people are relieved of the burden of decision while at the same time they are clothed and fed and given something to do. This must profoundly appeal to the weak and lazy who can simultaneously imagine themselves to be strong and powerful because their monolithic Sparta can and does follow its plans. The individual may be powerless and relieved of a sense of moral responsibility, but if he does what he is told, the social machine of which he is a part can generate power and use it, and the witless social fragment can proudly say, "Look what we did." Inasmuch as we are all at times weak, and at other times lazy, and since there is such a thing as joy in being a part of a team, glad to say *we* did something rather than to have to say *I* did something, there is a universal appeal in the sound of a drum that summons the town. I felt the pull of it myself during the war years, and would suppose that no one is immune to the blandishments of fascism, particularly in times of a vague national drifting upon a sea believed to be full of dangers.

I returned to the Army to be disappointed. In the normal course of military events, it was discovered that defective vision in one eye kept me out of pilot training, and that my arithmetic was too slow and too inaccurate to qualify me as a navigator. Instead of being trained for flight, the Air Force trained me to be a meteorologist and sent me to Utah to report that the air there was normally dry. For month upon empty month I contributed to our final victory by looking at the sky three times a day, five days a week, reporting the air to be dry and the sky clear, terribly afraid that the war would end before I would ever be sent overseas. I was waiting in Utah, as empty inside as the air and the state of Utah itself, when my son was born. The Army gave me a furlough to inspect him.

There was a glass-fronted room in Philadelphia's Germantown Hospital in which the new babies were displayed. There were some fine-looking babies in the front row of cribs, and I wondered which of them was mine. But those were apparently the display babies, like the fruit atop a wooden basket that conceals the spoiled fruit

123

beneath. A nurse drew a different baby from one of the cribs in the back and held it up to the glass window for me to admire.

I went down the hall to Margaret's room, wondering how to look cheerful. The little red-faced thing I had seen, with its angry, mashed features and its dreadfully shaped head, was a hopeless tragedy.

I remember kissing Margaret and holding her very close as one way of not saying anything.

"He looks just like his Daddy," she said happily. "He is very bright."

It seemed that she was delighted with our fine boy. The nurse brought him to be fed, and the nurse seemed delighted, too. Christopher puffed and sucked away and smelled bad. His skin was incredibly soft, and his feet were purple red and I thought they must be cold. I pulled a little woolen blanket over them and he kicked it off while continuing blindly to feed. Margaret looked down at him with lambent eyes.

The doctor told me the child was strong, healthy and alert. About the head? Oh, that, the doctor said, is the way they all look at first. The head is often a little squeezed going through the birth canal. Later, it rounds into shape.

I remember walking out of the hospital in wonderment, and later, when it was time to take Margaret home to the cheap apartment she had rented, there was the incredible joy of carrying our first-born in my arms. Apparently, I was a father, and no small part of the wonderment was wondering what it must feel like to be a father. I was too new at the business to think myself a part of it. A lover, yes; a bridegroom, certainly; a husband . . . well, not really yet a husband, because we had not quite got around to that phase of marriage, although we had seemingly arrived at parenthood. Margaret was very pleased when, toward the end of my furlough, we could push the baby carriage down the street to the grocery store. Walking slowly down the brick-paved sidewalks, pushing Christopher fat and full of milk and sleep ahead of us,

124

seemed a bit more like being a husband and a father, but there was always the Army walking silently along with us, and beyond the Army, the war it was fighting—the war that was seemingly without end. We were conscious of the days slipping away too fast from the marriage we had not yet begun to explore. The Army and the war made marriage seem improbable—a furlough was more like a date than a return to a home—and being married and having a child made the Army and the war seem improbable. And then, as suddenly as it had begun, the furlough ended, and I returned to the nothingness of Utah and to the inadequacy of writing letters to a mystery.

There was certainly nothing about my life or Utah that I could write to her, and I had no conception of what it must be to be a married woman living alone with a baby in a rented apartment, trying to make ends meet on the basis of my eighty-dollar-a-month Army allotment and the one hundred dollars a month she earned by typing at home. At a home, I should say, where the janitor was drunk at nine in the morning and where, in the same building, there was a Navy wife who entertained the shore establishment while her husband was at sea. There was very little that Margaret and I could really say to one another about our separate worlds, and this, I should think, was one of the horrors of war.

Nor was there very much that I could write to her about New Guinea, other than to describe some of the fruits and the Stone Age Papuans with their Semitic noses, reddish wool hair, odor of rancid coconut oil, great horny feet and bark penis shields. To be sure, books can be written—and have been—about New Guinea, its flora, fauna and natives, but the Army let me see little more of New Guinea than occasional aerial views of jungled mountains, and the everyday five-mile drive along the dirt road from our watermelon patch to our airport office. Nor was there anything much I could really tell her about the flights to Rabaul, because she could read all the war stories she wanted to read in the newspapers and magazines, and I knew she did not want to read those, because like most women, she was an enemy of war. Moreover, I could scarcely consider my military career to be a heroic one.

The truth is, as I was to learn, very few men in uniform ever see any fighting. For every man facing the enemy with a gun in his hands, there are at least ten men standing in a line behind him, handing him his ammunition, food, and equipment, training his replacement, fixing the ice cream machines, running the motion picture projectors, repairing shoes, drinking beer . . . More Americans have been killed during the commission of crimes than have died in all of our wars in the past 190 years of the Republic. During Hitler's war, the average American soldier's most sinister enemy was not the German, or the Japanese. It was boredom.

Flying occasional weather reconnaissance missions gave the next two years what military moments there were for me. In all that time, great armies were destroyed, fleets sunk, cities burned, the first jet aircraft shrieked aloft, the atomic bomb was devised and dropped, empires fell, and while all this was going on, most of the personnel of my organization spent an average of sixteen hours a day lying on our cots sleeping or reading, or sitting on cots playing bridge for utter lack of anything to do. For eight hours a day we performed our little specialty of discovering the tropical air to be warm and wet, thus becoming agents of history and materially aiding the process of Japan's incineration, but at the end of our working hours we returned to our cots because there was nowhere else to go, and the generally debilitating tropical heat made sleep seem inviting, and effort futile.

In the more than four years that I was a soldier, I should say I spent almost three days at war, if I were to add together all the hours that I flew on what were called combat missions. If I were to add together all the splintered seconds during which something actually happened on those flights, then it would be possible to say that I spent nearly two minutes in action—for the combat missions were long, droning hours over empty seas on the way to and from targets where, more often than not, no one shot at us.

126

Now, two minutes in action out of a total of more than four years in the Army does not seem to be an impressive military adventure, but I would say that it constituted a greater experience of battle than all but a tenth of the men in uniform ever had. Looking back on it now, I think that a reason why my American generation is so generally bellicose is that so few of us got anywhere near the war we waged. Together with those of us whose adventures in combat were as tentative as my own, most of us came away from Hitler's war with the notion that wars are not excessively dangerous, but are legitimate instruments of national policy—particularly because our experience told us that wars are always waged abroad and that our enemies always lose. While each man who fought may have his own memories of battle and his own ideas about it, I would say that what the millions of noncombatant soldiers remember about the war was not the stupefying boredom of Army life, but the fact that we won the war. Here, I agree with Frederick Manning's observation that what the world should know, and fear, is the fact that the next war is always made by the survivors of the last; by men who, having survived, cannot believe that wars are dangerous. One thinks of the American Legion, with its drum and bugle corps.

A different view is no doubt held by the wounded, the ravaged, and the dead. I do not know how I should have behaved in the war, or felt about it later, had I been flying daily in the murderous aerial combat over Europe, in which each man's life was a predictable number of hours long, or had I been an infantryman committed to incessant battle that could end only in wounds or death after a predictable number of days in action. Perhaps if I had survived that sort of thing, or had my home bombed and my family killed, I would not now endorse our current activity in Vietnam. Perhaps a reason why I do support the Vietnam war is that although I was badly frightened for two minutes, I was not driven mindless by terror, nor was I wounded, nor was anyone else in my immediate organization. The only dead and wounded I saw in the war were a group of soldiers who had been sitting in a latrine when a fighter plane crashed nearby as it came in for a landing, sending a wing section whirling through the air like a boomerang, scything through the nipa walls of the latrine and the people sitting there. Someone observed that it was a truly tough shit for them, and this callow remark was an exact demonstration of how little the war meant to those who experienced none of its action.

It was on other levels, in other areas than combat, that Hitler's war affected my generation and established the basis of our present society. Perhaps the most impressive lesson the Army taught us was that the America we had hitherto known as a land of bread-lines and uncertain economics was, in fact, overwhelmingly wealthy, productive, and powerful—once its resources were employed. The Southerners and Pittsburghers of my first infantry acquaintance discovered this the moment they entered the mess hall. For the first time in their lives they were presented with all the food they could stuff into themselves, and they ate quantities of bread, spreading it nearly half an inch thick with butter, which many had not eaten before, and marveling that they could have all the butter they wanted. Then there was the equipment that came flooding into the Army camps. In the beginning there may have been the blue-denim fatigues and the pointing of wooden cannons at trucks carrying signs labeling them tanks for purposes of practice, but new olive-drab fatigues, real guns and real tanks appeared in wholesale lots within the next few months, and by the time I went overseas, American production was the most important fact of the war.

What if our tanks, aircraft and guns were not as good as the Germans? We had more of what we had than the Germans had of what they had, and if we lost three tanks to every one they lost, the end of the battle would see no German tanks remaining while an immense number of surviving American tanks held the field. Students of military history will agree that all the races and nations of man are equally valorous, given an equality in leadership, equipment, and belief in what they are doing; and a narrow military lesson of the fighting in Europe was that the Germans, whose leadership, equipment and morale was often superior to our own, could be overwhelmed by superior numbers of American troops and the tidal wave of American military production. In the Pacific, the Japanese never had a chance, for the natural resources of their island empire in oil and steel, for instance, could not be compared to our own, and the dour valor of the Japanese peasant, willing to die for his God-Emperor, could not offset the superior technology and material resources of his American enemy. There was a joke about the Japanese being superior jungle fighters, but complaining that the Americans did not fight fairly because, instead of fighting in the jungle, the Americans simply destroyed the jungle with napalm and bulldozers.

Together with this spate of military equipment, America also drenched her soldiers with money and comforts. As far as money was concerned, the matter was comparative: an American Air Force sergeant received almost twice the sum given to a Royal Australian Air Force wing commander. Together with the English, no few Australians would complain that the only trouble with Americans was that they were "overfed, oversexed, overpaid, and over here." By virtue of the alchemy of war, the poor Americans of the hardscrabble farms and the unemployment offices had become the rich Americans of the infinite resources and the unbelievable numbers of dollars who, in the course of giving France back to the French and saving Australia from an Asiatic conqueror, wrecked the economy of every country they visited. In Australia, bankers' daughters were competing for jobs as waitresses in restaurants patronized by American soldiers, where they could earn more in tips than their fathers earned at their offices; the effect of American desires and American money on a rationed economy was to establish the black market. In New Guinea, an American soldier would trade an issue machete to a Papuan native for a few coconuts, completely unaware of the fact that in so doing, he had just destroyed twenty years of patient work that the Australian District

129

Officer had painfully completed in the direction of trying to acquaint the savages with the principle that all things excellent are as difficult as they are rare. In the Philippines, I did my part in helping the Filipinos to lose the victory. A woman came into our area, asking if she could do our laundry. I did not understand that this was her gift of love; that she wanted to do something for the Americans who had come as liberators. She was embarrassed when I asked her the price. Finally, she said she would take only enough soap to do my laundry. I gave her a bar of yellow Army soap, and she accepted it unbelievingly. I had no idea, then, that soap had become so rare during the years of Japanese occupation, that I had given her the equivalent of more than one hundred dollars. From such innocence to the black market was no step at all. Filipino businessmen immediately appeared, to offer supply sergeants $500 for a sack of flour; to sell soldiers Coca-Cola bottles full of "blackberry cordial type Scotch whisky, guaranteed not poisonous but 100 per cent satisfaction" for $10 apiece —which meant that the soldiers who were thirsty would have to sell their cigarettes on the black market to supplement their Army incomes. Within weeks of our arrival, the Filipinos were saying, "Before the war very cheap, now very dear," and were forming views of Americans that were quite different from the descriptions of Americans that they had read in their American schoolbooks during the prior forty years of our rule in those islands.

To find myself cast as a comparative Croesus not only in primitive areas but also in a country as much like our own as Australia was a provocative experience. I am told that the American wealth of money and supplies had the same effect upon our soldiers who served in Africa, Great Britain, India, Europe and Burma: that it made us all glad that we were Americans and not ragtag, rump-sprung and dirt-poor foreigners; that our military success was proof of our organization, methods and productive power; that we, who were only common soldiers in our own land, were as lords in the lands of others; that even the poor man in America had more material wealth than the middle classes elsewhere; that Americans

130

therefore lived a better life than other people; that it was therefore only right for other people to want to imitate us, and no more than our duty for us to help them to become more like ourselves.

Wherever we went, whenever we paused, we created little Americas that offered an infinity of comforts as compared with the lack of amenities in the surrounding areas. In our rear base camps, there were different motion pictures every night of the week; there was always a Post Exchange that sold everything from hair oil to Swiss watches; our Army brought along libraries, comic books, games equipment ranging from cribbage boards to football uniforms, newspapers, soft drinks, ketchup and cheeseburgers. Never in history has an army moved with such a baggage train and with so many hundreds of thousands—if not millions—of men to handle it. Europeans who saw this glut of luxury accompanying an unimaginable supply of treasure, an incredible complexity of communications, medical and engineering equipment, and an inexhaustible supply of weapons and munitions, could only hopelessly envy us, or hopelessly despair of us, but they could not hopefully oppose us. Neither our allies nor our enemies could do that. The world found itself confronted by the first modern state able to wage land, sea and air war simultaneously on all the continents and seas while, at the same time, providing food and weapons for its allies, and more than this, providing luxuries for its troops while also maintaining a high standard of living for its civilian population: in fact, the highest in the world, even with wartime rationing.

None of this was lost upon us, the common soldiers. We could see that we were not only a head taller than other races, but that we were profoundly richer in every material way—and, to our way of thinking, better—than any other people in the world. The thought made some of us proud to be Americans and others of us, wistful. The wistful, or sad, Americans would be those who suspected that health and wealth were not everything in life, and whose pity for the less fortunate nations led them to imagine that the Europeans and the Asians must somehow possess compensatory spiritual qualities superior to our own. For the majority, however, there was nothing spiritually appealing about muddy natives or exhausted Europeans. Most of us gazed down upon the ruined world from atop our mountain of treasure and said, "There, but for the grace of God, go I."

At the same time, being young and self-centered, we soldiers pitied ourselves. We reflected upon the American civilians who thought they had it rough, complaining about their shortages of sugar, meat, cigarettes and gasoline, meanwhile growing rich on wartime labor and contracts, whereas we were sacrificing years of our youth. It did nothing for us to discover that some of the cigarettes we bought contained wooden splinters and, worse, finding among the packages notes stating that these cigarettes were a free gift to us fighting men from such-and-such a civic organization or group of factory workers. Obviously, someone had cheated on the manufacture of the cigarettes, and someone else had taken what was to have been a gift to us and had sold it to us. Our view of the civilian world was that it was full of draft-dodgers, thieves and girls who wrote letters saying, "Dear John, I hope you won't be too sorry to hear that I am marrying a 4-F who has this fabulous job, but I'm not getting any younger and I don't know if you'll ever come home, but I'll always remember you as a good friend and hope you'll understand."

We were also derisive of that war-born anomaly, the Very Important Person, or VIP. What made him anomalous was not only the American libertarian tradition, but also Vice President Henry Wallace's insistence that this was the age of the common man, and the whole prior thrust of the social thought and legislation of the Depression years, compounded by the public feeling that the dangers and exigencies of the war should be fairly shared by everyone. It was obvious that some people must be more important than other people in the conduct of any large social affair, such as the conduct of a war, and libertarians though we might be, we accepted the pre-eminence of generals. Our complaint went to the Oriental nature of the preferential treatment accorded the Very Important Person, and to the Byzantine structure of his court. For example, it was difficult for us to see why we must leave our wives at home when General MacArthur was allowed to have his wife with him in New Guinea. While ready to grant MacArthur his stature as a military genius, and to acknowledge that since rank had its responsibilities, so too it might have its privileges, the justice of this particular privilege escaped us. It was as if a drill sergeant were parading his company while drinking a highball in a convertible, with one arm around his girl friend.

More immediately annoying were the privileges and prerequisites claimed by, or promoted by, the unimportant, whose success in the acquisition of some little extra comforts, special duties of dubious merit, or inveigled safe assignment in Sydney, made them at first apparently and then in fact more important than they really were. The rule was, in a world of uniforms and rationing, where everyone was presumably expendable and therefore individually unimportant, any special difference was a spectacular demonstration of status and was therefore envied and suspect. We talked scornfully of those who, as we said, were in like Flynn—a phrase that reflected our disgusted envy of a Hollywood actor's successful conquests of fifteen-year-old girls. Those were the people who had it made, we said, at once implying our moral superiority to such people and our acute desire to emulate them. If it had ever been true that most people believed there was nothing so valuable as a good name, that was true no longer. We were insensibly moving toward the idea that there was nothing so valuable as privilege and status; that status was defined by possession of comforts; that the man who had the most status was the man who had the most things; that the possession of power and material things implied notoriety and happiness; that their lack implied unhappiness and stupidity.

In sum, during America's experience of four years of Hitler's war, at least thirteen million of us were inchoately forming the future system of values of the postwar American world, which would include the following beliefs:

That America was the most powerful country in the world; that

133

Americans lived better lives than any other people; that America should therefore be the lawgiver and exemplar to the world; that since we could pour forth such a torrent of goods and comforts in a war, there was no reason why the national resources could not be mobilized to continue to provide everyone with everything when the war was over; that since we soldiers had devoted our youth to the state, the state could jolly well devote itself to serving us when we returned home; that obtaining comforts and privileges was a matter of first importance; that the only way of succeeding in the system was to find a way to use or cheat the system; that since life was absurd (as Camus would say) the only point of it was to look out for oneself.

Some of these beliefs were contradictory if not mutually exclusive, but no matter: we held them. The contradictions would be a source of tension in the postwar world, but I would say that our wartime experience led to establishment of the system of values that made possible such postwar phenomena as John Foster Dulles' Presbyterian brink-walking; Mr. Whyte's *Organization Man;* Mr. Riesman's other-directed man walking lonely in his crowds; Mr. Truman's Korean police force and Vietnam advisers; the success of Madison Avenue; the murder of Kitty Genovese; and the withdrawal that so unfortunately characterizes the current college generation. Here are matters we shall presently discuss, but I submit that the fall of Rome cannot be discussed except in the context of Rome's rise to power. I remember standing with soldiers in a truck driving north from Manila in the dust of the national road toward Lingayen, and thinking as we swept past the people who held handkerchiefs to their noses to keep out the dust that we were the new Romans with our soldiers, our engineers, our laws and our victories. Now I have an even clearer vision of a centurion polishing his helmet in his tent and contemplating his imminent discharge after twenty years' service and his return to Rome from the provinces, thinking of Rome while he blew on the bronze and shined it, and wondering to himself what there would be in the capital for him, and how he would get it.

I remember the way the war ended. We were living in a colony of tents pitched under coconut trees beside a lagoon on Palawan Island, and on a day like any other, hot and still, we were cooling beer by placing the cans inside a huge cardboard carton, sealing the carton, then cutting a hole in it to admit the nozzle of a carbon dioxide fire extinguisher. When you turned the extinguisher on, the carbon dioxide caused ice crystals to form inside the carton. While thus employed, we learned of the bomb that had been dropped on Hiroshima. We read the President's statement that this new weapon drew upon the same powers as those responsible for the existence of the sun, and we in the weather section had a sufficient technical education to be able to read much more between the lines.

There was a silence.

Then one of us said:

"If I ever have a kid and he picks up a test tube, I'll kill him."

It was obvious the war was about to end. Even without atomic bombs, Tokyo had been reduced to square miles of knee-deep ashes. What could the Japanese do? The second bomb fell on Nagasaki, and we wondered why. Of course we wanted the war to end and to go home. But we did not want it to end the way it was ending. We had no more control over the way the war ended than we had had over the way it began.

Some days later we were sitting in an outdoor theater watching one of those Hollywood films showing a leather-lunged girl who wore a tuxedo while singing, when the projector blinked off and an excited young corporal called over the public address system that the Japanese had surrendered.

"Yeah," someone said.

"Turn the movie back on," someone else called.

I understand that back in America, the nation got drunk and sang and danced in the streets and everyone who was in uniform had a girl that night. We walked back along the sand beach at the edge of the lagoon, after the show ended, and went to our tents to bed. I remember being glad the war was over. It had not ended with a bang or with Mr. Eliot's whimper; it had merely ended. I was glad that it had: only that—not deliriously happy, or joyful, or amazed, or discontented, or thankful, but simply glad the way you are glad when the curtain comes down on a particularly insipid play and you can leave the theater.

The only vivid memory I have of the voyage home, months later, was an officer telling me that it was a stupid thing, a criminal thing, for us to be going home when what we ought to do, if we had any brains and any sense of obligation to our children, was to keep the Army together and finish the job by invading Russia and wiping out Communism for once and all. Just two more years, he said, and we would really have peace, because what could they do, anyway, now that we had atomic bombs?

I remember, too, when moving through the separation procedures, that I felt a sudden fear of leaving the Army. I had not enjoyed it; I had often detested it; I intended throwing my uniforms into the trash can the instant I returned home. Yet, the Army had been my mother, father, big brother, and reason for existence for something more than four years. It was something familiar, something I understood. Outside yawned a vast uncertainty. If I stayed in the service, the Army promised to send me, Margaret and Christopher to Germany. Practically speaking, a free trip to Europe, all expenses paid. For the first time since my wedding day I seriously considered the fact that I had a wife and child and would have to do something to support them. The thought of finding a job was appalling. I was too young to go to work, in the sense that, before a young man goes to work, he should see something of the world. I had not yet seen enough of the world. The Army, however, would provide me with a grand tour of Europe; to re-enlist in the Army would postpone decisions. These thoughts winked through my mind in a momentary spasm of panic; it is only now that I can separate them for purposes of examination. At the time, there was only the instant's panic. When asked if I wanted to re-enlist, I said No.

With my discharge in hand, I joined the lines of men waiting at the telephone booths in the Post Exchange. Margaret had long ago sent me our telephone number.

A child answered.

"Chris?" I asked.

The last time I had seen him, he had been a slight, warm, sleepy weight in my arms.

"Is your mother there?"

When Margaret came on, I told her that I was now in Harrisburg, and out of the Army, and suggested that, unless she had some other engagement, I should like to see her that evening. She said that would be perfectly all right.

It is no great distance in time or space by train from Harrisburg to Philadelphia, but for me the trip passed as quickly as fighter planes close aloft: that is, there was no time for reflection—only for convulsive choice. But just as a pilot's decision is made on the basis of his long training and knowledge of the capabilities of his aircraft, so I should think that my choice was determined for me by my total experience. At one time in the Army I had got into a venomous argument with an older soldier about some Army task, and he had contemptuously asked, "What can *you* do?" I could not answer him then, but now I had an answer of sorts. The Army had taught me that I could do as well as or better than any man at most of its tasks, very nearly all of which could be learned on the job at need, for the work that men do is seldom complicated. If it were, very few people would be employed. True, some tasks require special training, but I was educable. In the Army I had reflected that all the men I saw about me would one day return to civilian life and eventually find jobs, and this was comforting, for I knew that if all *those* people could find work, *I* certainly would be able to do so. But what sort of work?

The answer came almost automatically. The one thing I had done well at school and college, and the one thing I had most enjoyed doing, was writing. So I would write. But I would need something to write about, and someone to pay me for writing it. If I worked for a newspaper I would be given subject matter, a salary and the possibility of travel. So I would become a newspaperman. There was something else that probably went into that decision. Perhaps I subconsciously understood that I had always been more of an observer of events than a participant in them; that I had never really felt a part of anything, nor ever had a strong desire to become involved in the things men did. For instance, while most of the airmen I knew wanted to *get into* action, I had wanted to *see* action: the difference is profound. Today I would say that this attitude is typical of our nation of spectators, and I do not recommend it. In the late fall of 1945, however, no such thoughts bothered me. I stared out of the window of a day coach, watching Pennsylvania going past, and decided to make a career of observation. The decision was as automatic as a conditioned reflex— which it very well may have been.

Then the factories bordering the Philadelphia railroad yards were clattering by, with signs on them reading WELL DONE and WELCOME HOME and THE NATION IS PROUD OF YOU. I could hardly believe they were meant for me, although I suppose in a way we had done well and no doubt the people who put out the signs were actually glad to welcome us home.

The taxi driver at the station was glad to see me. He looked at the service stripes and the overseas stripes on my sleeve, and at the campaign ribbons that bore battle stars for campaigns that the Fifth Air Force had fought and which were awarded to everyone in the Fifth Air Force even though it had been the few men in the air crews who had done the actual fighting, and he said that he had a kid in the service who was getting out soon and he knew how much he owed us so it would only be a dollar to Germantown for me; that when the meter said a dollar he'd shut if off. He said he'd like to do it free, because of what we'd done for him, but he had a wife and kids. I very wearily told him I completely understood.

Margaret and I embraced for a long moment, and it was as if I had never been away, or as if it had been yesterday since our last furlough. There was an old Army joke about the married soldier who returned home and said, "And the *second* thing I did was take

138

off my combat boots." I felt that way myself, but it seemed that I had responsibilities. We did not embrace too long and lovingly because of Christopher. Margaret had been very wise about this. She had written to me about the jealousies. It was going to be a shock to Chris, she had said, to have some stranger come into the house and compete with him for his mother's attention. It was not just Chris, but all babies, she said—all babies who had never seen their soldier-fathers. Also, I must not pick him up or fuss over him, because little children are put off by this, preferring to make their own way in their own time toward adults. So, instead of picking him up, I shook hands with my two-and-a-half-year-old son, and did not monopolize his mother.

By evening time, Chris had gathered the idea that I was someone special in some way or other, and he had consented to make friends with my brass buttons and varicolored ribbons. But he was a little puzzled when it was time for him to go to bed and I had not left. Turning to his mother, he asked:

"Is that man going to stay all night?"

It would seem that all the massive experiences of life are somewhat pedestrian at the moments of their occurrence.

7

Home Is the Hero

THE STORY of my generation in the postwar world is one of housing, jobs, children, education, and of haggard wondering whether or not our efforts have been worthwhile, and where, if anywhere, we might be going. Our lives have meanwhile all been touched by public events which we have felt powerless to control, and by social systems and attitudes that seem to have evolved for no particular reason but which have made it progressively more difficult for anyone to feel himself to be individually competent and free.

It was a strange America to which we veterans returned. Perhaps it seemed strange to us because, during our youth, we had no real experience of the ordinary stuff of adult life, but only vague and unfounded notions of what the lives of married citizens might be. Perhaps it was as if we had been guests in a house, enjoying the results of the work done by the servants, but taking these results for granted without appreciating the nature of the work that had produced them. Now that we had to do that work ourselves, in the course of bringing up children of our own, we were to find it often difficult and confusing.

Whatever the reason for my own mood at the moment of my reentrance into America from the Army, I remember that my country struck me as a rather disappointing one. The nation was to grow stranger still for me as it evolved into a land of brilliance that did not illuminate; of comfort that produced unease; of strength that could not be used; of purpose without meaning; of emptiness in the

140

midst of plenty; of hedonism without joy. The late, late show was to be one of its natural products.

For us, postwar life began on Christmas night, 1945, when Margaret, Christopher and I set off for Washington. That night, the train was as crowded as any train had been during the war. A soldier gave his seat to Margaret and Christopher, and he and I stood in the blinds outside the car all the way from North Philadelphia to Baltimore, smoking and watching the yellow window lights of the train flash past the snow fields. Enough people left the train at Baltimore for me to find a seat.

It was snowing heavily in Washington that night, and there were no taxis at the station. Nor was there any traffic at that hour on the plaza outside. My Uncle Louis could not come for us. He could not get out of that driveway of his. There were no buses at the station. Perhaps we could find a taxi in the areas of the better hotels fourteen blocks away.

So off we started on foot through the deepening snow, Margaret carrying the baby and I carrying everything we owned in a suitcase and a barracks bag. We walked all the way from Union Station to 13th and K streets before a D–4 bus came bulking through the smother. It was the only bus we had seen, and fortunately it was the only one that would take us anywhere near where we wanted to go. The driver said it was the last run that night.

The bus line ended a mile from the house off Conduit Road or, rather, MacArthur Boulevard as it was now called. I was having difficulty in understanding that I lived in a country that deified its living heroes. The America of Cincinnatus had become the America of Augustus while I had been away. The street, however, looked just the same despite its change of name, and Louis and my aunt, The Bear, lived in a woods well back from it. We were going to live with them, in a room over their garage, until we could find a place of our own. We climbed down from the bus into the snow, resting at least twice during that last mile through the drifts, and once again on the lane leading up to the log house in the woods. I thought of that Christmas during the Depression when Mother, Father and I had set off for New Jersey to look for Prosperity. It seemed there was now another family to which I belonged, seeking its fortune at Christmastime, mother, father and son. I thought: This is the ax my grandfather had. My father put in a new handle and I put on a new head. It was curious to be coming back to Washington. I had begun life in that city twenty-five years ago, and now I was apparently returning to it to start life all over again, almost as if my first twenty-five years had been a mistake. It seemed to me that I was always making new beginnings and incomplete endings, but at that time I had not yet discovered that personal life is not so much a series of new beginnings as it is a series of recapitulations.

Louis and The Bear welcomed us for what everyone thought would be a few days' visit. What none of us completely understood was that a housing shortage was the nation's most uncomfortable immediate postwar problem. But we understood it completely enough the moment Margaret and I started to look for a place to live. The city was no longer the sleepy Southern town I had left as a second-grade child. The old family town house on Kalorama Road, which had been sold at my great-uncle's death, was now officially tenanted by three Negro families and was believed to be unofficially inhabited by at least two more. During the past twenty years, Negroes had been moving into the city from the South; Roosevelt's New Deal had brought shoals of Government workers to the capital, none of whom had left, and the war had brought tens of thousands more, all of whom were still there, and now young families like my own were converging on all our cities, including Washington, where there had been no new building during the war except for Government-built housing projects for war workers. In Washington, housing space was still under wartime rent control, and all that space was taken. Our one hope, we were told, was to sign the waiting lists for Government housing where, as vacancies occurred, the apartments were rented to veterans. The average waiting time was nine months. There was also a compli-

142

cated formula governing rentals to veterans, one term of which specified that your salary determined the sort of accommodations you were permitted to obtain.

We learned of this from an old Army friend. He had gone to Africa and had married a French girl from Marrakech—a girl from a well-to-do family, used to a comfortable house, gardens and servants. She had looked forward to coming to America, that strong, golden land, lawgiver to the world, and now she and her husband and their infant daughter lived in a two-story wood-and-tarpaper former Army barracks called the Jubal Early Homes, situated in a reclaimed swamp under the noise of the landing pattern of the immediately adjacent National Airport. The French girl was distressed because she had found cockroaches in the baby's crib. While Margaret told her to put the legs of the crib in cups filled with water, I pursued the housing problem with my friend.

This, he said, was all he could get. He said that he was going to George Washington University on the GI Bill, a public law that provided college tuition for veterans who wished to attend, and he said that the pittance he received made him ineligible for the brick buildings of such Government housing projects as Fairlington or Maclean Gardens. We stared thoughtfully out the window of his one-bedroom apartment at a muddy yard full of clotheslines. The barracks block smelled of sour milk and diapers; the women took turns at the community washing machines; you could hear, through the plasterboard walls, the coughing of the neighbors. It was a place for veterans only. For poor veterans. For young new fathers who never had a youth, but who had left four years of their young manhood in Africa, Asia and Europe, who were now beginning to meet the girls they had married, and who were trying to raise children and, at the same time, go to college to establish the basis of their lives. Some loon in the Labor Department had said that a man with a college education earned during his lifetime an average of one hundred thousand dollars more than a man who had only a high school diploma, and no few of the veterans believed this to be a statement of cause and effect, rather than a

143

statement of coincidence. So they were going to college. They were all, like my friend, starting the race eight years behind any young-ster then being graduated, at the same time carrying more of a load, young without youth, stuffed into such places as the Jubal Early Homes. However, they may have been lucky to have been given such quarters, for elsewhere, as a Senate committee was to report, veterans' families were offered rental space in "garages, coal sheds, chicken coops, barns, tool sheds, granaries and smoke-houses. Such hovels are merely gestures of contempt toward those who are desperate enough to take anything which is offered," the Senate said. "Structures with no water available, heating facilities so bad that bottled drinks will freeze in the same room with a large stove, no sanitary toilet facilities, primitive food storage, no sinks, cardboard windowpanes and paper walls. . . . The plain fact of the matter is that the unscrupulous landlords who are extorting out-rageous rents for dilapidated, filthy hovels are doing so, in most cases, strictly within the limits of the law."

It was certainly lucky for me that I talked with my friend before I signed the waiting list for Government housing. I signed up for the reasonably comfortable brick garden apartments called Fair-lington, in Virginia, although my twenty-five-dollar-a-week salary as a copyboy on the *Washington Daily News* would have called for something on the order of the Jubal Early Homes. Without a qualm, I said I earned sixty-five dollars a week (then the top minimum salary for a reporter of three years' experience), and the clerk wrote this down.

Tell the truth, and live with roaches?

Tell a lie, and chisel in at the head of the chowline?

This was hardly the path of honor. In fact, I probably was committing some sort of Federal crime as well as a personal sin, but the Army had taught me that systems take no account of individuals; that they are unable to imagine exceptions; that the larger the bureaucracy, the less likely it is that anyone will ever read any of its pieces of paper unless something jams in the machinery. So there was a nine months' wait for a Fairlington

144

apartment? Very well, by the end of that time I would no longer be a copyboy, and I would have had to have found some way of actually earning at least sixty-five dollars a week, in which case my statement would not then be proved a lie and the machinery would not jam.

Meanwhile, we lived over the garage in the woods. There was nothing in this for Margaret. Nothing, that is, except for the acute frustration of living in another woman's house, when it is so important for a young wife to be mistress of her own establishment. If we had been Europeans or born into an earlier American generation, then Margaret might not have felt the same frustration, but would have fallen in with the custom of the bridegroom bringing his bride to his family's home. But that was neither the custom nor the dream of our American generation. To add to Margaret's problems, she was both pregnant and worried. She was worried because she felt economically insecure, which is the worst kind of worry a woman, particularly a pregnant one, can have, and she could look out the window each day and feel physically insecure as well, for there were bulldozers working in the woods. The city of Washington had decided to build a street through Louis's land, and the street was to come straight through the house and the garage where we lived, and each day the street came a little closer as the bulldozers ate their way downhill through the trees. When the street was completed, Louis's taxes would be increased because of this new improvement to his property.

As matters turned out, the bulldozers were still some yards away when, nine months to the day, a two-bedroom apartment at Fairlington became available. And the day after that, Margaret and I delivered our second child, our daughter Margaret, in our new apartment. There had been no time to reach a hospital, and the doctor arrived too late. He had lost his way among the five square miles of identical streets and buildings of the housing project. We were drinking coffee and the baby was sleeping in a clothes basket when the doctor arrived. We poured another cup for him.

By the time we moved into Fairlington I had added three side jobs to my normal occupation as a reporter, which brought my weekly income to nearly one hundred dollars, and as a consequence, nothing jammed in the bureaucratic machinery. My three additional jobs were identical. I was covering the city courts for my newspaper, and these institutions included the marriage-license bureau on their premises. Each afternoon I would gather up the marriage-license applications forms from the clerk, compare the names on them with the names in the stud book, as we called the *Social Register,* to see whether there was anything in the list that would interest the city editor, and then retire to a telephone to read the names and addresses to each of three different Washington photographic studios who would each pay me ten dollars a week for this information. The studios would then compete for the business of taking the bridal portraits and wedding pictures. My service saved them the time and expense of sending someone to the bureau to obtain the names and addresses. Why such a simple way of making money never occurred to the marriage-license clerk, I shall never know, but perhaps he did not have to find some way of buying food and rental space in Fairlington. Other men in that housing project worked as Government clerks during the day, went to George Washington University at night, and spent their weekends as salesmen in department stores. A first characteristic of the postwar world for my generation of veterans of Hitler's war, was an intense concern for making money. For us, the need to make money was greater than it had been for many people during the Depression—a rather odd statement that demands a brief explanation.

First, the nation was becoming prosperous, and as wartime price controls were progressively removed, the cost of daily living increased. Second, millions of young men married during the war or immediately after it, and now flooded toward the cities to look for work. During the Depression, people tended to marry later in life; they doubled up with their parental families at need; they postponed having children; they tended to remain in provincial towns and rural areas where costs were low. But after the war, the veter-

146

ans who had seen the cities during their Army careers now came with their brides to the areas of the once-again-busy factories and offices, each young couple now usually distant from their families and looking for single-family dwelling space, and condemned, as young people usually are, to poor housing and to the relatively low wages of their first jobs. Wherefore, a need to make money was the instant, overriding concern of my generation at that time, and I should suppose that our concern, and our experience, has colored our thinking ever since.

The facts of our Fairlington existence were also the facts of life for hundreds of thousands of young people like ourselves who came to live in the nation's apartment housing projects and in the housing developments of picture-windowed crackerboxes that were shortly built and sold to veterans for nothing down other than a promise to pay an inflated price for thirty years. People said we were lucky to live in Fairlington, and others said we were lucky to be able to afford it, but I did not think luck had much to do with it, and although I did not know it at the time, Margaret was finding Fairlington to be a fresh-air jail to which she had been condemned by circumstance. I was unaware of her distress, largely because she concealed it, partly because I was too new a husband to sense her moods, and chiefly because I did not live in Fairlington myself. Like the other husbands, I was an overnight boarder and weekend guest. During the day I was learning my job and discovering a postwar way of life that was absolutely different from any American way of life I remembered. The new world fascinated me. Margaret, also living in a postwar world that was different from any America she had know or imagined, was bored beyond tears and to the verge of hopeless desolation.

To deal with Margaret's discoveries first, I have no idea what she expected marriage to be, but I am sure that her concept never included a Fairlington. No such places existed when we were growing up. If viewed as a machine for living, there was nothing ostensibly wrong with it. The buildings were well constructed—better built than many apartment houses today. There was cross ventila-

147

tion in each room. The room size was adequate. The kitchen and bathroom facilities were good. The building line, no more than three stories high, was well within what architects call the human scale. Each apartment house contained six family units: two 2-bedroom apartments on each floor. Each building contained a laundry room equipped with washing machines and driers, and each stood on a bit of land and looked into a grassy courtyard. Duplex apartments, built to resemble two-story cottages, stood between the three-story buildings and added some variety to the scene. The architecture was twentieth-century Institutional Colonial—a by no means unpleasant hybrid. And the controlled rent, $68.50 a month, for a two-bedroom apartment, was certainly reasonable. In sum, Fairlington was clean, airy, adequate and relatively cheap, only twenty minutes by bus from downtown Washington, and its grassy areas, well removed from the quiet streets, indicated that the apartment project would be a safe, healthful place in which to raise small children.

Unfortunately, Fairlington demonstrated that people cannot live in machines that are run by systems. First, five square miles of the same thing, even of the Garden of Eden, is simply too much of whatever it is. Next, a great many systems impinged upon human life. One was the system that said Fairlington apartments would be rented to veterans who earned a certain amount of money. All this was very fine, inasmuch as the Government was trying to do something for young men to whom it owed its very survival, and it was trying to protect them against paying any more for living space than they could afford. But the practical effect of this philanthropy was to fill an immense area with the same kind of people. Everyone was of the same age, we all had the same number of small children, and the regulation as to income was a fair guarantee that we would all have much the same kind of problems and possessions. Moreover, since the principal business of Washington is government, most of Fairlington's young veterans were Government employees, and the salary levels indicated they all held much the same kind of jobs in their different bureaus, which in turn

148

meant they all had much the same kind of conversations and aspirations.

Another system, built into the plans, provided a choice of two shopping centers that were central to nothing. They were built on Fairlington's fringes, and in the first automobileless postwar years, this meant that nearly everyone had to ride the buses to reach them. A system having to do with the nature of shopping centers decreed that these market places consist of branch stores of national cheapjack chains, and that they offer a great deal of everything and the best of nothing. The pattern of life that says a man goes to work while the woman stays home meant that thousands of women and infant children were marooned at the end of a Virginia busline each day to stare at Fairlington's bland monotony and discuss the problems, such as toilet training, that they had only too much in common. The rule that says rules have to be made to govern for the common good, and that the more people, the more rules, resulted in such decrees as an absolute prohibition against planting trees, vegetables or flowers. The repainting of apartments occurred not at need, but according to a schedule as immutable as any devised by the Medes. The rules thereby denied the women certain opportunities to be homemakers. Finally, Fairlington raised the question of whether any child's best interests are served by bringing him up in a one-class communal kindergarten in which the only adults are women and in which there are no older children.

Fairlington's essential problem—that of all postwar housing developments—was that it was not a human community, in the sense that a community is an area in which people of all ages and different kinds of employment can each find privacy, work, recreation, education and physical variety. There were no corner stores, no piazza bordered by sidewalk cafes, no central business or shopping area, no convenient parks, no gardens, no schools, no civilized amenities; there were no public buildings, no traditions, no aged people, no adolescents, no throng to see in the streets, no differences. It was merely an adequate barracks in which people ate and slept out of the rain; wherein there was a constant neighboring without much real friendship; wherein people met each other because they lived next to each other and not because anyone had something to offer that someone else needed or wanted; wherein each stranded woman had a choice of two conversationalists: her prattling babies or another stranded woman who prattled about *her* prattling babies. Finally, there were only two gods in Fairlington's pantheon: the weekly paycheck and the Spirit of Friday Night.

Margaret was later to say that the three years we lived there were three years taken out of her life, just as I regarded the time spent in the Army as time taken out of mine. She was willing to accept the fact that a mother may expect to serve some years as the prisoner of her children. But while a more diverse community of people and buildings can give a mother some variety during her period of servitude, Fairlington provided only a soul-numbing monotony. In this empty world of women and babies without men, the quality of bitchery became such that a woman who left her wash in the machine past her allotted time would be literally afraid to retrieve it until a late hour of the night. Then she would find it sodden in a corner where it had been hurled by an enraged young woman whose violence was in no small part an expression of her general despair.

It would have been better for Margaret if we had had an automobile, for then we could have taken little weekend drives into the country. But, assuming there had been any automobiles to buy at the still-controlled price, we had no money to buy one. Our great Sunday recreation was to take the bus into Washington, there to do all the things that were free—such as walk around the Tidal Basin or the Lincoln Memorial, or visit the Smithsonian, and eat a picnic lunch of tunafish sandwiches and Coca-Cola on a bit of Government lawn. We could see no possibility of a change in our lives in the immediate future, for despite my extra jobs and the fact that we lived a frugal life virtually devoid of such little luxuries as an occasional motion picture and dinners out, we could save no

150

money toward an automobile or toward an escape into a more expensive apartment in the city or a house in the country.

I suppose I could have changed jobs easily enough. In the post-war period, jobs were simple for white men to come by. Instead of depression and unemployment, there was now a burgeoning pros-perity and an acute labor shortage as America, with its war-expanded and undamaged industrial base intact, turned from the manufacture of munitions to supplying goods and food for a domestic population ready to spend its war-saved money, and for the huge empty market that was war-gutted Europe. But Margaret knew that I did not want to work just for money's sake, and that I was happy in and good at the only kind of work that appealed to me, and that it was better for us to have me doing something I liked to do than for me to do something I didn't like, even if it was bad for her to live where and as we did. Her chief trouble was that she could see no way out of our trap. She could take what consola-tion she might out of the fact that almost everyone we knew was in much the same fix, but that was a most depressing sort of consola-tion. The Government may have been right in reporting that Amer-ican savings accounts were at record levels, but we did not know a soul our age who had such an account. In fact, we knew many who did not have a checking account. The people who had stayed home during the war had made money, but not the veterans. We were very conscious that veterans constituted a special class in society. At our infrequent occasions, everyone brought his own bottle and contributed something to the hors d'oeuvres. In our set, BYOB was more common than R.S.V.P. on invitations, and the bottles usually contained the cheapest beer.

I cannot look back on those days with misty sentiment for young, struggling people happily working their way through adver-sity to mature prosperity. For Margaret, the early years of mar-riage were hardly those of joyful love in a rose-covered cottage. They were more like being jailed in a barracks for unwed mothers. For my part, matters were more supportable, because I spent my days out in the world, learning my trade. But my trade dealt almost exclusively with what was wrong with America, not with what was right or good about it.

In all that follows, it is probably well to bear in mind that not only was I an only child, and an outsider by temperament and choice, but also that newspapers insist that their reporters stand outside events in order to preserve an objectivity, and that news by definition is that which is unusual, and that what is unusual is usually bad, or at least that which is bad news is usually more readable and interesting than good news and therefore receives wider coverage. Moreover, reporters are trained to be suspicious. For example, I remember going to the scene of an accident to find a frail grandmother lying on the pavement while a white-faced driver shakily tried to explain matters to two stolid policemen. I felt a pity for the woman and for the driver—an emotion which did not change until much later when the same cast was reassembled for Act Two in the courts. Then, to my youthful astonishment, it turned out that the sweet little grandmother had a trick knee, a set of X rays of someone else's broken hip, and was an accomplished acrobat and amateur actress who was what the police call a professional flopper, employed by a crooked lawyer who made a living suing insurance companies. Such discoveries are sobering, and in the newspaper business one unfortunately makes a considerable number of them, with the result that the reporter becomes unusually dubious of his fellow man. So what I have to say should be measured against your own experience, for mine may have made me an outsider, much too suspicious, and too prone to say that within every silver lining there is a black cloud. Having delivered this caveat, I now submit that the most impressive thing about postwar America to me was that I had entered a nation that looked upon its laws as constituting an obstacle course. The trick was to run the course without encountering the obstacles. The people who did this were regarded as clever.

Much of the general moral leprosy stemmed from the shortages of everything. People were waiting in lines for soap flakes at the

152

supermarkets (supermarkets had apparently been invented while I was away), for tables at restaurants, for buses on street corners, for refrigerators and automobiles and for living space. When goods are scarce and wartime price controls are in effect, black markets flourish. America's contribution to the art of black-marketing was to take narrow advantage of the letter of the law, in order to cheat the clear intent and purpose of the law—a contribution more corrosive of morality, I should say, than plain, simple, broad-daylight thievery and sale of stolen goods.

For example, automobile dealers had a great many more customers than there were automobiles. A man who wished to buy a new car at the controlled price could expect to wait thirty-six months for his name to arrive at the top of the dealer's list. Or, if he wished, he could find a dealer who would sell him a new car in the next five minutes. All he had to do was agree to buy an automobile festooned with spotlights, slipcovers, windshield visors and sundry other unwanted and unnecessary accessories that, by a perhaps-purposefully-left-open loophole in the law, were not subject to price controls. The accessories were sold at prices which allowed the dealer to make a profit of up to one thousand dollars over and above his legitimate profit on the sale of the car. There was nothing illegal about this, any more than there was anything illegal about the rental of a chicken coop to a man who was willing to consider it a house.

Neither seller nor buyer was concerned with the fraudulent aspects of the agreement, nor with its offense against public morality; and so many people were willing to pay such premiums for new cars that some dealers had two waiting lists: one arranged in chronological order of application by regular or naïve customers, and one arranged in arithmetical order of willingness to pay. There even appeared agents—men who said they were the friends of dealers—who received a fee from a customer for introducing him to a dealer and a second fee from the dealer for having brought him such a sheep for the shearing. Those who paid the prices flattered themselves on having been clever enough to obtain a new car while their neighbors had to wait, and the dealers congratulated themselves on having been businessmen of vision.

Less Levantine, but as corrosive of decency, was the manner in which many a Washington housewife bought her nylon stockings. The normal process was that women would queue up early in the morning outside stores where, rumor said, a shipment of nylons had been received. Within a few minutes the stock put on public sale would have been sold. Later in the day, the private sale to selected customers would begin, at prices paid to sales clerks but never reflected in the store's accounts.

I knew that this sort of flummery had been going on during the war. I had seen black markets in Australia and in the Philippines, but I nevertheless had somehow naïvely thought it was only foreigners and soldiers who engaged in them. It was something of a shock for me to discover that there really had been a civilian *American* black market in rationed gasoline, meat and cigarettes, and that the nation had been living for years on Prohibition's basis of "Joe sent me."

In the Federal courts, I listened to the story of a Congressman who conspired with two sharpers to profit from the sale of defective munitions that the two sharpers had manufactured; to the tale of an Air Force general who used his special knowledge as procurement officer to make a killing in the stock market; to endless accounts in small-claims court of the shabby practices that businessmen perpetrated upon the uninformed poor. And, as an assiduous reader of our own newspaper, and as a listener to the conversations of other reporters, I was quite aware of the flavor of gimmick and deal and jockeying for power and advantage that was so much a way of Washington's public as well as private life. It was amusing to hear stories of how rival women in society would compete to give cocktail parties for the nation's men of power. It was less amusing to be told that you could learn more at such a cocktail party, by overhearing conversations and by watching who talked with whom, than you could by asking these officials public

154

questions in their public offices. And it was not amusing at all to speculate upon the possible uses the hostesses made of that which they overheard.

Nor was a reportorial acquaintance among politicians always an improving one. The first impression that speeds to a young reporter's mind is that "politician" is another word for "liar." It was maddening to talk with them. For example, the residents of Washington are not allowed to vote for a city government. They are governed, instead, by a committee of Congressmen. If you asked a Congressman why this should be so, he would smoothly say it was because Washington is a Federal city, and therefore belongs to all the people of America, and that it is therefore both right and proper that its government be representative of all the people—which is to say, Washington should be governed by the people's representatives, the Congressmen. But when he said this, you and he and all the residents of Washington, and the majority of Americans acquainted with the facts, knew very well that the real reason for Washington's lack of suffrage was not an antique law no longer germane to the facts, but was because the city has a Negro majority. Enfranchised, the residents of Washington might vote themselves a Negro-dominated government. A second reason, just as real and just as immoral but much less important, was that a voteless Washington provided Congressmen with an opportunity to pay off political debts by finding city jobs for their constituents.

Washington was a splendid city for anyone to lose his intellectual virginity in, replete with local rapists as it was, and serving furthermore as the news center of other, national affairs. Like the local news, the national news seemed to indicate that America had slipped its moral moorings. My newspaper work gave me a view of the nation as being engaged in a kind of yacht race, in which the rules demanded that everyone steer as close as possible to the shoals of the law. And everyone, from local loan sharks to politicians to the presidents of national corporations, seemed to be engaged in this singular pastime. The number of those who steered too close, and piled up on the rocks, included some of the great,

155

but for everyone who came to grief, dozens more seemed to loophole safely through and around the shoals, with the district attor-
neys well aware of what they were doing, but without a means to
stop them, and the moral seemed to be: Go thee and do likewise if
thee expects to get thy share. When I discussed the matter with a
lawyer, he shrugged and said that he did not think of himself as
cheating the law when he found a loophole for a client but, rather,
that he was helping the Government by pointing out that a loophole existed; that if the Government wanted to plug it, the Congress would enact remedial legislation. Another lawyer said that the
very multiplicity of laws, rules and controls invited inventive
circumvention; that it was human nature to resist systems; that
some people thought it was just as important to know how to use
the rules of a game as it was to know what they were.

The second lawyer, I now think, was exactly right. Today I
would say that what I was disgustedly observing as a young reporter in postwar America was the human result of the application
of the idea that what had been good for the Army was good for
General Motors and everyone else besides. What Hitler's war had
done for us was to subject the nation to a forced growth toward
the corporate-welfare-garrison state it has become. Certain rather
admirable American traits had come to front center at war's need:
our pragmatism, our genius for organization, our impatience with
inefficiency, our willingness to try something new, our concern for
immediate results, our fondness for tackling a big job. So we
mobilized the immense latent powers of an industrial society to an
extent never seen before on this earth. This fact had not been
apparent to us who ate C rations and drank General Issue lemon-
ade in God-forgotten Asiatic jungles from one rotting year to the
next, and if anyone had then told us we were the best-supplied and
fastest-moving troops in history, he would have run a serious risk
of personal injury. Yet our informant would have been quite correct, and our boredom could have been seen as one result of the
very efficiency he was describing, for the facts of life of an Army,
as of an industrial plant or state, say that efficiency is achieved

156

through specialization intricately organized and centrally controlled. Seen from the vantage of high command, a complicated social machine is very beautiful and there is no question that it is remarkably efficient and productive, but seen from such an eminence it is difficult to remember that the machine is composed of people. During the war, people did not count, and no one counted them. But after the war, when people thought they ought to matter once again, it was hardly possible for them to believe that they did, because the systems that had been devised for winning the war applied to the uses of peace. Indeed, the systems proliferated. There was a postwar emphasis on expanding and compartmentalizing the organization of whatever it was, be it the Cub Scouts or the American Telephone and Telegraph Company; there was continued emphasis on the creation of specialists and specialized departments and hierarchies of command. You could see this emphasis in every sort of activity from junior high school football, complete with recruited ringers, ninth-grade beauty queens, cheer leaders and marching bands, to the creation of supermarkets and to the administration of the Government. Everyone seemed to be busy building empires or systems that used people as integers instead of as individuals, creating complex structures that narrowly defined people's roles for efficiency's sake. No one seemed to speculate what the human cost of the resultant efficiency might be, but we had a phrase in common usage during the first postwar years. We spoke of life as being a rat race. Apparently no one thought it odd to equate Americans with rats.

I did not conceive myself to be involved in any such race. My view was that what I was seeing was interesting, as a drop of swamp water interests someone with a microscope, and I thanked God that I was not one of the animalcules in the evaporating drop. Reporting on the lives of others, I found the conviction growing in me that what most men did every day was exceptionally dull when it was not actually stupefying. Be they factory workers or tax lawyers or throat specialists, what did most men do? Whatever it was, they performed their little specialty, or function, over

157

and over again every day in the same place all their lives, like the professional football player who does not really play football, but who only kicks field goals. First they stuck at it, and next they were stuck with it, and finally they either gave it all they had or it took all they had whether they wanted to give it or not, until retirement and the congratulatory traveling bag did them part, and that was life. In such a plight, people said, "Thank God for Friday" and looked forward for fifty weeks a year to the two-week vacation with pay, and the vehemence with which they greeted Friday, and the poignancy with which they looked forward to the rented rooms by the lake were quite accurate indications of their boredom and need for release.

Was this, at last, the real life to which I had been looking forward since childhood? To live in a barracks instead of a town and be a function instead of a man? Such apparently was the fate of millions of my generation who passed from a depression through a war and returned to an impersonal America of mass housing, mass markets, massive corporations, massive Government, mass media and massive boredom. I wondered what had ever happened to the notion that each man must do his own work, stand on his own feet, make his own way. Perhaps the concept of the rugged individual had always been just that—merely a concept, never a reality. In any case, it was also quite clear to me that very few people of my acquaintance wanted to shift for themselves, much as they might complain about department policies and rules. More often than they complained, they would talk earnestly about security, pensions, and chronological promotions. They did not speak of what they did, but rather of what they had. At least in the Eastern cities, the pioneer spirit was quite satisfactorily dead. Those in private business seemed exactly as unadventurous as the Government workers. Instead of speaking of the pleasures of responsibility, they talked of the value of teamwork; of going along with the group; of how some dubious course of action had been none of their doing, but that of a committee to which they belonged. It was as if they were all delighted to have found in the

158

civil world a simile of that all-providing, many-breasted mother, the Army—in whose impersonal arms they would be safe for ever and ever, so long as they were never caught making a mistake.

Sensing the national mood, *McCall's* magazine minted the word "togetherness." Togetherness indeed! There was something else in that welter of togetherness that also seemed familiar and Army-like. It was the buck passing, angle shooting, ass kissing, chowline cheating and goldbricking of the dearly beloved who were gathered together. The veteran was not finding the transition to civil life unduly difficult. Very well: consider inventive circumvention to be a human response to an inhuman system. As it had been in the Army, the purpose of that human response was quite familiar. It was a pathetic attempt to identify the practitioner as a Very Important Person in a world where no one was important. Accordingly, each clerk was jealous of his insect authority and he wielded it arrogantly whenever it was safe for him to do so. Acting also on the theory that the VIP was identified by his possession of things that others lacked, and urged by the mass media that the ownership of the new and different guaranteed "the bang of living it up," each nondescript status-seeker, subconsciously oppressed by the crushing weight of togetherness, equated position with possession, accepted accretion as a reasonable substitute for ambition, and confused purchase with happiness. I was startled to find people looking on shopping as a pleasure instead of regarding it as a chore to be performed at need. The simple act of buying something gave them a happiness that often lasted nearly all the way home, and best of all, it was practically free! People no longer asked "What does it cost?" but "What are the monthly payments?" Apparently it was possible to become a Very Important Person by installments. "Fly now, pay later," the advertisements said, and no few just flew away without a thought of the future. This again was all very Armylike, for in the Army everything seems free and there is no future. In the new civil life, as in the life we had known, there was little demand that my generation distinguish between its wants and its needs, but an enormous assumption that position and possessions were optimum goods, to be acquired by almost any means.

Thus, while Margaret was finding life in Fairlington to be a dreary thing, I was finding life in the somewhat wider, more exciting world to be nearly as depressing. It did nothing for me to realize that I was committing many of the same sins I deplored in others. For instance, there had been the way I had applied for the Fairlington apartment, rationalizing this by believing we needed a decent apartment more than we needed a scrupulous consistency. Together with other reporters, I had accepted Christmas liquor from lawyers. Next and worse, there was the matter of the car.

One day a public relations man from the Ford Motor Company approached the *Washington Daily News* with a promise to provide new Fords immediately at the controlled factory price for any reporters who wanted them. In return, the *News* was asked to look with favor upon the Ford Company whenever it could. There was nothing about this proposal that smacked of honor, any more than there is about Democratic Presidents using Fords in their inaugural parades and Republican presidents using General Motors products in theirs. If I had been without sin I would have had no part of the thing. But it so happened that a relative of Margaret's had died, and we had unexpectedly come into money enough to buy a Ford, which in all sober truth we needed—or so we said. We needed it to escape from time to time the nothingness of Fairlington; to get free of the bus routes; to go far beyond the bulldozed plains on weekends.

No doubt we could have continued to live without a car, and no doubt we could have put our name on a dealer's list and waited our turn.

But we believed we needed one right away—or so I rationalized when I told the city editor to include me among the reporters ordering Fords through the company.

I did not, however, bother to rationalize the pleasure it gave me to listen to a Ford dealer's curses as, at company order, he turned over to me at list price a new car he could have lathered with

160

gadgets and forced on someone else. It was a real pleasure for me to listen to him belch about people who had pull. Nor did I look for excuses for the joy it gave me to own a new automobile at a time when most of our acquaintances could not obtain one. I positively wallowed in this distinction, just as any other successful cheat did. At the same time, though, it was depressing to realize that, no matter how much I might think myself outside it, I was bound up in the system; to understand that I was both a victim of and a participant in the gathering sickness of the age. As the Beatles would later sing, I was just a nowhere man, living in his nowhere land, no more and no less of a brother rat than all the others in the race.

8

The Scapegoat and Its Kid

DURING the late Truman and early Eisenhower years the nation and I continued to prosper. The factories were busy, the stock market rose, and I acquired a house in rural Maryland and a summer island in Canada. But during these same years, I never crossed the Canadian border without feeling I had just escaped from a psychiatric ward full of dangerous lunatics, and I never re-entered the United States without misgivings compounded of fear and disgust, because for all its riches, the nation was terrified.

First of all, there was a panicky fear that the Russians would shower us with atomic bombs without warning at any moment. Washington was so jittery during those years that one of our *Washington Daily News* reporters turned pale every time the siren sounded in the firehouse across the street from our office. Each time, he feared it would be the air raid alarm. Another of my friends on the *News* seriously measured the distance between the Pentagon building and his Virginia home to determine whether his family lived sufficiently far from the presumable Ground Zero of the first incoming Russian rocket. Another friend told me I was lucky to have moved thirty miles out into Maryland. Real estate agents were selling houses in Maryland and Virginia to people who wanted to live outside what everyone called the disaster area. One reporter figured out an escape route from Washington based on fifteen minutes' warning. It avoided the main access roads, which already bore signs designating them as emergency routes to be used by Civil Defense vehicles in event of enemy attack. A manufacturer of paper cups donated a supply to be kept near Annapolis to be used by any survivors there might be. In the Washington area public schools, children practiced air raid drills, which called for them to curl into fetal positions in the corridors. Civil Defense was unaware of any irony thus symbolized.

Concurrently, Senator Joseph R. McCarthy was bounding about in the gutter, darkly claiming private knowledge that our State Department was riddled with Communist agents, and that it was the pinko intellectuals and homosexuals in Government, who were either Russian spies or domestic traitors or the witless dupes of diabolically clever Communists, who had betrayed our secrets and our strength and who were responsible for all of Communism's political victories and Russian military power. He did this in such a way as to imply that anyone who had a thought in his head was either a Communist or was controlled by Communists, and by hints and innuendoes he called into question the loyalty of anyone who disagreed with him. He had the visage of a thug, the eyes of a basilisk, the mentality of a Spanish Inquisitor, and the mood and manner of a large policeman with a rubber hose left alone in a locked room with an undersized suspect. More will be said of this statesman in a moment, but at this time I wish only to say that Washington was so afraid that it was about to be attacked by Russian nuclear rockets that men jumped when fire alarms went off, and that it was simultaneously so frightened by McCarthy that some entirely innocent and quite ordinary citizens would use pay telephones to talk with friends for fear their own telephones were tapped by McCarthy's agents.

Before examining that incredible era in further detail, I should like to suggest some reasons for it. A foreign observer, for instance, newly arrived among us from a still-devastated Europe with his sense of history intact and excruciating personal memories of his immediate past, would have been astounded to discover the well-fed and fearsomely potent Americans so terrified of imminent destruction from without and of betrayal from within. He would have thought we were crazy, and so, I think, we were. I think that our terror could be attributed in great measure to our horrified discovery that, after Hitler's war, we had become a great power. As the smoke lifted from Hitler's battlefields, there, across the way, brute and terrible, we saw our quondam ally Russia, coldly ready to seize Europe and Asia. And, looking hastily about, we realized that we were the only nation that could oppose her and that it was absolutely necessary that we should. There ensued a sharp series of Communist political victories on both continents, and then the bitter discovery that the Russians had unlocked the secrets of nuclear fission. We were appalled. How could all this have come about? Had we not won the war, and were we not now, after years of depression and war, to be allowed at last to broil steaks on our new outdoor fireplaces and otherwise enjoy an affluence we had never before experienced? Was there to be not peace but only a more monstrous violence? It was almost as if a wicked old witch had stolen all our Christmas presents some time between Christmas eve, when we had seen them under the tree, and Christmas morning when we woke. A common reaction was a helpless, petulant anger and a chill terror, and a desperate wonderment as to who could possibly have been responsible for such a mess.

It was at this point that Senator McCarthy contributed his all-inclusive explanation that blamed the Democrats, the Communists, the Russians and the intellectuals for everything, exactly in the manner of Hitler telling the Germans that they had not lost the Kaiser's war, but had been betrayed by the Jewish-Communist-plutocratic-intellectuals in their midst. If any ordinary citizen had uttered such nonsense, the press would not have noticed him and the local authorities would doubtless have questioned his sanity, but McCarthy happened to be a United States Senator. As such, he was presumed to know something, and in fact he had power. The press reported his remarks (a) because he was a Senator and (b) because what he was saying was so unusual that it seemed to constitute news.

In retrospect, it is easy to see that Hitlers and McCarthys are never the creators of moral swamps, but are merely the odors

164

emanating from them; that Hitler was less of a leader than he was an agent for the sick frustrations of the Germans; that McCarthy capitalized upon a mood and gave it furious voice.

I would say that, just as marsh gas is not an element but a compound, so the mood upon which McCarthy capitalized, and which he did so much to deepen, had many components. For example, I would say that our fear that someone would drop an atomic bomb on us stemmed, in part, from our guilty knowledge that we had dropped atomic bombs on someone else—on a someone who reportedly had been trying to surrender at the time.

Then, there were McCarthy's political bedfellows. One would be the plumber who put George Washington's theories on foreign entanglements into more basic English when he told me, "I can't see why the hell my kid has to go get shot in some asshole country that nobody gives a shit about." Having been in one war himself, the plumber wanted no part of another, and he was well within an American tradition when he spoke for isolation. He agreed with right-wing politicians who opposed foreign aid and participation in the United Nations, and who demanded stricter laws concerning the admission of immigrants. The policy of isolation has never lacked for adherents since Colonial times, but not until Hitler's war was over did the United States decide to act the part of a world power at stage center. Millions of Americans, particularly those of older generations, thought this was a mistake. They would include those who had opposed our entrance into the Kaiser's war, and who at the end of it supported the high tariff and had been glad when the Senate refused to allow President Wilson to take us into the League of Nations. They would also include those whose opposition to the draft was so clamorous that the draft act was passed only by one vote in Congress on the eve of our entrance into Hitler's war, and the multitudes who were listening to America First speakers even as the Japanese fleet was steaming toward Pearl Harbor. The isolationists would have included all who, in Adlai Stevenson's phrase, had to be dragged, kicking and screaming, into the twentieth century.

The unlikely allies of the isolationists were those of a precisely opposite persuasion—the latter-day followers of Theodore Roosevelt's policy of gunboat diplomacy. They were the people who said, "The only thing the Russians understand is force," and who argued that we had the power to do what we wanted, and what was the good of having power if we did not use it. They were quick to say that people who disagreed with them were soft on Communism. A common ground that the gunboat diplomatists shared with the isolationists was a nostalgia for a simpler time and an enthusiasm for the Republican Party. The bankruptcy of their position added a measure of hysteria to the quite general and legitimate fear of war.

Also contributive to the intensity of our terror was the sickening feeling that there was nothing anyone could do to control events. The more complex a society, the more widespread such a feeling is bound to be, and our highly organized industrial state was no exception to the rule. Given a society predicated on the notion that the team is greater than the man, and that everyone's different roles were small and special, it was no step at all for Everyman to believe that nothing he did either could or would affect whatever "they" decided. If his own corporation was an impersonal "they," then surely the Federal Government was a perfectly Olympian "They." And given that feeling, it was easy for Everyman to think They were his enemies. Given also many kinds of examples, such as those discussed in the preceding chapter, to the point that each man would cheat the system if he could, Everyman became suspicious of Their honesty, and when he found out that Government favors were bought and sold for mink coats and vicuña jackets in cliques close to the Presidents, his fears were confirmed. Next, when it was revealed that a Soviet espionage apparatus reached into Government offices and filched atomic secrets, and that despite our strength we could not for some mysterious reason use it, but were bogged down in a peninsular Asian war that apparently could not be won, the end result was an inchoate frustration and resentment of the crooked and stupid Them.

In this context, no small part of the national frustration during the McCarthy era derived from our American belief that we were the strongest and the best of nations, but that somehow we were not winning. The point is that all of us felt this to some extent, not just the gunboat diplomats, and this was maddening, because we Americans love to win at everything all the time by the biggest possible score. Europeans with two thousand years of history behind them may understand that each nation will win some of the time and lose most of the time, but we Americans who are less than two hundred years old think we should win all the time because, so far, we have never lost. During the McCarthy years, we began to find out that we had embarked upon a confrontation with Communist powers that may well persist for decades, in which there can be no such thing as winning, not even in a war then confined to the Korean peninsula, and millions of Americans angrily wanted to know how we got into such a mess and why we could not shoot our way out of it.

This anger was sometimes an expression of fear, as anger often but not always is, and our anger was sometimes, but not always, poorly informed. I would say that President Truman and General MacArthur, who were brave, well-informed men, shared a feeling of frustration but held quite different opinions as to how to exorcise it; that a follower of Senator McCarthy and I would be poorly informed men who shared the same feeling but reacted differently. Indeed, I can no more imagine America's losing at anything than can a member of the John Birch Society—although I would certainly have different ideas as to how we ought to go about winning. For purposes of discussing the McCarthy years, however, I would say that these were the years when it was first put to us that there might be no immediate victory, and that the nation greeted this notion with angry amazement, and that millions of us raged in helplessness and decided it must somehow be Their fault.

Finally, nagging at the back of all our discomforts and fears was the Depression-born suspicion that our emergent affluence was too good to be true and that it could not last, based as it was on inflation and upon the installment plan. To think such a thing was to entertain the fear that They might once again be at fault, which raised a question: If They control your life, whom can you trust if They are stupid or crooked, or both? A distrust of our own Government intensified many an American's fear of imminent war and it also opened the suspicious man's ears to McCarthy's message.

Since fear is largely the result of the exercise of too much imagination, while frustration represents the application of too little, it could be said that the national mess was more a mental disorder than an objective reality. Unfortunately, the Government itself deepened our neurosis and lent McCarthy credence. It did this by saying not that McCarthy was crazy, but that the Government was identifying more Communists than he was. The Truman administration publicized its investigations into the loyalty of Government workers, eliminating any Federal employees who might possibly be conceived to represent what the Government called "security risks." It remained only for McCarthy to lead the public mind to equate "Government worker" with "potential traitor," and "security risk" with "convicted spy."

Perhaps we who lived in the Washington area were more caught up in the McCarthy ugliness than other Americans, for Washington's news and conversation are almost entirely political and the city is sufficiently small for almost anyone—particularly for anyone who is a newspaperman—to have some personal knowledge of the people involved in political events. In our case, Margaret and I were among the friends of a Government physicist who was dismissed from his job on grounds that he represented a threat to the national security.

Naturally, our friend wanted to know why. He was not told.

Who had testified against him? He was not told that either.

He demanded to have his case reviewed, and this was granted—perhaps only because one of the secretaries of the Defense Department was a friend of the physicist's ancient, prominent and wealthy family. Later, I read a transcript of that loyalty review board hearing, the highlights of which were these:

Our friend had played a part in the development of a secret weapon that was largely responsible for our victory in Hitler's war. There was no evidence that he at any time had told anyone about his work—not even his wife.

His ancestors had arrived in the New World among the first Puritans, and members of his family had played important roles in the establishment first of the Colonial, later of the United States, government. His own record was one of contribution to his country, without the slightest blemish on it.

It was at length decided by the review board that he, personally, was not a disloyal person, and the charge that he might be such a person was stricken from his file. But——

His wife was descended from dissidents who had gone off with Roger Williams to form Rhode Island. One of her maternal ancestors had been a suffragette. Her mother believed in birth control, and so did she. She believed that the public schools should be integrated and that Negroes should otherwise be admitted to the duties of citizenship. She had entertained left-wing sympathizers in her home, including some people suspected of being at least the friends of known Communists if they were not Communists themselves. Obviously, the physicist's wife had been descended from a family of odd people, and she held peculiar views herself. There-fore——

At some future time the husband might inadvertently say something about his work to his wife, perhaps in his sleep. She might perhaps repeat this to her friends, some of whom seemed radical. These friends might pass it on to people who could very well be Communists, and they in turn might relay it to Russians, who could send it to Moscow. Wherefore——

It was decided to uphold the physicist's dismissal from Government service on grounds that while he himself was a loyal person of good family, the same could not be said with utter certainty of

169

his wife or her friends, and it would therefore be risking the security of the United States to retain him in the secret work he had been brilliantly performing for more than a decade.

While no one doubts the Government's right to hire and fire anyone it pleases, according to any criteria it wishes to establish, the manner in which the "security risks" were fired was plainly violative of every precept of common law. It can certainly be argued that firing someone is an administrative procedure, not a judicial one; but the Government after all is supposed to be based upon the law, and is supposed to uphold and protect it. To find the Government acting in a manner far removed from the spirit of that which gave the Government its very meaning was frustrating. Worse, the administrative act of firing a man for reasons of security was to inflict upon him the effect of a judicial punishment. Specifically, the punishment was to deprive him of his means of livelihood.

In my friend's case, the result was that he never found subsequent employment in his field. He applied to, and was turned down by, eighty private physics laboratories. Some of those who refused him held Government contracts and could not hire a man judged to be a security risk. The others were hoping to obtain such contracts. In the end, our friend became a teacher in an old, famous private preparatory school that he and his ancestors had attended. He was very lucky to have found this sort of home to return to at need, and to have had a private income to supplement his teacher's salary, because other security risks lost their homes and careers and were forced to look for any sort of work they could get from anyone willing in the age of McCarthy to hire suspected or potential traitors.

While this kind of thing was going on in the Executive department, circuses were taking place in the Legislative. McCarthy in the Senate, and the Un-American Activities Committee in the House, were in full cry, all teeth and lolling tongues, baying and snapping at witnesses, insinuating that the wretches before them were Red Judases; that their guilt was plain because of their association with others said to be Communists; denying the witnesses the right to know and cross question their accusers; gaveling them down; taking a Constitutional refusal to answer questions to mean both contempt of Congress and a tacit confession of guilt.

One result of such investigations—which, by the way, produced no revelations that could not or should not have been brought to light by the FBI and presented to the courts in an orderly way— was to strike such a pitch of public fear that a woman in Maryland suddenly broke off a conversation with a friend, saying, "For all I know, you may be one yourself. I don't know that I should talk to you. I don't know if I can trust you. I don't know if I can trust anyone."

One result? That woman had a great deal of company. It became increasingly difficult in the days of McCarthy for the ordinary citizen to speak his mind.

For instance, one librarian told me that a thought had come to him while shaving. It was to take such works as *Das Kapital* off the shelves, and to put a collection of anti-Communist books on special display, as a public service. Naturally, I wrote what I thought was a merry little column about the kinds of ideas that just sort of occur out of the blue to librarians as they hold razors to their throats in these times of McCarthy. The editor, throwing my column into his wastebasket, seriously asked me if I were insane. He did not disagree with my point of view, he said. Indeed, he agreed with it. He just wondered if *I* was crazy enough to think that *he* would be crazy enough to print it.

To my mind, the niggling consequence of the anecdote demonstrates its crucial importance, and helps to illuminate the following one.

A Pennsylvania schoolteacher was castigated for criticizing McCarthy's lack of ordinary decency. The principal said he felt the school's parents might erroneously think that the teacher represented the views of the school, and for this reason the fellow should be fired. No one asked if the principal meant to say that the school officially applauded the Senator's activities. Instead, every-

171

one seemed to think the principal was quite right; that teachers should not become involved in controversy. So everyone thought —everyone, that is, except the faculty, who threatened to resign en masse if their colleague was dismissed. But such bravery was very rare, and the teacher did not press the point. Instead, he resigned, much to everyone's relief—including the faculty's.

In those times, controversy was a dirty four-syllable word, and the fear of controversy was generalized into a fear and suspicion of any difference. It was a time when a Virginia householder reported to the FBI that his neighbor habitually wore his pajamas, and nothing else, when he went outside on Sunday morning to collect his newspaper from the lawn. The informant received a polite note from the FBI, congratulating him on his vigilant Americanism. In another Virginia suburb, a housewife placed a Grecian statue in her back yard, whereupon the neighbors pulled it down at night, littered her lawn with garbage, and wrote her ugly anonymous letters. Everyone in that community felt safer when she moved away, although, as one reporter discovered, those who felt most vehemently about her had never met the lady, and the only thing that anyone could find to say against her was that she was artistic. A friend of mine who wore a neat Van Dyke because he was one of the very few men in this world who happens to look much more presentable with a beard than without one, had to pay a price for his difference. Every time he entered a railroad station, plain-clothes policemen of various private, civil and Federal agencies would demand to see his identifying papers. He said it was damned annoying to be stopped when he was trying to catch a train, but that it was amusing (in a horrible kind of way) to know that he was a citizen of a country whose police assumed that anyone who had a beard was (a) suspiciously different and (b) therefore potentially dangerous.

The most dangerous difference was an intellectual one. In those days, there were people who seriously believed that plans to put fluorine in city drinking water were Communist plots. They refused to believe that fluoridated water inhibited dental decay, preferring

172

to believe that Communists were trying to poison children, and that the intellectuals who favored fluoridation had either been fooled by the Reds or were Reds themselves. It was a time when foolish people believed that the nation's schoolteachers were either agents or dupes of the Kremlin, and in popular mind, Harvard was not regarded as the leading university of the Western world, but was thought to be a nest of dangerous radicals. During the Mc-Carthy epoch, the following syllogism was widely believed:

A. Our Communist enemies are diabolically clever;

B. Intellectuals are clever people;

C. Ergo, intellectuals are our Communist enemies.

What made the intellectuals so particularly vulnerable to suspicion was that so many of them had played a part in the social experiments of the 1930s, and that they had been so successful. President Franklin D. Roosevelt had enlisted the intellectual community to seek cures for the Depression's ills. He had brought what he called a brain trust of quick minds with him to Washington, and students from nearly every college had gone to Washington upon their graduations to take part in the creation of the welfare state. By the 1950s, the radical proposals of the 1930s were now largely the law of the land, and it had been the New Dealers who guided the state through Hitler's war and into the nation's commitments in the frightening postwar world. The postwar political reaction that McCarthy exemplified was, therefore, also a reaction against intellectuality—almost as a matter of definition. The facts that Roosevelt's administration had recognized the Soviet Union; that the New Deal had been supported by the Communist Party; that Alger Hiss had been an architect of the United Nations; these facts and coincidences lent color to the syllogism in the minds of McCarthy's followers.

It was also terribly easy for the McCarthys of the land to accuse a man of having had some connection with Communists during his collegiate past, for I should say it would have been virtually impossible for any intelligent person of my college generation not to have met at least one campus radical during his school

173

days. Nearly every bright student would have joined in the discussion of political ideas, if he had not actually taken part in a radical activity. This would also have been true of writers and artists, for the central theme of the plays, novels and pictures of the Depression years was social protest. So it was easy in 1950 to accuse a man of having been the associate of "known Communists" in the 1930s. Such an accusation could almost have been made simply on the basis of his Intelligence Quotient. What was not so easy to prove, particularly for the accused who was put in the position of having to demonstrate his innocence, was whether the "known Communist" John Doe was actually a Communist, or was known to be one, either in 1950 or when Doe had been an eighteen-year-old college freshman fifteen years earlier. Nor was it easy to prove what the relationship between the accused and Doe had been, and what—if anything—the actual result of their acquaintance had been with respect to constituting a danger to the peace and good order of the United States of America. But anyone who had gone to college during the Depression, or who had worked in any New Deal department, or who had taken part in the performing or communicative arts, or who entertained educated people in his home, had very likely met several John Does of various shades of Pink or Red, and could now be accused of guilt by virtue of his past association with them.

Apart from having made themselves vulnerable by reason of their political success, the left-of-center intellectuals were also the victims of the success of their social philosphies. They had preached the need for all men to work together, to form unions and committees, to appreciate one another's functional significance in the interdependent technological society. Much may be lost in translating sociological theory into common speech. To some people, the message was that intellectual do-gooders, parlor pinks and New Dealers, were just a bunch of Goddamned Nigger-lovers who wanted to destroy the private enterprise system that had made this country great.

More general, however, was the public acceptance of the essen-

174

tial social message of the 1930s; the message that said all of us should have a concern for the group. As noted, there had been a necessary emphasis on teamwork during the war, and an equally strong, if not so necessary, emphasis on it in postwar life. For instance, there was an emphasis on group activity in the new crackerbox suburbias, where social occasions took the form of block parties. Everyone on the block was invited—which is to say no one was. Bright young city planners spoke knowingly about traffic flow and land uses without much concern for those who currently made use of the land, but with great concern for their own conception of an over-all social good. Manufacturers began to regard public opinion as the sole mother of invention; corporations refused to hire or promote competent men if it was felt that their wives did not promise to fit in well with other corporate wives, and the communications media constantly felt the public pulse to determine what would be profitable for them to print and depict. Just as the mass-produced shoddy was driving the unique specialty off the grocers' and the merchants' shelves, so variety was going out of American dialogue as people increasingly held it to be a virtue to accept the opinions of the group. In other words, the whole thrust of social, political and educational thought from 1930 to 1950 was in the direction of concern for the group at the expense of the individual, with the result that one exceedingly sour, and unexpected, fruit of the radical thought of the 1930s was, in the 1950s, conformity.

In all, having inadvertently helped to create the conformity which now made conspicuous intellectual activity unwelcome, and having taken part in creating a state whose policies were now in question, and being vulnerable to the accusation of having met on the frontiers of thought with those now identified as our enemies, the intellectual was a goat practically bleating to be stoned—and McCarthy had a supply of stones as well as an insatiable, if not demonic, desire to throw the first one.

While I am quite sure that the McCarthyites were a minority of Americans, I am also sure that a timid, uneasy, apathetic majority

175

allowed them full rein. The situation was made no better when General Eisenhower, running for President and helping McCarthy win re-election in Wisconsin, sat silent on the speaker's platform while the Senator traduced the honor and patriotism of General George C. Marshall, one of the most distinguished Americans of any age and the man who had plucked Eisenhower from relative military obscurity and had made him commander of our host in Hitler's war. In effect, it was General Marshall who had made Eisenhower a Presidential candidate, and yet Eisenhower sat there on the stage and allowed McCarthy to blackguard the character of his friend, former commanding officer, and benefactor. In those days, when even the President kept silent, you would hear worried people say such things as these:

"Well, yeah, McCarthy's a rough guy, but where there's smoke there's got to be fire, I guess," and "We wouldn't have all these air raid drills and things if They didn't know something *we* don't know, would we? And They'll never tell us what's going on." But much more often, people said "Look, I don't want to be involved in anything controversial. I'm not going to stick my neck out."

During this time, one newspaper sent reporters out to try to gather signatures to a petition. The petition happened to be a copy of the Constitution's Bill of Rights, and the overwhelming majority of those to whom it was presented refused to sign it, saying they did not want to get mixed up in "controversy." Many thought the paper a Communist document and accused the reporters of being Communists.

The plight of the intellectual was made no better by a series of trials in Federal District Court that followed the refusal of left-wing supporters of the Spanish Loyalist cause, and of several Hollywood writers, to answer questions put to them by the investigative committees of Congress. There is no doubt that they did refuse to answer the questions, and that this refusal did legally constitute contempt of Congress, for which they were duly punished. But there is also no doubt in my mind (and I speak as one who covered all the trials) that the defendants were being punished not so much

176

for refusing to answer Congressmen's questions as for having had radical friends, or for having held views that had come to be regarded with profound suspicion. I believe that the Congressional committee's activity had almost no legislative intent and that it was not even concerned with exposing Communists to public view. I think it had everything to do with a political reaction against the whole course of recent history, and that this reaction took an anti-intellectual form for the simple reason that the intellectual community had been bound up in the events and policies against which there was now a revulsion.

No doubt it was historically fortunate that Eisenhower was elected President. There would later be a joke about the Eisenhower doll: *It was the kind of doll which, when wound up, sat on a shelf and didn't do anything for eight years.* It might have been even more fortunate if we had elected a President of more forceful character, but I doubt that it would have been possible for us to have done so. Adlai Stevenson's unsuccessful campaigns demonstrated the futility of trying to talk sense to an American people who had been led by events to be equally suspicious of politicians and of eggheads, as intellectuals were derisively called. The electorate evidently felt it to be a virtue of General Eisenhower that he was neither one nor the other. Our next-door neighbor said he voted for Eisenhower because Stevenson told jokes, when what this country needed was a military man who could deal with the Russians, get those Reds and pantywaists out of the State Department, and clean up the mess in Washington. In the event, President Eisenhower did none of these things to anyone's particular satisfaction, but it was probably good for all of us to have a lackluster President who did not want to become "engaged in personalities" and who seemed to be a benign, permissive father who helped to provide a kind of placebo for a neurotic nation. A critic called him a wad of chewing gum rolling about in the jaws of history, and I should think the description accurate in a much less pejorative sense than the critic had in mind, for in retrospect, it would seem that a wad of chewing gum was exactly what was needed to keep

177

the teeth from chewing something else. Eisenhower was someone whom both the left and right wings could deplore, but he seemed to be such a pleasant, well-meaning, honest fellow that no one could hate him, and after a while, the Eisenhower administration began placidly to provide something for everyone, and nothing much for anyone.

For example, while the gunboat diplomats were given John Foster Dulles' policy of taking us to the brinks of wars, the isolationists could at least console themselves with the fact that the Korean war ended in a truce and that it would therefore seem that Mr. Dulles did not really mean to go over any brinks, but rather, to shrink from them. The military establishment was vastly enlarged, which made the admirals and the generals happy and was very good for General Motors. The Communist-hunters could feel that the Republican administration would weed out those radical New Dealers and strictly supervise the loyalty check programs; the left wing might take what comfort it could from the fact that the new Administration preserved and expanded its welfare-state concepts, and that it continued President Truman's commitment of America to an international role. Meantime, no Russian bombs fell on Washington after all, and everyone made more money and increasingly turned away from adult concerns to take up an undue interest in the affairs of their children. And the press, having created McCarthy, at length pulled itself together and buried him. Telecasts of the Senator at work pitilessly disclosed his emptiness; the general public thereupon either caught on to him or got tired of him, or both; and a certain editorial bravery ensued. Eventually the Senate censured him, and that was that, at least so far as McCarthy's personal role was concerned.

I remember the sky clearing somewhat toward the end of McCarthy's influence.

One of our reporters had prepared an article detailing—and questioning—the sources of the Senator's income and McCarthy's somewhat peculiar way of accounting for it. Somehow word of the preparation of this article got to McCarthy, who immediately dispatched an emissary to our editor. If we printed the article, the editor was told, then McCarthy would accuse the *News* of having a Communist on its staff. The presumption would be that the Communist had planted lies in the *News* in order to do harm to Communism's greatest enemy, Senator McCarthy. And who was this Communist agent? Well, it turned out that *I* was. I have no idea whether McCarthy's none-too-scrupulous staff had come across some mention of my expulsion from Michigan, or whether they just chose a name from our reportorial staff at random, but the threat was typical of the Senator, who was careful to make his accusations from the Senate floor were he was immune to suits for libel and slander, and we had no doubt that he was perfectly capable of carrying out his threat. On the other hand, the facts were that I was not a Communist and that I had had nothing to do with the preparation of the article. It was also a political fact that by this time McCarthy needed the press too much to attack any part of it, and, considering one thing and another, our editor very sensibly decided to publish it and let McCarthy be damned. I regarded this as a distinct improvement in editorial frames of mind; an improvement over the days when editors questioned the sanity of reporters who wished to call attention to the terrors of librarians.

The fears and hatreds of the McCarthy era by no means vanished at the moment of McCarthy's censure, however. They continued to smolder like a fire deep beneath rocks and pine needles that feeds on roots, and like such a fire they would erupt again at later times, given the opportunity. But during the Eisenhower administration, the brightest flames were allowed to burn themselves out, and the President could therefore seem to have been a fairly effective fire chief. The President chose another image. He spoke of himself as a driver who wanted to keep America in the middle of the road. No doubt in horse-and-buggy days the middle of a high-crowned country lane was a safe place to be, but on a busy modern highway he who holds the middle of the road blocks traffic in both directions.

179

In any case, stasis, and an avoidance of extremes, and a bland refusal to take sides on public questions no matter how important, or to discuss personalities even when personality was precisely the issue, or to engage in controversy, were all believed to be among the virtues of President Eisenhower—and perhaps they were. The President's brand of know-nothingism was at least more benevolent than McCarthy's version, and ultimately indifference may have triumphed over evil.

To my mind, however, the final measure of the McCarthy-Eisenhower years could be found in the description of its college students as constituting a "silent generation." Surely those children were coming of age during the high moments of the witch hunt. Just as surely, they must have absorbed as adolescents the full effects of a public school education that only too often penalized individual enterprise and rewarded what many a teacher called "good followership." And certainly they must have met adults everywhere whose one desire was to find security and who reasoned that the best way to do so was to play on the team and not look to right or left and to say nothing for fear of being understood. One could scarcely imagine that inspiration would come from bullied faculties or a body of parents afraid of distinctions. As it was, an entire college generation crept away from its graduation ceremonies during those years intent on entering corporation offices, there to acquire charcoal-gray suits, black Homburgs, bland faces and briefcases. They looked forward to the paid vacations, the expense accounts, the company pension plans and medical insurance. When asked what they wanted of life, they said "security." They looked forward to the houses in the suburbs that they would share with the girls who would wear the car coats being worn by every other suburban wife who had gone to college to find a husband who wanted to be a business executive dressed in a dark gray suit. It was not much of a generation; but then, it was not much of a time. If I have failed to express the full terror of that time, perhaps it is because I suffer the difficulty of trying to describe emptiness.

Permit me a final attempt to describe it.

Margaret and I had moved to Maryland during the McCarthy reign of terror, and when our children entered school, we attended meetings of the Gaithersburg Parent-Teacher Association. Much about public education struck us as being unlike anything we had remembered, but we withheld asking questions until we were sure what questions we wanted to ask. By the end of our first Maryland year we had a number in mind, and took our seats expectantly as the last meeting of the year was called to order.

"I think we all ought to be congratulated," the PTA president said, smiling as he opened the meeting, "on the fact that *this* year no controversial issues came up."

There was a delighted applause. I can still see that man's honest joy and hear the battering handclapping of thanksgiving. I suggested that there were several dozen questions that had by now occurred to me, but I was quickly told that the only purpose of this final meeting was to elect a new PTA president. Afterward there would be refreshments.

The impressive thing to me was the depth of genuine relief that the applause expressed, and the speed with which any questions were found to be out of order. In sober truth, everyone was eager to get to the refreshments. It was the public mood, not the words, that bespoke a nervous fear. The emptiness was that of the soul, apparent not only in jittery Washington but also in the innocuous affairs of an obscure rural school district.

For the rest of it, I must say that our private life was fairly full and placid during the McCarthy epoch. I have noticed that the material fortunes of my own family have followed almost precisely those of the statistically average white-collar worker, and by and large our concerns were then also his. We lived in a ten-thousand-dollar white clapboard three-bedroom house in the country, raised chickens and vegetables, and had three children. I drove an hour each day to work in Washington, and an hour a day back to my house. Margaret had an automobile of her own—a 1939 Dodge we bought for two hundred dollars from my uncle Louis. We had a concern for the costs of the house, the cars, and daily living; we

181

had a concern for the quality of the public education our children were receiving; we had a concern for my advancement in my profession, and Margaret was taking part in civic affairs of the county government. We were on good terms with our neighbors with whom we had very little to do, and our closest friends lived thirty miles away.

We visited with our friends, at their house or ours, on an average of once a week—usually on weekends. These occasions would see us all in the kitchen inventing things to eat, sitting long at table with a gallon of California wine afterward, talking of food, music, writing and painting. I liked to think that our conversations were not the average ones. At least, we flattered ourselves that they were not, although such a presumption may have comprised a somewhat short sale of our fellow citizens whom we otherwise in so many ways resembled.

The one thing that may very well have not been average about us was our ownership of a summer island in Canadian water of the St. Lawrence River. There is always a kind of special magic about an island, and to me, our island was something more than black oaks, yellow birches and white pines growing among the summer grasses atop a bulk of lichened gneiss set in water as blue as the Mediterranean. It was where we lived. No one else lived there. It was a place where the rules and laws were those of our own devising. It was where a man and his wife and their children could be alone together. It was a place where the rhythms of our life were regulated only by the speed of the wind, the water level, the state of the mile of open water around us, the temperatures of air and water, the changing seasons. Natural facts, and these alone, determined our responses. On our island there were no newspapers, no magazines, no telephone, no radio, no television; just blueberries, raspberries, grass, trees, and great stones, and all around us deep, clear, potable water filled with fish, and over us swinging gulls and the deeps of the sky.

During the years of fear of McCarthy and fear of the bomb,

friends would sometimes say we were lucky to have the island. We could always go there in case anything happened, they would say. We would be safe in Canada, they said. While I did not think of the island or Canada in precisely these terms, I admit to sharing enough of the common fear to have felt a distinct relief every time the Canadian customs and immigration authorities allowed us to enter their country, and to a feeling of having drawn up the bridge and slammed down the portcullis once I had the stones of my island under my feet.

More important, however, and certainly more intellectually defensible, was our use of the island not as a hiding place but as the center of our life. I dare say that we all share Antaeus' need.

After three weeks of what Margaret called "communicating with Nature," we were much better prepared to cope with the next forty-nine weeks of Washington's lunacy, for the island gave us perspective as well as renewed strength. It reminded us that not all the eternal verities are man-made, and our association with Canadians reminded us that not all mankind was preoccupied with what Americans and Washingtonians thought was important. At the end of our insular vacation, I could drive back into America in Mencken's mood of a man going to the zoo. I remember once crossing the border and turning on the car radio to find out what time it was, and hearing an excited man frenetically advertise the bargains to be had at a clothing store. For the next two and a half minutes a girl shrieked something about love, shrilling over trumpets, drums and saxophones. Then the man's voice breathlessly told us that today, for a limited time only . . .

"Do you think that has been going on ever since we have been away?" Margaret asked, shutting off the radio.

"Day and night, twenty-four hours a day," I told her.

We laughed, and realized that while we had come back to America again, there really was no need to know what time it was; that we would be driving in the car for so long as it took us to reach

Maryland; that we would make what time we could and eat when we were hungry and that it was possible to live without time signals and news broadcasts every hour on the hour; that there was time and a way to think of love in terms other than those the shrieking girl set forth, and that life's real bargains are not offered for a limited time only for ten dollars down and twenty-four weeks to pay. The constant noise, the incessant chatter, the fancied need to do it now, for time is precious, the haggard feeling that there is nothing you can do about it anyway; all these voices . . .

Margaret, and our island, shut the car radio off.

Still, despite the relief our island gave us, and no matter to what extent it enabled us to say with Puck what fools these mortals be, it was a fearsome zoo to which we would return: to the zoo that was our America—strong, rich, violent, suspicious and afraid.

I have always wondered (for I know of no way we can be certain now) what effect America's miasmal climate of that time has had on our children's generation. If psychiatry is correct in assuming that the child's first experiences are his most formative, then it would seem that the responses of those now leaving college should in some way have been conditioned by the air they breathed as children. An air (I would say) heavy with the dank fragrance of *McCall's* togetherness; redolent of conformity and of fear of controversy, of witch hunters, spies and traitors; an air that smelled of money and automobiles and of a concern for having money and buying things; an atmosphere periodically sliced into pieces by the howls of sirens ordering children to curl into fetal positions in corridors shielding their eyes against an expected light that would be brighter than the sun.

Today's generation is not a silent one, like the classes of the 1950s. But with due allowance for exceptions, it is a singularly cool, wary one, not noticeably eager to have too much to do with the rest of us. In certain ways they seem emotionally stunted, for if their relationship with us is a suspicious one, their relationships to one another are usually shallow and exploitive. In their own words, they guard against blowing their cool, and I wonder to what

184

extent their lack of trust in us, and in one another, may not stem from their having grown to puberty during an American time when men feared being drawn into controversy or into a discussion of personalities; when the roaring voice in the land was McCarthy's, and when the President held to be virtuous those responses that so particularly distinguish the ostrich.

9

Second Childhood

WHEN OUR YOUNG nephew heard there was to be a birthday party at one of the summer islands, to which forty children had been invited, he could scarcely believe it.

"Oh my God, that lucky kid!" he said. *"Forty* ten-dollar presents!"

Yes, and party favors for each guest, and boats to water-ski behind, and prizes for swimming races, and beer for the teen-agers and ginger ale for the young, and sometimes at such parties a magician, and always someone to do the dishes and clean up the litter, and if someone ran a boat into a rock the insurance would always pay for it so do not worry, and the boys and girls would always be healthy and tan and very beautiful and very, very happy.

And the happy parents of these fortunate children would sit on the broad, screened porch with the hostess drinking a little too much once again, and she would gladly if somewhat thickly say that the children are a lot better off these days and have a lot more things than we ever had.

I remember thinking at that particular party for the forty children that the hostess was quite right. We had given them the atomic bomb and television along with the twenty-eight flavors of ice cream and the water skis and the ten dollar presents, and we had given them a series of appointments instead of a childhood. We never had any of these things, ourselves. We were not given so much. I think "given" is the key word. We have given them practically everything.

I sat watching the forty children speeding over the placid water like so many motorized Christs without problems, and it struck me that they were not part of a process but its end result; that they were glad to be isolated in a golden playpen and hoped they would never have to leave it; that they were just as estranged from society as children had been when I was growing up, but for different and often opposite reasons.

It also occurred to me that I was watching a religious spectacle: the worship of youth. It is an American religion, old as the New World itself. In superstitious days, at least one Renaissance explorer came here looking for the magical fountain. Next, youth was worshiped as a matter of necessity: a young continent demanded young strength. We began to sing of this, eventually producing our great novel about a boy who runs away to float down the Mississippi on a raft to encounter reality. We still say we should all *think young,* and in contradistinction to Europeans, we Americans do not believe in age and death. We refuse to think of such things. We call our soldiers "boys," and congeries of widows at bridge tables, with their blue hair, scarlet lips and clattering bangles, call themselves "the girls." We have produced the familiar American boy-man and girl-woman who wear sports clothing into their dotage. And we shower gifts upon our young.

Now, there is nothing necessarily wrong or foolish about a desire to remain young and vigorous for as long a time as possible, but it can be disruptive of a sense of priorities if carried to extremes—as a good many observers suggest it has been. Nor is it necessarily a bad thing to give our children as much as we can, although a plethora of gifts may confuse the recipients—as a good many recipients have been confused. As preliminary to sorting matters out, I suggest the following statement:

The affluence which has been growing steadily since Hitler's war has given us the means to gild the temple of youth, at which we have always worshiped. Meanwhile, we have added special services every day for children, adapted from the Gospels of St. Karl and St. Sigmund, as written by Dr. Spock in collaboration with the authors of *Fun with Dick and Jane.*

It will be seen that we are dealing with simultaneous and inter-related matters here, so that there is no true, single starting place; but purely for convenience I will say that the circumstance that set in train all our giving to the young began, for people of my class and generation, with lack of physical space.

In our first suburban houses or apartments, a mother, a father and their children were constantly within sight and hearing—if not actually within touch—of one another. In our household, for ex-ample, there was no Rose to put Christopher on his pot, or to feed him at a little table of his own in an upstairs room until he was old enough to join the family as a silent, obedient participant at a family meal. For one thing, we had no money to hire a Rose; for another, the Roses of America had by that time disappeared; for a third, there was no upstairs to our two-bedroom apartment, or even a farther room. We had no relief from our children, nor they from us, and the constant needs of childhood made the children the focal point of a family life that took place in what—to Ameri-cans—were cramped quarters.

Concurrently, the children of the suburban housing area became the focal point of what passed for our social life. The children's friendships with other children often determined the mothers' ac-quaintance with other mothers. In Fairlington there were so many children of an age, all living so close by, that there was an average of one birthday party a week in our vicinity, to which all the children had to be invited as a matter of diplomacy. Preparations for these, and many other occasions, threw children and mothers into the enforced intimacy of a tribal life on a very small island, and gave some children the idea that they were equally welcome in every apartment at any time. One of our friends, who lived in a duplex apartment, could never leave it without first searching from top to basement to flush out small children who, having entered to play with her youngsters, remained to amuse themselves. Every-

188

where in Fairlington, other people's children, as well as our own, were literally under foot.

Later, when the children grew larger and needed more space than tiny suburban yards provided, and more things to do than could be done in the restricted areas of their regimented cubicles, the maternal car pool was created for them. They were car-pooled to the country, to the zoo, to the Smithsonian, to the parks, to ballet, skating, badminton, riding, ballroom dancing and music classes; to the Cub Scouts and the Bluebirds. A brand of station wagon was advertised as being able to carry an entire football team of twelve-year-olds, and it was another of those advertisements that mirror, rather than create, reality. In summer, the children were car-pooled to suburban-area day camps if they were not packed off to Maine, and all in all the children must have gathered the impression, as they were car-pooled about on their appointed rounds, that fun was something that happened elsewhere than at home, and that you needed an automobile to get to where the fun was to be had, so that "they"—the parents—*had to* take you there. The idea of not having fun all the time was unthinkable, and fun was something you had only with other children your age.

All this was quite different from my own prepubescent childhood, and may in part account for some of the differences in outlook between my generation and our children who, having grown up in suburbia, are now leaving college to enter adult life. For instance, we were unregimented children of space. When we lived in the country, I had the freedom of woods, fields and Chesapeake Bay; even when I lived in cities there were school yards, parks or vacant lots within walking distance of our residence, and I took myself to these alone. Instead of being urged to be one of a group, and car-pooled about in a group to planned entertainment, I was sent out to play, and the assumption was that I would be able to do so. "Don't ask me what to do; find something to do for yourself," either of my parents would say. I received the same admonition on rainy days. I was supposed to be able to amuse myself in a responsible way, out of sight of adults; but then, our living quarters were large enough to permit everyone his privacy. My children, however, were brought up in a shrunken America that not only lacked both space and privacy, and streets in which they could safely play, but was given to a basically inhuman style of life—one that was very different from the style of life in which their grandparents had been raised.

For example, in my father's youth the grandparents, parents, children, aunts, uncles and cousins lived and worked hard by one another. Each had has different work to do, but when both sexes and all ages lived and worked near one another, there was a sense of duty, of place, of family, of permanence, of community, of human continuity. If a child came last in every pecking order in this society, he could at least see himself as part of a human process. In my youth, this style of life began to change, as we have seen in my own case, and nowadays it is just a mother, a father and their children who eat and sleep in rooms in an impersonal metropolitan area (it is no longer a city or a community, but merely an area), from which the father travels miles each day to work somewhere in a glass and concrete anthill while the mother amuses herself with the housework in her bedroom-restaurant, while the children are loaded into Hallowe'en-colored vehicles that roll them away to a third world of their own—to a building that looks just like a factory in a new industrial park for light industry. Meanwhile, the grandparents have been shot off to a barracks for the aged five-hundred miles out of mind, there to do the generous thing, which is to die before all their money is wasted on medical bills. In this new style of life, there are no real chores for a family to share (assuming that you are willing for the sake of argument to call these dissociated blood relatives a family), for service industries, agencies and machines dispose of the garbage, collect the trash, deliver the milk, maintain the buildings, supply the light, heat and water, while the food rains down out of the gravity-feed racks into the shopping carts in the supermarkets. There is nothing in this that enables anyone—man, woman or child—to feel himself a part of anything.

190

I therefore suggest that the child-centered aspect of suburbia may have represented, in part, not only worship of youth in general and an answer—or an attempted answer—to some needs in particular, but also our reaction to a sterile pattern of life: that when we deluged our children with toys and tried to find things for them to do, and joined them in the doing, we were trying to save them and ourselves from boredom; that, in self-defense, we were trying to give ourselves and our children *something* in a nothing world. But I would also say that additional factors compounded our child-centeredness, and that two of them were mutually reinforcing, and both had to do with money. It was as if in reality we were the ones who wished to play with the toys; as if when we car-pooled our children to an event, we were hoping to enjoy the event vicariously through our children; as if we were at last enjoying a childhood we had never known during the Depression and the war. I would say that the Little League is a precise example of fathers playing a child's game through their sons; that any too vehement parental sponsorship of team sports at least through the high school level reflects the fathers' desire to play the games by manipulating living counters.

What is true of this parental interest in sports is also true of the parental interest in the children's cultural and social success. It seemed to me, in the earliest years of my parenthood, that the nation was playing with dolls—dressing them, walking them around, talking to them, allowing the children no more lives of their own than dolls have. I think this is still quite true: What is one to think of the mother who sends her sixth-grade daughter off to dancing class wearing lipstick and sheer stockings? Who is going to that dancing class? An example of our concern for children—an example that is as exaggerated as it is true—would be the Pennsylvania housewife who took a job as a barmaid to supplement her husband's income in order that she could provide her twelve-year-old daughter with a horse, a stable and feed for it, and membership for the girl in a riding club. The child goes off to the club in her riding habit, and the barmaid happily says that her daughter is having social advantages that she herself never had, and it is very clear as she says this, while wiping down the bar, that the mother is riding in her dreams with the wealthy young gentlemen she never met. If the example seems extreme, what was by no means extreme was that a major portion of the suburban family's daily time schedule was built about the comings and goings of the children, and that much of the family budget was devoted to their clothing, toys, fees, food and transportation.

The second factor, reinforcing parental desire to give and also dealing with money, is what merchants call the youth market. The relationship between the two may be like that between the chicken and the egg, for if the postwar parents spent a great deal of money on their children, the nation's merchants encouraged them to do so, and devised and marketed fads, fashions and activities for children. I do not think the nation suffers when people make money, but I would say that one result of the merchants' efforts has been to subdivide the population. For instance, there was no such animal as the teen-ager when I was growing up. There was also no such thing as the teen-age market. Both appeared, together, in the postwar years. I am speaking here of a matter of degree, for of course there have been adolescents and also different fashions, fads and games for people of different ages, ever since man came came down out of the trees. But the matter of degree became enormous during the postwar years—enormous and divisive. I think one reason is that, after Hitler's war, when more Americans began earning more money and began to live closer together in both a physical and a sociological sense, there formed a vast, anonymous middle class which for the first time in history, presented a true mass market. With typical American organizational genius, the merchants divided this population into separate markets by age groups, and hired sociologists and psychologists to help them provide the badges, trinkets, toys and trivia appropriate for each group, capitalizing upon Anonymous Man's real need to distinguish himself somehow in a classless society of interdependent

192

functionaries who lived in an impersonal urban sprawl. But in so doing, the merchants helped further to divide the Americans into the separate and hermetically sealed categories we find them in today: into the babies, preschoolers, lower-graders, upper-graders, junior high schoolers, teen-agers, young people, college students, graduate students, young marrieds, parents, middle-aged and what are euphemistically called senior citizens. Within each group we find both horizontal and vertical divisions based on sex, residence, activity and income, and the compartmentalization is now so complete that it is difficult for the inhabitant of one compartment to know much about the inhabitant of any other, or even to speak to him—as the social critic Russell Lynes has suggested. Among the many factors responsible for this fragmentation of American society, mercantile technique is not the least of them, and for the purpose of immediate discussion, I will say that the invention of the commercial youth markets steadily contributes to the sense of estrangement the current generation feels; that it relegates children to the status of dolls; that vast numbers of products designed for different mass markets do not give anyone a feeling that American life is a process, but rather that it is a series of experiences in separate buildings in an amusement park.

In this context, the one building that nobody really wants to enter is the one where they give you a green suit, ten general orders to remember, a gun, a mattress cover to serve as your shroud, and free transportation to a rice paddy.

That room comes as quite a shock to the young.

Nothing in their car-pooled experience has prepared them for it.

I should say that their lack of preparation can be charged to the psychological, social and political theories under which they have lived from cradle to legal age. I should also say that these theories formed the context in which all of our attentions to youth may be found. For example, I believe that the first, greatest single source of difference between my generation and my son's is that, whereas

193

we were brought up to understand that children were separate, inferior, apprentice people to be seen but not heard, my children's generation were raised according to a quite different theory.

The modern theory of child-raising holds that babies and children are intelligent, sentient human beings; that their earliest experiences are formative; that they have more need to feel important and loved than anyone else, and just as strong a need to feel that they belong to, and are a part of society. The new policy calls for the child to be given tender loving care. It assumes that mothers are the best-qualified people to give a child such care, and that fathers should be the great chums, or buddies, of their young. If a baby cries, the mother is supposed to pick it up, tend it, cuddle it, and shove a nipple in its mouth.

The new policy is thoroughly consistent with modern sociopolitical thought, for the whole burden of legislation, from the New Deal to the Fair Deal to the Re-Deal to the Ideal to the Great Big Deal, is that if anyone cries, the Government should come along, all warm, tender, and dripping milk, and pick up the discomfited citizen and shove a nipple in his mouth. In the public schools, practice of the same theory takes the twin forms of making education seem like lots of fun and of shielding the child from what might make him cry—namely, failure. If it seems that the student might fail at something, then the school tries to find him something else to do at which he can succeed, meanwhile promoting him each year from grade to grade, whether he has learned anything or not, for the sake of keeping him happily among what his teachers call his peers. In short, the schools act exactly like a mother offering a baby another toy if the first seems displeasing; like a mothering Great Society giving aid and comfort to those who do not or cannot make their way under their own power. Common to all aspects of the new theory, whether it be raising babies, educating them, or nursing them through their adult lives, is the notion that everyone should be made to feel an important, respected member of the family; of the school community; of society.

194

One wonders what the result of all this cradle-to-grave diaper-changing and breast-feeding will be. The weight of modern psychiatric, educational and political thought holds that the end result for America will be excellent; that all this coddling will produce a freer, happier, more effective and productive race of individuals than Darwinian Nature, red of tooth and claw, could ever produce. One hopes this will be so, but the results will not be apparent until the next century—provided, of course, the car-pooled and breast-fed generation will quickly adjust itself to the rice paddy and perform so effectively therein as to ensure that there will be a next century. If there is one, we may be able to see whether *our* way of raising children was actually one whit more beneficial to the child than the sternest, most austere Victorian upbringing; whether the country then will be any less of a mess than it was when my generation inherited it.

I should also say that we are currently experiencing real difficulty in establishing a sense of priorities appropriate to youth and age. It might have been one thing if, in playing dolls with our children, we had sought to bring them into the family, clearly setting forth everyone's different duties and responsibilities. But this was not the case. Rather, we made the children acutely aware of the fact that they were children. At the same time, we gave them the idea that we were not their parents but their pals—perhaps misreading the new theory.

Certainly a neighboring family would seem to have misread the book. They asked their children not to use the words "Mother" and "Father," or anything so sickening as "Mumsy" and "Dadsy," but to call them by their names: Bob and Mary. Wasn't that sweet. Next, after the parents had established themselves as just friendly, older children, the situation deteriorated to such extent that the youngsters could scarcely call their childhood their own. They finally began to entertain serious doubts as to who, if anyone, was minding the store, for Bob and Mary asked them to help make decisions. They claimed that theirs was a democratic family.

While not every suburban family carried concepts of democracy

195

to such lengths, it was perfectly true that all too many people of my generation asked their children, at home and at school, for their opinions—treating them as if they had sufficient information and experience upon which to form judgments. The idea here, consistent with modern theory, was to solicit and respect each person's thoughts in order (*a*) to get him used to thinking things through, and (*b*) to assure him that he could speak out freely, confident that his contribution would receive serious attention.

A brilliant teacher, using this theory, would be a Socrates who asked such questions as would lead a child to discover the answers the Socrates had in mind. But no matter how dedicated to their profession all teachers might be, the number of resident Socrateses is always small. Therefore, when the general run of teachers invited juvenile opinion, they commonly received half-baked answers from children who believed they had as much right to their opinions as adults did. Then, whenever these youngsters discovered that not all opinions are equally valid, but that—according to the test—there had been only one right answer all the time, an uproar usually ensued. The brighter students somewhat bitterly concluded that the teachers had just been playing games with them without having explained the rules. One result of the general practice of the so-called discovery method of teaching is a complaint voiced by intelligent college youth today: *You can't trust anyone over thirty.*

A point which seems to have escaped the parents and teachers of my generation, but which is clear enough to psychiatrists, is that children very badly want and need to know what the rules are, and just where they fit into them. To be asked to help formulate the rules can be most confusing to the child, particularly if he subsequently discovers that his opinion was not solicited in good faith. In the first event he might very well question the competence of his parents and teachers; in the other, their honesty.

Be this as it may, while our children were wallowing through adolescence, many communities established teacher-parent-child committees to work out codes of conduct. For example, in the

196

Philadelphia, Pennsylvania area thirty-five public and private suburban schools created (and still follow) a document called *We Can Agree*. It is published by an interschool council, and it says, "Parents need fortification to combat the pressure, exerted by the plea of their young people, that EVERYBODY DOES IT." Of course no parent in his right mind and in full command of himself should be at the slightest loss to tell his child flatly what that child may and may not do, with no regard for standards other than those of the parent's own intelligent, conscientious devising. But the *We Can Agree* people are different. Significantly, they speak of children as "young people," as if the only difference between child and adult were a matter of chronology. Significantly, they speak of the need for fortifications—which are defensive positions. To protect themselves from what "everybody" is alleged to do, these people have to form a little "everybody" all their own, in order that nobody will have to be somebody. Their pamphlet, which discusses social behavior, asks if everyone cannot agree that "an ill-behaved guest should not be permitted to spoil a party," and that "appropriate dress is a mark of good taste." It reads as if it were a primer addressed to the singularly backward citizens of an emergent nation; to a people who had never heard of manners nor of common decency. Perhaps it was, for all sorts of people made money and moved to suburbia after Hitler's war. In any case, the *We Can Agree* people solicit the opinions of their children in the formulation of the rules to be agreed upon, which is a means of abdicating parental responsibility by diffusing it among the children. As in the case of Bob and Mary's children, the *We Can Agree* children might very well wonder who is minding the store.

Pathetically enough, a curious thing about social codes mutually arrived at by committees of teachers, parents and children is that the children normally demand more stringent enforcement of more rigorous codes than either parents or teachers suggest. So it was in this case. The children's demand indicates the truth of psychiatry's observation that children badly need to know their limits.

Even more curious, considering America's political traditions, is

197

that nowhere in such mutual agreements as *We Can Agree* do we read that anyone, child or adult, should have the slightest sense of individual responsibility for his actions. The omission would seem very strange to anyone of my father's generation, although it is in accord with the teachings of the present day, and thoroughly at one with current American social and political thought. In grade school, our children heard many a teacher say something like this: "Because two of you were talking, the whole class will have to stay after school." The teacher thereby established the principle of mass guilt and mass punishment, as opposed to that of individual responsibility. A proponent of the new concept would be the California junior high school principal who said, "We may be sure that the group will bring the deviate into line." He said this during the piping days of Joseph McCarthy, when our three children were growing up, and at the time his dictum rang with a terribly clear, bell-like sound.

Our gifts to our children will therefore be seen to have included giving them a confused, if not inflated, view of their proper place in the scheme of things, and, simultaneously, a charter to kick one another into some common shape which they hope we will find pleasing. Also at the same time, we positively deluged them with material goods, attention; we became their chauffeurs, played their games with them, waited on them, lived vicariously through them, popped nipples into their mouths whenever they opened them, fixed things at school so that it would seem as if they could never fail, took up their words and phrases, dressed little boys in long trousers just like their fathers, strained the family budget to ensure their great fun and social success—and we did all this with a most bizarre result:

We marooned our children in a gold-plated playpen.

Surely, this was the last thing we intended, for our thought was—as an educator would say—to prepare the whole child for life. Nevertheless, we did maroon them, because while we seemed to be giving them everything, we actually failed to give them a room in the house of man. For that matter, given the fragmented

198

nature of our industrial urban society, we have no such rooms ourselves, but this, too, is our failure, for we created the society. Our worship of youth did not fail to give youth the idea that it was somehow a very good thing to be young, but it also succeeded in giving youth the idea that they had been set apart from ordinary humanity. Wherefore, some of the young demigods feel markedly superior to the rest of us, and say as much. A few cry out with the boy who said, "They give me everything I ask for. I wish they would punish me; if they would only punish me when I'm bad, I'd know that they loved me." But most of them, like the forty water-skiers at the summer birthday party, just bop about in their golden playpen without a passing thought.

In all that I am saying here, it is well to remember that, even if millions of Americans are doing something at any one time, it is probably a minority activity. For instance, one impressive fact about a magazine that has a readership of six million, is that one hundred ninety-four million other Americans evidently do *not* read it. Just so, while I am talking about suburban Americans, who constitute a large minority of Americans and whose effectiveness in society is disproportionately great, considering their number, I cannot claim that a feeling of estrangement pervades every sub-urban household and every suburban child. Nor can I say that irresponsible hedonism characterizes suburbia, although hedonists are not rare.

What I will claim, however, is that disaffection, or unease, and a disinclination to commitment and an inability to make decisions are quite general among those suburban youths who seem to have been given the most of everything—those fortunate ones who have good brains, who come from affluent homes, and who with such high parental hopes are shoved into the best of schools and later stuffed into the Ivy League colleges and the select women's colleges of the East Coast. When these students complain, as they do, that their school or their college is not "real," it is as if they who have everything believe they must lose it all in order to gain possession of themselves. Which might very well be true.

I speak as one who himself was given every possible advantage by his parents, and who felt that it was all unreal and that he, like Stephen Dedalus, had to go into exile in order to encounter the reality of experience and forge in the smithy of his soul the uncreated conscience of his race. Today larger numbers of youths are receiving the gifts once bestowed upon a relative few. If rebellion is the province of adolescence, and if the circumstances of the rebellious adolescent are affluent, why, affluence is what he must rebel against. Yet, there is a very great difference between a thing given and a thing gained, and this may be the truth that disengaged youth perceives, and which may have escaped us, the suburban givers.

By the same token, there is a difference between a pleasure worked for and an unearned pleasure, and this truth seems to have escaped even the most perceptive youths who, like the forty oblivious water-skiers, somewhere along the line apparently picked up the idea that they should always have whatever they want right away. Such an idea is infantile, but we cannot plead surprise if they entertain it, for what can a child-centered society produce but children?

10

The Hope of the Future

I WISH I COULD CHANGE the subject, but I cannot. Our children have been my generation's principal topic of conversation ever since we returned from Hitler's war to raise them. We have spent more time and worry over our children's education alone than we have on all our other obligations of citizenship and all the other events of our time combined. I think there is involved here something more than the normal concern of parent for child. I think there has been another reason, lying beneath our consciousness—a reason more subtle than those outward reasons for our child centeredness that I have so far adduced. I believe that we have subconsciously been using our children as a means of escape.

Of course this is a theory I have no way of proving, but it is a theory suggested by sundry observations. For example, issues and events of our postwar years would include the politics of the cold war, fear of nuclear disaster, the rise of McCarthyism, war in Korea, the despoliation of our countryside, pollution of our air and water, the manifold ills of our cities. And what was our response? I would say that it was largely to skitter away to the suburbs and play with our dolls, on the ground that there was little the ordinary citizen could do about any of these things happening outside the doors of his house, and on the further ground that he did not want to think about them anyway.

The Korean war is a curious case in point. Normally, you might suppose that a nation's citizens would take some interest in a war that their country was fighting. Yet no one of my acquaintance among my contemporaries took a personal interest in the Korean war. When we thought of war, we thought of the war *we* had won. That, we said, was a real war—not some kind of obscure Asian skirmish that President Truman called a police action. The President's choice of words suggested a business no more weighty than sending a squad car to a barroom brawl. To my mind, the interesting thing is not so much the President's description of that war, as our acceptance of his description as being accurate. Our principal reaction to the whole affair was to share a low-grade angry puzzlement as to why the cops did not promptly square the bad guys away; but serious interest there was not.

Understandably, the common citizen of an industrial state might very well think there is nothing he can do about great events, but a glory (and a danger) of the American system is that legal means exist wherby the governed may actually determine the actions of their government. Yet, just as in the case of the Korean war, my generation took almost no constructive interest in the cold war, nor in the dialogue concerning nuclear armament. Again, what interests me is not that we did not make an effort to take part, but why we refused to think about making any such effort. And, while Senator McCarthy was speaking, who of my generation was speaking against him? Surely the Senator's activities would seem to have been of much more immediate concern, and much more controllable, than events overseas, but who among us stood up to call attention to the fact that this particular emperor had no clothes? Damned few—until McCarthy attacked the Army in which we veterans had a nostalgic interest.

By and large our response was massive, fearful withdrawal.

For evidence of this, I refer you to the contents of our national magazines prior to the Kennedy administration. The editors of our mass-circulation magazines are extraordinarily skillful at deducing what their readers are willing to read, and the articles of this period were uniformly bland, and essentially concerned with giving advice that would enable you, too, to have family fun. As a free-lance writer who offered articles to the magazine market of that time, I

202

very soon learned what would sell and what would not—and what would *not* sell was any article the editors called "strong" or "controversial." I believe the editors were quite right whenever they said, "People don't want to read about that," and the question then and now in my mind was why there was no readership for articles of any weight that dealt with matters that should have been of common interest. For example, today a national magazine will print a report on the shrinkage of our water supply. In the 1950s, they would not, for as one editor told me, "Who the hell wants to hear that, five or ten years from now, when he turns on the faucet nothing will come out? Right now all he wants to hear is how to build an outdoor fireplace." He was right. But why?

I suppose the simplest answer is that we were all like the Hemingway hero who, tired of what he has had to do, just wants to have fun with his girl and not think about anything. Or, more precisely, like Candide at the end of his moil, we just wanted to cultivate our gardens. I suggest that our withdrawal from events was a fact, and that it was the kindergarten that we cultivated.

In this regard, my own household was more normal than unusual. I cannot claim that Margaret and I played the public citizen's role to any greater extent than anyone else. We, too, allowed the great issues and events of the days to wash over and around us without trying to do anything about them. We isolated ourselves with our children in the country and, in summer, on our island, and very largely let the world go hang. We took an enormous interest in our children, however, to such extent that we let them determine our budget and our style of life, and dictate to us where we should live.

Looking back, I can think of no home of our acquaintance where the quality of the school curriculum was not in question, and with very few exceptions, our friends were all concerned with wedging their children into college because they had been to college themselves and did not want their children to descend the social ladder. But now it seemed that *everyone* was trying to get his children into college so that they could subsequently earn good

203

money; and since there were more applicants than there were desks in colleges, the colleges were taking only those with the best preparations. Wherefore our friends, the social collegians, as well as those of our friends who might be called the intellectual collegians, were jumping up and down on their local school boards to jazz up the high school curriculum, or were moving to other school districts where a finer high schooling was rumored to be available.

For example, when we moved from Fairlington to the Maryland countryside, we looked for a country house only in Montgomery County for the sole reason that its school system was superior to any other county's in the Washington area. Later, after I became a free-lance writer, we moved to Philadelphia only because we had reason to believe that Montgomery County's school system was none too good, no matter what the National Education Association might think of it. We would not ordinarily have traded woods, fields and clean air for a grubby city full of gasoline fumes, but we thought it important to enroll our children in one of Philadelphia's excellent private schools. We chose the school not because of any particular belief in the intrinsic superiority of private to public education, but because of the state of the family treasury. There were many excellent public schools in the nation, and as a freelance I could live in one town as well as in another. But we could not afford the price of a house in the areas of the excellent public schools. On the other hand, we could afford to buy a house in what is gently called a changing neighborhood in Philadelphia and have money enough left to pay the private school tuition.

This decision must sound strange, coming as it does from one who had little use for formal education himself, but as I said, Margaret and I were no less child-centered than anyone else of our generation. Caught as we were in the contemporary mood, our thinking ran as follows:

As parents, we took the view that our children would not necessarily closely resemble us. It was therefore possible that they might find college more enjoyable than I had. As parents, we had a re-

204

sponsibility to present them with all the opportunity we could contrive to give them; in this case, to get them into a school that would—providing they did their part—give them a preparation sufficient to meet the entrance requirements of the most exacting colleges. What colleges they chose to enter, if any, would be their decision; our responsibilities began and ended with the business of putting them in a position to make the best use of whatever brains they might have. Finally, we did not want them to have a qualitatively worse secondary education than we had, and it seemed to us that if we left them in Maryland schools this would be their fate. It seemed that we would have to go to unusual lengths, not to push our children ahead of our neighbors' children, but simply to find for them basic high school standards equal to those of the 1920s and the 1930s.

One trouble was, the standards had changed. In accordance with modern theories of social welfare, every child in the nation was now going to high school at least until age sixteen, as compared with the less than half the school-age population who attended high school in the 1930s; now, no less than half of all high school graduates were going to college, as compared with perhaps the 3 per cent who went during the Depression. Understandably, as public education became more public, it became less educational—particularly in those schools addicted to theories of social diaperism. In our well-regarded Maryland school, for instance, the eleventh-grade English class read the *Reader's Digest* in order to stimulate interest in literature. We opted for a school where the eleventh grade made a structural analysis of *Moby Dick,* and we did this not for reasons of intellectual snobbery, but of intellectual decency.

Our decision might seem logical, even laudable, up to a point. I am not so sure, however, that we would make the same decision today. If we had it to do again, I think we would allow the children to suffer through a Montgomery County education, teach them *Moby Dick* at home if it seemed all that important, continue to enjoy living in a fragrant countryside, and devote the seventy-five

205

thousand dollars that we spent on their school and college to taking trips to Europe. Or, if we were to do it again, we might choose to live abroad for several years, confident that the change in culture would be not only most enjoyable for us but also more educational for our children than the American schooling we gave them.

The public search for quality in education may have begun for panicky, wrong reasons, i.e., for snobbish or mercantile reasons as contradistinct from intellectual ones; but I should say that he who toys around with quality is sooner or later infected by it. One result of what I have elsewhere called a sheepskin psychosis was that the quality of national public education *did* improve, and another result was that those children who were capable of learning something began to jump through intellectual hoops that most of their parents could not have got through themselves. Never a nation to do things by halves, we Americans reversed our anti-intellectuality and went on to make a fad out of a concern for affairs of the mind, with, I should say, the repudiation of McCarthyism and the election of John F. Kennedy as among this fad's subsequent by-products.

Now, having said this much about monetary considerations as having inspired the rush to college, I think it necessary to add that this was merely the most visible reason why parents pushed their children to obtain diplomas. There is plenty of evidence to suggest that it was the controlling reason: Everybody said that no one could get a good job without a college degree, and since everybody said this, saying it made it so.

But people seldom have just one reason for doing anything, and the most apparent reasons are not always the real ones. For instance, if anyone had sat down calmly to study the facts, the connection between degrees held and money earned would have seemed tenuous, if not spurious. It would also have been seen that, inasmuch as only 7 per cent of the population held college degrees, the work that Americans currently did was scarcely so complicated that only college graduates could do it. Finally, if anyone had interested himself in the facts, it would have been clear that to

206

require diplomas of job holders henceforth would be tantamount to condemning more than 50 per cent of Americans to unemployment, inasmuch as only 50 per cent of high school graduates were now going on to college, and of those who were, 40 per cent were dropping out.

I think it important to ask why no one was really interested in getting at the facts and thinking this business through. I also think the answer is this:

The equating of diploma with money was a convenient rationalization that permitted us to continue to play dolls with our children.

I do not believe that we can consider this matter, or any other historical event, out of context. And I believe the context is that of America's historical worship of youth; of Jefferson's vision of an enlightened electorate; of our historical concern for free public education for all; of recent decades so raddled by disasters, wars, perils, regimentation and affluence as to make pediacentricity both appealing and possible. Finally, I would say the context would include that foolhardy perennial, American optimism.

Briefly, we've loused the deal, but the kids will fix it up.

With specific reference to our children, we Americans have always felt that way about them. I assume that at every commencement exercise ever held on these shores someone has always told the graduates that they were the hope of the future. But never before had so much hope been invested in so many. I think all the reasons for our child-centeredness were operative here, including parental desire to go to college vicariously, now that the Den Dads had gone through the Little League; to all this we added an almost religious conviction that our little children would lead us all to salvation.

I am saying that our intense interest in our children may have been not only an escape but also an admission of defeat.

I can think of no other general theory that would account for the fact that we not only thought of our children first, but thought of them first all the time, to the virtual exclusion of all other adult

207

concerns, and that whenever we thought about them in any way more serious than wanting to play with them, we thought principally in terms of their education.

Nor can I think of any other theory that would also so well explain the depths of our despair when we found out that not all these dear little plants grew into beautiful flowers in our kindergarten. Surely the most poignant cry echoing through the graveyard of our hopes is the one we most commonly voice: *Why do these children, who have everything, behave the way they do?*

Before we can go an inch further, I must make it very clear that I am about to discuss only the fifteen-to-twenty-two-year-olds from comfortable if not affluent homes, with special emphasis on those of college age, and that I am more particularly concerned only with those among them who are giving a tone, or style, to their generation. I am not conerned with the unimportant majority. Most of the members of any new generation will gladly do all the tricks asked of them and they will wag their little tails in appreciation of the head-pattings and sweetmeats that reward such an exemplary performance. Nearly all of these will lead useful, intelligent lives, and some of them will even lead important ones. They will be our solid citizens, the squares, and they will serve, as they always have, as a brake on progress. There are many times when a brake is essential, but brakes never determine the style of the machine. The style is set by what is highly visible, and in a social context, it is only the different few who stand out. As matters usually work out, the attitudes of those different few become the mores of society twenty or thirty years later. Thus the world changes, sometimes for the better.

What therefore should concern us is today's rebel, not the Eagle Scout. Like any other rebel, he rejects the society around him—in this case, the one we have given him. But unlike any prior American rebels, the current ones are *not* optimistic. They have no program to offer. Some express their rejection through a degree of violence never seen before in this country. Others commit slow suicide. A few—and the rate is going up rather rapidly—commit quick, messy suicide. Many are totally withdrawn. Even the constructive rebels among them are unprogressive, for rather than setting out to change the order of things, they are merely trying to make the present structure work. Oddly enough, those who most totally reject our standards are found in what we like to believe are our best schools. Our standards are obviously those of making money, acquiring things, and seeking status within a money-oriented social order; but at the best of schools our youth learns that business is a nasty, grabby affair, that there is something inherently evil about money, and that anyone who seeks status suffers from an inferiority complex. (I am sure no such lessons are taught explicitly, but I am equally sure that such are the impressions acquired.)

Among our visible youth, then, we find a few surviving beatniks at one end of the scale of dissent. Truly apathetic, the beatnik quite literally wants to do nothing. In his view, a lunatic society has beaten him into immobility. He wears the uniform of another generation—one that, in the 1920s and 1930s, lived in the Latin Quarters of the world. But while the earlier Latin Quarters had their quotas of useless hangers-on, they also contained a good many youngsters who had a specifically different view of the world and who were working hard to perfect that view and bring it to the world's attention. The beatnik's point, however, is that nothing makes sense, so all effort is futile. His philosophy is: sufficient to the day is the evil thereof. To offset the evil of each day, he accepts whatever pleasure someone may wish to give him—his role in sexual intercourse is passive—but he will not say "Thank you" for a gift, because he reasons that the giver had the pleasure of giving, so that if anyone should be thankful, it should be the giver. If he is accorded a curse and a blow instead, then he will say, "Such is life." The beatnik may tell you that his philosophy stems from existentialism or from Zen, or from both, but it will shortly become apparent that he has comprehended the meaning of neither. Most likely, he has not really tried. He is as close to a human zero as it is possible to come and still be alive, and the fact that this

209

type of person can exist in any appreciable number is wholly due to charity received either from worried relatives or from that perpetually flowing wet nurse, the Great Society.

At the upper end of the scale of dissent we find the bright young man who stands at the very pinnacle of socially accepted adolescent achievement, but who sees no way to go from there except down, and who does not want to move from where he is. He is a boy who has stayed right on his tracks from childhood, earning top marks in the best of schools, and who has emerged with honors from an Ivy League college. Now, looking around from his point of vantage, he feels the world's humdrum tasks are beneath him. He sees his father monotonously catch the 8:15 every day to do something that strikes the son as being insanely stupid. For pleasure, the father plays golf, which the boy regards as surely one of the world's most pointless wastes of time. Nothing seems worth striving for. Social position? He already has that, and is not impressed. Creature comforts? He has them; he has had them, right up to the ears. He has been driving the family Cadillacs for years, and now has a new Porsche of his own. As one such boy put it, "So this is the big deal? I mean, it isn't all that great." What does he want to do? "To tell you the truth," the boy said, "I really don't know. I guess I'll go to graduate school—it helps postpone a decision."

A second Hamlet of our time, also an Ivy League senior, said, "You must understand that ours is not a hungry generation." He said that his parents of the Depression and wartime generation had things much easier than he because, since they lacked everything, they "had to go to work." But his generation, he said, did not enjoy the luxury of being under the lash. Instead, they were crushed beneath the burden of free choice.

A third boy said the choices were none too good. "We've been told America is the greatest country on earth and we have the best of everything and all that jazz," he said, "and frankly, if this is the best, you can have it. Besides, what is 'good'? What is 'truth'? Truth is relative."

Each of these three college seniors, each extremely intelligent

210

and capable of playing all sorts of intellectual games, said he intended to go to graduate school and then into either teaching or the Peace Corps. Each felt that such activities were honorable, whereas business was not. Be that as it may, it was quite apparent that their desire to remain in the academic world, or to enter that of professional altruism, was a way of avoiding the workaday world. And, more specifically, each felt it was a way of avoiding the draft. One of them was terrified by the idea of serving in the Army, although the others regarded military service as merely an unpleasant waste of time to be escaped if legally possible. Meanwhile, all of them found some aspects of their present existence delightful. Theirs was the world of girls and Volkswagens and ski weekends and intellectual mumblety-peg, with all expenses paid. As one of them said, "I don't want this to stop just yet." Although each felt that one of these days he would have to do something mundane, none wished to dwell on such a sordid subject. Until the evil time of decision, the three boys will remain within the free-masonry of disengaged youth. And their number is not just three but legion.

Between the two extremes of the bright escapers-into-farther-Academe and the beatniks who prefer oblivion to thought, we find all manner of youngsters whose actions range from stupid to the depraved. They are semibeatniks in the sense that, while they agree that most human activity is square, they will energetically seek pleasure. We as their parents or we as the taxpayers give them everything they basically need, but what they want is the wild, new, far-out kick. By "far out" they mean something far beyond the pale, and these are the youths who make the headlines. As, for example, the Hell's Angels make the headlines.

Hell's Angels are a group of toughs anywhere from twenty to forty who drive motorcycles, terrorize small towns, beat up police-men, otherwise seek to skewer the bourgeois, and they swagger about in costumes that Hermann Göring might have designed. Listen to this view of themselves, as reported in a Los Angeles newspaper interview:

211

We're goofing through life on our hopped-up Harley 74s, riding to the brink of it, twisting the tail of it until it screams.

We've punched our way out of a hundred rumbles, man, and stayed alive with our boots and our fists since we set up the Hell's Angels in '54.

We've littered beer cans on a score of beaches, man, and we've rode our bikes over the cliffs, taken the hard falls, and rode 'em back up again.

You know how it is, man, with your knees locked on the gas tank and all that power between your legs.

Man, don't talk to me about your doctors' bills and your traffic warrants. I mean, you've got your woman and you're on your way.

We're the one percenters, the one percent that don't fit and don't care.

Our motto, man, is All on One and One on All. You mess with an Angel, man, and you've got 25 of them on your neck.

Don't push me on who we are, man, because we're nobody and somebody wrapped in one.

A far-out crowd indeed. As is the custom with certain New York street gangs, if a girl wishes to ride with the Angels, she is expected to service not just one but all of them. What is particularly disturbing about these young men, and their girls, is that they are not unintelligent, and they are certainly not lazy, and they do not come from the dregs of society. ﹏ut their intelligence has gone very wrong, their energies are those of the Vandals and they are estranged from their homes. They seem to furnish proof of the theory that violence is the last fruit of affluence. Anything but beat, they roar about flaunting their unwelcome difference, and there are not just twenty-five of them. Some three hundred Hell's Angels gunned their motorcycles into several Monterey Bay, California, towns over the Labor Day weekend of 1964, bawling obscenities, beating up the citizenry and the local police, looting and raping.

While the Hell's Angels are so special a minority as to be almost outside our interest here, they are by no means an unimportant

212

minority, for they represent only the most extreme attitude of thousands of youngsters who might as well be called Hell's Cherubim. These latter are those fine young American boys and girls who amuse themselves by engaging in pitched battles with the civil authorities during Easter, Fourth of July and Labor Day vacations. On one such occasion in 1964, Ocean City, New Jersey, got off relatively easy. The police were able to keep control, jailing thirty-nine youngsters for offenses ranging from drunkenness to assault and battery.

But a resort town at Lake Winnipesaukee, New Hampshire, was not so fortunate. There, a swarm of motorcyclists ran wild, terrorized the townsfolk, set fire to buildings, smashed windows, overturned automobiles, and fought an all-night guerrilla against the hastily summoned National Guard. At dawn, the town's main street was littered with debris, more than seventy persons had been hurt, and forty motorcyclists jailed.

At Seaside, Oregon, the National Guard was also called out for two nights running to fight a mob of sweatshirted youths who showered them with stones and sand-filled beer cans; ninety-five were arrested. At Orchard Beach, New York, more than one-hundred teen-agers stood off the local police with beer cans and garbage; the National Guard was called out at Russell's Point, Ohio, and had to resort to chemical warfare to gain control; at Arnold's Park, Iowa, after the bars closed at 1:00 A.M., collegians rioted and set a tavern afire and damaged more than one-hundred automobiles; at Rockaway Beach, Missouri, youngsters climbed the dance-hall roof and kept the police out of the building by bombing them with firecrackers.

At Hampton Beach, New Hampshire, a few hoodlums sparked a riot that soon involved more than seven thousand high school and college youngsters, who began chanting obscenities. Then, as the mob moved on to the police station, the chant changed to "Kill the cops!"

"It was one of the most appalling things I've ever seen," said a terrified restaurateur, who climbed up onto his roof for safety.

213

"Girls and boys as young as thirteen and fourteen were chanting in a near frenzy."

The police had to resort to fire hoses, dogs and shotguns filled with birdshot and rock salt to prevent an attack on the station, but all night the young rioters held the streets, breaking windows, setting fires, and hurling stones, beer cans and garbage. The New Hampshire governor called out the National Guard, and at the end of the riot twenty-two persons had been wounded, and 139 college and high school students jailed.

In 1961 more than fifty thousand collegians arrived in Fort Lauderdale, Florida, to celebrate the Easter vacation and the good townsfolk gleefully raised the price of beer to fifty cents a bottle and packed their guests ten and twelve at a time into hotel and motel suites at ten dollars per night per person. But there were too many visitors for Fort Lauderdale to accommodate them all, even in this brutal way. Some eight thousand youngsters with nothing to do and nowhere to stay eddied about aimlessly in the main streets, battling for three nights in a row with the town's hurriedly reinforced police units while still other collegians stole buses and put six-foot sharks and alligators into hotel swimming pools. The war cry of the rioters was, "We want beer!" and more than five hundred of the ringleaders were jailed before a semblance of order was restored.

Anyone who is not an American businessman might suppose that, with such examples before them, the city fathers of Daytona Beach, Florida, would have thought twice before soliciting the college-student trade. But in 1962, the city advertised that the students would be welcome, and the following year they came to take the place apart. Back again in 1964, they enjoyed a wild two weeks that left the city's motel owners petitioning the city to keep the students out. "This college student invasion," their petition said, "will, unless checked, expand like a cancerous growth . . . to a point where it will destroy the prosperous business created by the many Easter vacationing families."

I could multiply the examples, but I think it apparent enough

214

now that the kind of thing I have been discussing is not a local phenomenon, but is occurring north, south, east, west—anywhere there are adolescents. No doubt college vandals constitute only a minority but they are certainly not an insignificant minority. As the *New York World Telegram & Sun* remarked, "Nobody, of course, teaches the youngsters to stage these mob riots, but apparently, nobody has taught them not to, either."

It is too easy to say that the rioting collegians are largely those who come from a lower-class stock that has been jumped up too suddenly into middle-class affluence and, before it had learned its manners, had sent its children off to state universities. While this may be true enough, it is also true that we find similar examples of mob behavior occurring among upper-class youths. At Princeton University, for example, some students ran wild, and in the course of battling with police, setting fires, and generally amusing themselves as young gentlemen will, they pulled up the fence that bounds the grounds of the college president's house. And, not too long ago, another swarm of bluebloods made a complete shambles of a Long Island mansion in which they were the invited guests. The occasion was a debutante party, and the damage occurred after the party was technically over. The dance orchestra had gone, and sixty-five collegians repaired to the beach mansion that, standing apart from the main house, was serving as a dormitory for the boys.

"We had been drinking for two straight days, with no sleep and a liquid diet. We weren't the same people we are today," one of the boys subsequently told a Long Island judge. "Some Harvard gymnasts had been doing stunts. The gentleman from Harvard who was on the other gentleman's shoulders was swinging the chandelier back and forth. I was up on the mantelpiece, watching people crawl on the rafters. One of the other boys up there swung to the floor on the chandelier, and about ten minutes later I guess I wanted to be a gymnast, too."

At that point, the chandelier came crashing down. Meanwhile another young gentleman was on the mantelpiece, holding a ship's

215

wheel and pretending to be the skipper of a yacht in a storm. Thereafter, someone soared through the closed French doors, and after that, the party guests began breaking windows. They broke every one. They destroyed the furniture, smashed whatever they could, and in all did six thousand dollars' worth of damage to the house. The result of all this was that the host had to appear in court as a "reluctant" prosecution witness—one wonders at his reluctance—and the boys' families paid for the damages. Not one of the defendants received the punishment that might have been meted out to a poor boy who threw a stone through a schoolhouse window by accident. But perhaps the words of one of the defendants had weight with the judge. He said:

"I am not ashamed of what I did. . . . I agree that someone has a moral obligation about this damage, but I don't know who is responsible for the atmosphere that caused what happened at the party."

While it can be maintained that the aristocracy never sets standards of behavior that are worthy of emulation, it is certainly true that the next class down, the upper class of any society, always sets such standards as are followed. Wherefore, I would say that we are in trouble, because we now find the most visible among the upper-class youths engaged in shenanigans not wildly different from those of their social superiors and inferiors. At least one psychiatrist says that, in so doing, they merely caricature the emptiness of the society they see about them in their suburban homes and schools.

I wonder if he could have been talking about us?

If you talk with the police, you will learn that there is no more and no less delinquency among suburban youths than among slum youths. In affluent suburbia there are youthful gangs that commit burglaries, stage gang fights, peddle pornography, experiment with narcotics, engage in sexual orgies, drink like sewers, and wreck houses. They are called "groups" or "sets," not "gangs," but the distinction is a fine one. Metropolitan police chiefs speak of such activities as the "hidden" delinquency of suburban youth. It is usually hidden under a thick layer of dollar bills, for the police are reluctant to heave into jail the children of their social superiors. Instead of the crime's being recorded on the police blotter, the usual solution is to call the boy's home, whereupon the father comes to take his son in charge. Bills for damage are quietly paid, fines are paid, and in flagrant cases where juvenile court action would be necessary, the young offender is most often taken direct from the police station to the friendly neighborhood psychiatrist, or packed off to a military boarding school rather than to a state correctional institution.

Whenever instances of hidden delinquency come to public light, as in a case of vandalism, it is all too often supposed that the whole thing came about because the youngsters "had too much to drink." This argument is often put forth to explain the town-wrecking exploits of middle-class college youth, but too much can be made of the point. Upper- and middle-class youngsters normally start drinking during their sophomore year in high school, and most usually the children receive their first drinks from us, their parents. By the time they enter the age group that concerns us at the moment, they should have had sufficient experience with alcohol to know how to handle it. If they drink to excess, the question to ask is not: Was drunkenness responsible for the subsequent activity that brought the cops on the run? Rather, it is: What caused them to drink too much in the first place? To drink until "bombed out of their minds" as they revealingly say, is no longer a childish experiment to them. Instead, it is—as a psychiatrist pointed out—evidence of a death-wish. They want to leave this world. A suburban police detective said:

"The youth today, even those that are active, seem bored. They seem bored with life. I don't know what they expect of it. Nothing seems to give them a kick. It's a sign of the times, I'll tell you that."

In one suburban community, a high school crowd broke into a house whose owners were away for the weekend. They slashed fine paintings, smashed bottles of aged brandy in the fireplace, stole the

217

lady's jewels. They did not try to fence the jewels: the boys merely passed them out to their girl friends. It was, a policeman said, as if they wanted to be caught and punished. Asked why they had done this, most of the youngsters said, "I don't know." Others of the group said, "For kicks," and some said, "to get even." To get even with whom? For what? Why?

"I don't know," they said.

I think it highly significant that these people "don't know" why they do what they do; that when they are apprehended, their stock excuse is, "everybody else was doing it and I went along with the group"; and that there is so often a pathetic kind of desire to be punished. It is almost as if youth, from the Hell's Angels on up through the social scales to the house-party wreckers, is trying to tell us something. Consider the case of a college boy who made a telephone call not to his parents but to an aunt:

"Come get me out of here," he begged, gave the address, and hung up.

The aunt went to the house, owned by a couple then in Florida, and found it filled with smoke, alcohol fumes, and a welter of glaze-eyed youngsters in various stages of nudity. One couple was copulating on a sofa when she entered; the others were milling vaguely about. Her nephew was slumped beside the telephone table, waiting.

Outside, on the street, the boy explained that he "didn't have the guts" to leave the place by himself. He said he had been sickened by the whole affair, which had been going on for three weeks.

Of course he was lying to himself as well as to his aunt. Why did he go to the orgy in the first place? Why did he not walk out of it the moment it revolted him? Why did he have no guts? Why did he need to have some member of his family come and be a witness? Why the choice of an aunt rather than his parents? Was he not somewhat like a five-year-old who, having broken the cookie jar, runs to find his mother and sobs, "Look what you made me do"?

Apart from the vandal and the delinquent, there is another seg-

218

ment of intelligent youth that merits inspection: those who, in their language, are "cool." Like the apathetic beatniks, the cool care absolutely nothing about such concepts as patriotism, honor, glory, duty, religion, community responsibility or the dignity of labor. Like all other disengaged youth, the cool can see that a distance lies between what we adults preach and what we practice. But the cool are not beat. Nor are they wreckers. Nor are they builders. They are aloof consumers. Nothing impresses them, for to be impressed would be to "blow your cool." The cool would not be caught dead in Fort Lauderdale, any more than they would wear black leather jackets and tear around on motorcycles. They regard these activities, and the depredations of suburban youth, as juvenile. They stand upstage, calm and sardonic; they are a kind of Greek chorus of our time, one that views stage center with satirical condescension. They are absolutely amoral, and are possessed of a singular style that is not without charm.

Indeed, the cool are the high stylists of their generation, and something of their example is imitated to one extent or another by all their contemporaries, including the square. In purest form, the coolest of the cool is handsome, nylon-smooth, and dressed just a bit beyond the height of fashion, but just this side of Carnaby Street. He—or she—is athletic, brave and intelligent. Most of them have been to college, many are graduates, and some of them have serious intellectual specialties, such as mastery of medieval musical notation or fluency in a language as esoteric as Arabic. They may be knowledgeable in an astonishing number of areas, but regard their accomplishments with amused contempt, as if to say, *"anybody* can put *that* up." Their public pose is that they prefer pop and camp art and the popular music of the 1920s. With equally grave satire, they say they enjoy peanut butter and raisins fried between two pieces of scrapple, washed down with beer-and-tomato juice. Their dramatic hero is Humphrey Bogart as seen in his more implausible roles. To them, Sean Connery as James Bond is wildly funny.

The coolest of the cool comprise a kind of talent elite of disengaged youth, and they can come from any social class. As one of them told *Life* magazine writer Robert Bradford, who reported on their "fatalistic, private world" at the Aspen, Colorado, ski slopes:

"Anyone can be accepted here if he shows internal fortitude. There's a misconception that ski-bumming surfers are uneducated troublemakers. That's not it at all. We just have this drive *to do everything*. We don't want to get fixated. We took up skiing because it's a new challenge. This keeps us vital."

"To do everything" can be translated as "to do nothing in particular" and "to seek any pleasure." The cool are the great experimenters with hallucigens. They live at speed in sports cars, on skis and surfboards. Their pleasures, which they pursue with singleminded selfishness, and on which they spend nearly all their money, are often quite as expensive as they can be physically dangerous, and the cool are not unduly concerned about the ways in which they acquire their money. Some of the girls coolly become whores at need. Some of the boys who drift from resort to resort, following the seasons and serving as beach boys, as swimming, surfing, tennis and skiing instructors, also serve as gigolos to lonely middle-aged women and/or lonely rich men. Some of them supplement their tips and incomes by stealing money, travelers' checks and jewels from hotel rooms, and if they do, the cool make no moral judgment. To get away with something is regarded as cool. To be caught is stupid.

As Mr. Bradford reported of the cool surfers who took up skiing at Aspen, many of them have been married and divorced. A cool youth—boy or girl—does not necessarily oppose marriage as being square. He or she may say it is perfectly all right to *try* marriage. If it works, fine, and if not, "you can always get divorced." But most of the cool simply live together as long as their first enthusiasm lasts. Then they drift away to find other partners. It cannot be said that they have shared relationships, or even that their heterosexual intercourse is truly heterosexual. Rather, they coldly use one another as masturbatory devices.

The essential characteristic of the cool is their rootless, drifting hedonism.

"My life is a gas," one of them told Mr. Bradford. "In the spring I'll take my mountain junk and drop it off in Laguna. Then I'll grab a pair of Levis, a T-shirt, swim trunks, socks and tennies, and head for Mazatlan, Mexico. Then back to Laguna for surfing and volley ball and maybe back here [Aspen] in the Fall. I'll see what the crowd is doing."

The drifting does not last forever. Usually, by age twenty-five, they drift into something more productive than sliding down waves or mountains. The point is that the cool take full advantage of the opportunity to drift around in that gold-plated playpen to which we have so largely relegated the adolescent, and while they drift, they formulate the styles, outlooks and attitudes they will carry into the adult world of their, and our, future. The stylists of any generation do this. When the stylists of the 1920s became adults, they brought a new freedom into American life and set the stage for those of us who were the radical stylists of the 1930s. We in turn have given birth to the detached cool of the 1960s, and in 1980 their children will almost certainly inherit something of the tradition and characteristics of the unconcerned.

Standing to one side of the beat, the rioters and the cool—but just as much inside the gilded playpen as they—are the youths who wish to be engaged in our affairs. These will be the youths of good will who join the peace marches, the civil rights demonstrations; who volunteer to work and teach in the slums of our cities and in what are coyly called the developing nations. No one can question the bona fides of the altruistic young, but what seems tragic about them is that they are not an advancing army. They are an under-manned occupation force that would like, please, to be allowed to try to consolidate a gain. The youths of good will seek, essentially, to make us do what we say should be done, and for their pains they are derided by the cool as being out of it, and by many of us as being draft-dodgers. Our view of them suggests that we are just as disengaged as any beach boy.

Granted that the various types of rebels I have been describing are a distinct minority; they nevertheless constitute—to my mind —the only youth who should concern us because they are the stylists of their generation. They also constitute a large enough minority to require the occasional attention of the National Guard and the constant attention of police, school boards, college administrations, civic organizations of all sorts, mental health agencies and, appropriately enough, the nation's alienists. And their number is growing. Most serious crimes are committed by young people; the average age level of the criminal is dropping. There is no doubt that a relationship does exist between crime and poverty, but there is also no doubt that another exists between violence and affluence. I regard it as ominous when a psychiatrist in private practice can tell me that high school and college youngsters now comprise three-fourths of his clientele, whereas ten years ago they did not. He added that his professional colleagues report a similar phenomenon.

We cannot ask ourselves who these youngsters are, for the answer is plain enough. At one time or another, in one way or another, I can recognize my own son and daughters as bit players in the shifting scene. At such times I have asked myself how in hell our bright children got mixed up in it.

What explains one youngster's behavior at any one moment may not necessarily explain any other youngster's behavior at that same or any other moment. Nevertheless, the question clamors for answers, and sundry of us have suggested a great many. For instance, a sociologist took the view that the Fort Lauderdale rioting was "a mere variation of spring sap running," and the city's merchants, gleefully counting up the three million dollars that the youngsters had left behind in the wreckage, instantly agreed with him. Yes, sir, that's all it was, they said, stacking up their dollar bills. No more than a little normal boyish enthusiasm, like a panty raid on a girls' dormitory, or a bonfire after a successful Princeton football season . . .

222

But other observers were less sure. One psychiatrist found great significance in the fact that, during the similar but smaller-scale mob violence that demolished the Long Island mansion, one of the boys had seized a ship's wheel and pretended to guide a vessel through a storm. He also thought it significant that the boys had destroyed a *house*. The question in his mind was whether, symbolically, it was not the house of society that they were wrecking. "As a psychiatrist I know that nobody wrecks a house the way those boys did without having reasons," he wrote in *Life* magazine, and he suggested that their parents should be more concerned about learning those reasons than about having to pay for the damage. By wrecking the house, he said, the boys were "unconsciously taking revenge." But revenge against what? The doctor suggested that affluent teen-agers' quarrel is often that their parents do not discipline them enough; that they desire to be disciplined, and that when they behave in a socially unacceptable way, this at once speaks of their need to be punished and at the same time punishes those who have so far failed to discipline them. This theory has numerous adherents, and might seem applicable to the boy who summoned his aunt to rescue him from the orgy.

Commenting on the depredations of Hell's Angels, one psychiatrist said at the time of the Monterey forays that their brutality "probably reflected a feeling of disengagement from society because of the complexity of modern life—[and] a desire on the part of the demonstrators to express a feeling of control over their own destinies." His point is echoed by a number of educators who believe that the impersonal nature of modern urban life and the impersonal nature of most jobs diminishes the importance of the human individual. Whereupon, they say, the individual casts about to find something that will rather loudly announce his presence. Here, we can say it is particularly difficult for youth to find a socially acceptable activity that will demonstrate who he is, because the late adolescent is not socially accepted in the first place—unless he is in college doing his lessons.

But these various explanations do not explain why a search for identity must take the forms of criminal nihilism.

Regarding the hidden delinquency of upper-class youth, at least three psychiatrists agree that these children need a sense of identity, but say this is the one thing their parents cannot provide, inasmuch as they themselves have none. Delinquency, one of them said, "is a growing problem, and I don't see it stopping. If anything, the kids who get into trouble get younger and younger. The adults themselves don't really accept what they say are the standards—their lives are full of evasions."

One suggestion, almost as simplistic as the spring-sap theory, is that all blame for the waywardness of our youth can be laid at the parental door. There is much to be said for the notion, but it implies that children are little more than extensions of our own personalities and will share exactly all our attitudes and responses. Such is by no means the case. As one Oklahoma farmer said on being apprised of the fact that his son had just murdered nine people in cold blood and for no apparent reason: "You can't tell how they're going to turn out."

There is also the possibility that something is wrong with the question: Why do these youngsters, who have everything, behave this way? The key words would seem to be *who have everything*. Let us take another look at what we have given them.

Although they have food, clothing, money, creature comforts of all sorts and leisure enough to drive the devil mad trying to think up enough work for idle hands, our children have a desperate feeling of living on borrowed time. It is not so much nuclear holocaust that threatens them, for we have all refused to think about that, even as we build antimissile missiles. One thing the young man has constantly hanging over him is the fear that at any moment he will receive greetings from the President. This is also a cause of concern to the young man's girl. It is not sufficiently clear to young Americans why they are being killed in a remote Asian jungle; nor can they see why, if America is as strong as the Pentagon assures us it is, we allow this lethal neither-war-nor-peace to drag on. Neither their schools, nor their parents nor their Government have explained the facts of history and geopolitics to them in any way that makes sense. At least, in a way that might make sense to them. It is frightening to think that we cannot do so—that our effort in Asia may not make sense. What they do know is that while their military service will most probably not put them on a battlefield—because most soldiers never see one—the fact remains that it might, and that being the case, they want to know what they will be fighting for. A sick society? Who can answer them?

Fear of the draft may not be the overriding constant concern of all youth, but it is one of their fears, and it is certainly contributive to their sense of estrangement. The draft applies to no one else. It is the skull in the playpen.

We have also given youth a world in which pleasure seems the goal. As one young man said:

"Anybody of any intelligence at all knows, by the time he is six years old, that he is going to die. So what difference does it make *what* you do until then? You might as well do something pleasant and amusing. You can try to get to be President and run the country if that amuses you, but what difference does it make whether you're President or not? Who cares? Why sweat? You're just going to die anyway, like everyone else."

Surely this is the voice of affluence. To a young man of an earlier time, laboring on a flinty frontier farm, the point of life was terribly clear. A great many youths are now busily toiling away on our present-day frontiers of science, art and human relationships, but a tremendous number are not—and one reason they are not is that they do not have to, and therefore cannot see why they should, and no one has really asked them to join the party, anyway. Instead, we have played with them and then in effect patted them on the head, given them twenty dollars and the key to the family car, and told them to go away, have fun and not bother us.

Another part of youth's inheritance is a society that seems in

225

constant flux, that lacks coherent class structure, and is largely without guidelines. This may help to explain, but not excuse, youth's subsequent behavior. If everyone else in the world is out for himself, as is so obviously the general case, why should youth not be out for itself, particularly when youth is left so much free choice?

One of the very few things we have *not* given our children is a clear idea of what to do once they are out of school or college. Confusing them with ourselves at the moment of their school or college graduation, we proudly say, "There! Now you're all grown up and on your own!"

On their own *what?*

All along the way we held their hands and wiped their noses and shoved nipples in their mouths, and whenever they got into trouble, dear old Den Mother or Den Dad came charging in to rescue them. We sent them to schools that taught the vital importance of good followership and of getting along with everyone and of going along with the group, and no few of us echoed this nonsense at home. We taught them at home and school *not* to be individuals, and our businesses and industries have the same lesson to teach. Our very laws reflect it: for example, the tax codes give advantages to employees of corporations that they deny to the self-employed man. With this sort of conditioning both behind him and ahead of him, what is a youth to think when, on leaving school, he is told he is now on his own?

Particularly, what is he to think when he finds out that we have no place for him to be on his own, and nothing much for him to do, until he is some years older? Why should he not feel beat, or decide to drift, or play it cool in the company of his fellows who are marooned with him in the playpen we have created for the late adolescent?

Youth has been conditioned to be a group, and a special group, and it is inevitable that when we seek to cast them loose individually they cleave to one another in a continued estrangement from

226

the adult world. They say they are happier in the company of their contemporaries. Many of them say the only reason they go to college is "because all my friends are going," and they stay in college past graduation because "I want to be with my contemporaries."

The separation of late adolescents from our world, into a world of their own, is largely an artificial one that no one sat down to create, but which for a multitude of reasons developed like a cancer. But the point is that a separation does exist; that they have been forced to one side by virtue of our constant attention to them, and they cling to one another exactly as we trained them to do. Fifty thousand individual college students did not go to Fort Lauderdale. A group went there, and a group did the damage, and we tend to think of them (and they of themselves) not as our sons and daughters, but as something called fiftythousandcollegekids. Every single one of them has the perfectly natural human desire to be a recognizable individual, and every one of them who threw a beer can at a policeman may psychologically have been trying to do something that would call attention to his individuality and his need to be recognized, but all the circumstances of their lives have made them an anonymous group, and their responses at Fort Lauderdale were the responses of a mob.

All that is generally true of American youth is also generally true of the youth of all other industrial nations—a fact that suggests there may be something about an industrial state that produces the phenomena. I should think the general explanation is this:

All industrial societies create modes of living in which their populations are compartmentalized and systematically administered to; they all tend to create a constantly diminishing need for human labor. This latter effect has, as one of its results, the creation of devices to keep people out of the labor market, and in turn one of the devices we have so far hit upon has been to keep children in schools and colleges on the pretext that the jobs are

227

becoming so complicated that a great deal of education is necessary to their mastery. In every industrial society we see evidence that adolescence is becoming increasingly prolonged, and in our own country I think that we have special reasons (which I have been trying to adduce) for prolonging it.

In this context, it will be seen that adolescence is not a matter of chronology bounded by ages twelve and twenty. It is a time when four major steps are taken. These are (1) emancipation from parents, (2) choice of vocation, (3) acceptance of heterosexual goals, and (4) integration of the personality in the direction of altruistic goals. I would say that the youth I have been describing —the weeds in our little kindergarten—have a considerable distance to go in all four respects.

I would add that we Americans have created a society so undemanding as to stretch adolescence beyond the twenties, for however long anyone wants to remain in it; we certainly do not have a primitive or medieval society wherein the problems of survival are rather bluntly and abruptly presented from the moment of walking. It is very easy to be a boy for a long while in our fair land today, particularly if you are given money enough to run up fifty-four-dollar telephone bills, buy automobiles and wet suits and skis and airplane tickets to Paris, all without having to do anything for the money, and most particularly if you come equipped with a couple of parents who give you all this because they want to live their own lives all over again through you, and who never, never want to let you go.

Whenever we discover weeds instead of flowers in our kindergarten, our anguish is in direct proportion to the emotional investment we have made during the course of playing with the little dears and we experience a cold fear that our chosen saviors may prove to be incompetent. If our children are not better than we, what becomes of the American belief in progress? To ask this much is to suggest that we may once again have to return to the bitter business of trying to save ourselves and stop nattering on so about the young.

228

It is also to suggest that we may have to take America completely apart and put it back together again in such a way as to create a world fit for human habitation; to create a society in which no one would be in doubt as to who he was, or what he must do if he would call himself a man.

11

The Trash and the Dream

COME WITH ME for a moment into the supermarket that, by reason of its commercial efficiency, has driven all the butchers, bakers and greengrocers in my neighborhood out of business. It is now my sole source of supply.

I enter its electrically operated doors thinking of ham. Perhaps a brine-cured ham this evening? Or pepper-cured? A good, hard country ham, such as those that used to hang in farmers' smokehouses in Possum Road, Maryland?

Well, no. None of those is available. The only ham that is available is, to all intents and purposes, a machine-made product from Chicago. It has been tenderized, as some of us say, by the injection of water into the meat. While the water no doubt decreases the resistance of the meat to the teeth, it also dilutes whatever flavor the blandly cured and too fat ham might have had. But, because public-opinion sampling has indicated that most American housewives prefer tenderized hams to all others, this is the one that is mass-produced and nationally distributed. Because of shelf space, time and cost formulas, the supermarket stocks nothing but the watered hams, and the Possum Road farmers cannot get their meat to market.

As with the meat, so with the fish, the vegetables, and the fruit. So also with what are called the gourmet foods at the Gourmet Counter, where we discover the French snail kits in bottles, and the frozen Swiss fondue. We find ourselves trapped by our own success. There is plenty to eat; plenty of choice. Thanks to our efficient marketing system, we Americans are taller and stronger than the citizens of any other land. We have provided more food, of more kinds, for more people, at lower cost, than any other nation—a not inconsiderable achievement. But the hams are not really hams; the brook trout turn out to have been raised in a pond and fed on liver and do not taste like brook trout; the allegedly fresh corn may have been grown a month ago in Texas or in Latin America or possibly on the dark side of the moon—in any case, it is not fresh corn. Nothing is quite what it is advertised to be in that supermarket, and it comes down to this:

There is plenty of whatever we want to eat, provided we are willing to agree with the manufacturers and processers that the names of the foods we eat are actually descriptive of what we are eating. There is so much of everything that there seems to be no reason why we should defer any pleasures, or look forward to them, because we can enjoy whatever we wish, right now—as long as we are willing to accept an apparently reasonable substitute for the genuine article. And, because so many of us *are* willing to accept the substitute right away, this creates a profitable mass market, with the result that the substitute often drives the genuine article out of existence. Wherefore, we cannot say that we eat as well, in terms of human gustatory pleasure, as a thin Italian who has no refrigerator, who buys each day what that day has freshly brought forth, and who must wait for the arrival of the Sicilian oranges, the vegetables, the grapes, the figs, and the game, each in proper season.

What is true of food in this respect is also true of nearly everything else in an industrial society operated largely on the installment plan. It is true of our houses, our schools, our automobiles, our entertainments. It is as if we were a race of children, all playing Let's Pretend. The pretense in the supermarket is that the hams are hams. Note that the ham is made easier to swallow in both a literal and a figurative sense: the housewife can buy something she can petend is a ham, but which she will not have to take pains to prepare for table. Likewise, the nothing-down ranch house with the picture window that millions of us live in is more of a show than it is a house. It is not on a ranch, there is no picture worth seeing from its window, and its lineal ancestor is the Western building with the false front. So, too, the American automobile is more of a show than it is a motorcar. It looks as if it were a safe, powerful, efficient and reliable means of transportation. In fact, it is none of these things, but merely a contraption deliberately designed to fall apart within a predictable time profitable to the manufacturer. Our education is also nine parts P. T. Barnum. The show here is that our children attend colleges and earn degrees, but the colleges are in the main trade schools and the doctoral degrees require only a demonstration of how to use the library, and not an original contribution to knowledge. Our businesses and industries and labor unions constantly put on shows of one sort and another, pretending that their employees are "associates" and that the union members are "brothers" whose single purpose is to serve the public which, in fact, they systematically fleece. I think it extremely discouraging that we are so prone to accept appearance for substance. I think it significant that we speak lovingly of show business, for almost everything about America is a show of some sort, and at the same time, it is most certainly a business—when it is not also a game.

We speak, for example, of the game of love. And so it is—and very good fun. But we also treat sex as if it could be programed for a computer. Then we widely analyze and exploit sexuality for commercial reasons involving everything from the sale of soda pop to washing machines to marriage manuals. The end result of our thinking about sex is that making love in America assumes certain aspects of buying tickets to play house with a prepackaged construction kit that has more pieces than a Monopoly game and which comes complete with instructions to paint only within the numbered areas and to see your psychiatrist twice a year.

In all, we are a nation of showmen—a fact that has something to do, perhaps, with foreigners' suspicion of the depth of our friendships. For instance, I think I am being friendly when I invite

232

a new acquaintance to dinner at our house. But a Frenchman might take a different view of the matter. One European told me, "American friendships are too easily granted to be taken seriously. It is nothing but a pleasant acquaintance for you. But to be invited to dine in a friend's house—that, for us, is full of meaning."

We might think the European wrong in his assumption that our friendliness is always superficial, but he at least suggests a question that we do not always ask ourselves: Can anything mass-produced, or easily had, be as valuable as something thoughtfully made by one man for another, or acquired only through some expenditure of time and effort? Nothing is more foreign to Americans than thinking in these terms, however, because our entire orientation from Colonial times to date has been toward inventing means of saving time, trouble and expense. Do it now the easy way, we say. You, too, can have the newest thing today—it's as easy as breathing. Given an inventive turn of mind, we have got farther along the road toward a fully automated welfare state than any other nation, but given this approach to life, acceptance of appearance for substance comes easily, particularly in a country so inured to constant change that the value of anything seems transitory. I should think the constant, easy availability of approximate values (such as the enormous supply of brook trout that are not really brook trout), and the commercial context in which everything, including love, is presented as a kind of cute, happy-making show, tends to give us each day our daily disappointment.

I should also think that our daily disappointments reinforce our awareness of a certain emptiness; of a certain ambiguity in our lives. To get at this in another way, let us now look at some pictures in an exhibition—for any nation's artistic productions offer clues to the national character.

The work is that of Andrew Wyeth, our most popular living painter, who depicts the America he sees. More than two hundred thousand people recently filed through a Philadelphia gallery that showed a collection of his work, and the consensus was that the paintings were not only beautiful but restful and serene. "It's like it

233

has always been there," a woman was heard to say. "So peaceful."

Now what Mr. Wyeth had meticulously painted was scene after scene of death: of hooks, knives, vultures, ropes, chains, despair, nostalgia, empty buckets, beached boats, empty fields in winter, muddy roads, loneliness and insanity. Ragged curtains blew in a window of a deserted house. When there were people in the pictures, they usually lay defeated and depleted on attic beds, or stared into nothing, facing three-quarters away from the viewer. A woman sat in a catatonic trance. A painting the artist called "A Spring Evening" showed a nude—it was not easy to determine that it was probably a woman—lying alone in a rumpled bed, facing into a corner formed by two blank walls. Another painting, called "A Kitchen Garden," showed a winter scene: deep snow, a frozen pond, nothing growing. Mr. Wyeth's skies were usually devoid of sun or cloud. The clear, almost surgical-theater light in his paintings had no apparent source. There was a painting of a ruinous graveyard. Someone had placed what were now dead flowers by a gravestone. The painting was called "Perpetual Care."

To be sure, any beholder reads much of himself into what he sees. It is always possible that what Mr. Wyeth painted suggests death only to me, which would provide a clue to *my* character. But it is just as possible that the public did not see what Mr. Wyeth was painting, and it is just possible that Mr. Wyeth himself did not know what he was doing when he selected his subject matter and his colors. We all unconsciously express our subconscious selves in what we wear, do, say, write—or paint. I can only say that every picture in that exhibition had something to do with dead things or with a dead past, and at least one psychiatrist agreed with me that Mr. Wyeth's production seemed to be that of a man who believes that life is a tragic business, if not a down-right desperate one. The psychiatrist said he did not find a single happy picture in the entire display, and he wondered if Mr. Wyeth's popularity did not suggest something about the public.

The only other critical comment I heard came from a painter who did not care one way or another about Mr. Wyeth's subject matter, but who said Mr. Wyeth's technique was a facile thing of no depth: that when Mr. Wyeth painted a dead deer hanging from a hook, the deer had no weight. Not being a trained painter, I cannot say whether this criticism is valid, but if it should be true, then I would not be surprised, for Mr. Wyeth strikes me as being a thoroughly American painter, and facile superficiality is at least as much a national characteristic as open hospitality.

To my mind, Mr. Wyeth's importance as a painter lies in his easy availability. He is not describing anything new, nor is he seeing what other contemporary artists do not also see. Other modern painters give us visions of distorted shapes, of splintered and mangled people, of abstractions upon abstractions. Some of them quite logically wind up by dripping paint on canvas from overhead trestles. Our sculptors poke through junkyards looking for bits of things to weld together, searching in our kitchen middens for that which will encapsulate and explicate the contemporary condition. Whereas Michelangelo apparently believed that a figure lay hidden within the stone, waiting to be called forth by the genius of man to the greater glory of man and of God, our sculptors now seem to think that the meaning of man may be found in his junk. Our leading playwrights concern themselves almost exclusively with crazy people; our music is increasingly one of cacophony and dissonance; one of our first-ranking novelists turns from fantasy to describe in loving detail the actual slaughter of a farm family by two mental defectives; our best-selling literature is sadistic pornography. What is common to all this artistic production, including Mr. Wyeth's, is a brooding sense of disintegration— usually, of violent disintegration. I should say that it takes an effort of will to face up to the fact that our artists are commenting on the quality of ordinary, daily American life; to remember that artists today do what artists have always done, which is to tell us what they see and regard as true of the world. It is just here that Mr. Wyeth's contribution is most disturbing, for his immense popularity may depend upon the people's not seeing what he is plainly showing them.

For example, when Mr. Wyeth shows us his dead deer, no one has to wonder what it is—as they very well might if an abstract artist painted one. There is the Wyeth deer. It may have no weight, but it is a perfectly recognizable dead deer, sure enough, and people look at it and say, "Oh, look at the dead deer," and move on to look at the two dead crows, at the dead tree with the fungus on it, at the deserted church with the broken window, at the old chair abandoned in an empty field. All these objects have been painted with quasi-photographic fidelity, which makes them available to every viewer, and everyone says Mr. Wyeth's paintings are lifelike. No one seems to think it odd that every single picture tells a morbid story. When Mr. Wyeth paints a picture of a farm being auctioned off, who stops to ask himself: Why does Mr. Wyeth invariably concern himself with the deaths of farms? Where is there a painting of anything growing, of something living? Why has he chosen to paint boots crushing dead weeds—particularly boots that have not been seen on mortal man for these past hundred years? Why does Mr. Wyeth show us emptiness, torment, and death, and why do we, looking at these images, say, "How lifelike"?

To my mind, the overriding question to ask about Mr. Wyeth's work is: What makes it so popular? The easiest, least comfortable answer suggests itself: Mr. Wyeth has painted an American reality with which an artistically untrained public can easily identify.

But the realities Mr. Wyeth depicts have to do with death, despair, loneliness, madness, the results of violence, nostalgia for a bygone age impossible to restore, and the destruction or decay of material objects—surely a catalogue that is a mirror image of that which is presumably typically American: jolly good fellowship, preoccupation with youthfulness, refusal to think about death, joy in material possessions, enthusiasm for the new, good common sense, and a steadfast belief that today is better than yesterday and that tomorrow will be better still. No other American painter has made disintegration so popularly appealing to a nation of optimists. Perhaps a reason for this might be that Mr. Wyeth touches upon reality in so slight a way that his work leaves our optimism undisturbed—much as if Walt Disney had guided the hand of Goya in illustrating *The Ladies' Home Journal.* In any event, an American reality that might have been excruciating if done by another painter emerges as something people can find serene and restful if done by Mr. Wyeth, and I suggest a reason for his popularity may be that Mr. Wyeth's work perfectly expresses a schizophrenia that to one extent or another afflicts all of us. I further suggest that Mr. Wyeth's concern with death may represent his reaction to an ugly America that most certainly exists.

I think the element of nostalgia for a Colonial past that he introduces into his work may represent his lament for the great, good America of Revolutionary promise.

I believe the disintegration that he and most modern artists depict is something we are subconsciously aware of, and that his nostalgia is something we all feel. I would guess that Mr. Wyeth's popularity may stem from his having combined both a well-known American fact and an equally familiar American dream on the same canvas in a slick-magazine-illustrator way that makes no demands upon the untrained viewer, so that most people can see a Wyeth painting as a celebration of the virtues of Colonial life, even though the depicted fact is that the family farm is going under the auctioneer's hammer.

The point is, there are two Americas.

One is great, good and pregnant with a new Renaissance.

The other is full of trash and violence.

These two Americas are not only coexistent but are inextricably bound together, and this has much to do with our difficulty in feeling at home in our own country. For example, I am sick of the trashy America of the commercial hokum and the substitute values, of the disappointing foods and the ugly cities and the general disintegration that our artists depict. But there is another side to the coin. Together with everyone I know, I am hopeful that tomorrow will be a great deal better in every way, and that we will in due course provide ourselves with incontestable reasons to believe that

237

we live in the greatest country on earth. I recognize the fact that the America of the Revolutionary vision produced, through free enterprise, the America of the junk and violence. But I am sure we will do something about this situation. I think we all sense imminent change, and I am sure that the direction of change will be toward humanism, because I cannot imagine in what other direction we could possibly go, now that we are nearing the materialistic millennium. After all, a Great Society cannot be measured solely in terms of gross national product: it must mean something more than that to people. So, amid my daily disappointments, I maintain my allegiance to the textbook concept of Revolutionary America, the great and good.

It does not seem coincidental to me that Mr. Wyeth's macabre Colonial nostalgia should be having a current vogue, because I think that members of my generation are now asking what there might be in the old American dream that could be applied to ameliorate the contemporary condition, and how it could be applied. How, for instance, to preserve the freest possible enterprise, and competition, and personal liberty for all citizens while at the same time ensuring that whatever men do, or build, will at least do no harm to others, and at best will be beneficial? How to prevent a real-estate developer from making a public mess while at the same time allowing him his freedom; how to grant an industrialist liberty while requiring that he not poison the air and the water and while also telling him whom he cannot refuse to hire and how much he must pay his labor and under what conditions their work will be done and, possibly, what price he will be allowed to charge for his goods and what percentage of profit he will be permitted to keep for himself? How to bring Mr. Wyeth's Colonial farm back to life and into the foreground, while moving his vultures into the background so that they will no longer dominate the scene? An enormous difficulty is presented by the fact that constant change, constantly accelerating, is the fundamental condition of American existence. This being the case, it is not easy for us to establish a proper sense of priorities for the expenditure of our energies. In such a fix,

238

many of us throw up our hands and conclude that we must each look out for ourselves as best we can in the midst of all the death, violence, disintegration, despair and drift.

I think most of us, however, come at last to conclude that man's home does not exist solely in the physical environment, but is chiefly to be found in certain qualities that have always been specifically human no matter what the external conditions. I further think that the human qualities necessary to the life of Western man turn out to be those which our ancient legends have always celebrated: self-sacrifice; honesty; a willingness to get at the truth no matter what; responsible individuality; charity; wisdom. Only through their employment can we alter the environment, devise legislation, and change the modes and conditions of education and work to the end that the business of becoming Western man can be more easily got at by the maximum number of people.

And I think that my generation did not come to this conclusion until John Kennedy was shot.

In reviewing the episodes of our experience, I think we came back from Hitler's war in a mood to stop thinking. We were tired of depressions and wars. So tired that we largely hid away from McCarthy and let events wash over us as we played with our children and concentrated on production and consumption. But during this fallow time, I think we began to discover that two cars and a backyard swimming pool could not long remain the center of our attention; that there surely must be something more to life than making money and having things and playing dolls. After our years of opulent, fearful drift among dangers, John Kennedy's appearance reminded us of the textbook ideals of our youth. Because he was our classmate, his candidacy gave us reason to believe that we might be able to put them into effect after all. He stood in high relief against the public-relations materialism of the time. I am sure that most of us remember that he said we should ask ourselves what we could do for our country, and not what our country could do for us. He said we must get America moving again.

When he spoke, I somehow heard in memory's ear the echo of

239

stories about young heroes who, with a ready grin and a friendly wave, set forth from the village and down the high road to slay the local dragon and rescue the magic princess. And I also heard echoes of a Revolutionary drum in Boston town, and voices speaking in Independence Hall, framing a new social contract for the human race. John Kennedy seemed to be saying that men can do what they set out to do, and he seemed to be a young Athenian with a concern for affairs of the mind and a sense of responsibility for the state.

I remember with what great hopes we elected him, and then how appalled we were by what happened soon afterward in Cuba.

I think we were all on the verge of uncertainty when he was shot. But that, I think, brought us at last to commitment.

I think that the meeting of John Fitzgerald Kennedy and Lee Harvey Oswald dramatized the choices available to us. It would be difficult to pose a wider contrast than that presented by these two young men, and I should think that the flood of Great Society legislation that poured through Congress after the assassination represented our awareness that somehow or other the country did have to get moving, rapidly, and in a direction as contrary to the likes of confused defectives as possible. John Kennedy was not going to save us. He had never been able to, in any event. He could only remind us that we could, if we worked at it, save ourselves, and when he was shot the point became abundantly clear: no one else was going to.

Much of the new Great Society legislation may seem to be concerned with nose-wiping and diaperism, but be this as it may, it is at least a human concern. It has more to do with the quality of human existence, for example, than it has to do with business, commerce and industry as such. If it is in great measure maternalistic, it may very well be because a large number of us are still comparative children through no fault of our own, and the rest of us are trying to put the children into a position from which they can grow to man's estate. When we are all grown up, then I should think the next business of the Great Society will be to add meaning to existence. And this, I think, is what our Revolution, and any Renaissance, is all about.

We are now busy trying to recover America for human use, as a step preparatory to enjoying it. For example, the conservation of wilderness areas and the extension of national parklands and the creation of green spaces in our cities are all intended to do for everyone what my island does for my family—to make it possible for people to satisfy their human need to be one with earth, stones, grass, trees, air and water. The requirement that a certain percentage of building cost in Philadelphia be devoted to incorporation of fine arts in the construction is another example of trying to meet human needs. So is the tendency to find ways to keep automobiles out of our cities, in order that our streets may be used by people instead of by machines. An equally obvious concern for humanity governs the changes we are trying to effect within the interior environment. We are trying to find ways to reconcile efficiency with mercy in caring for the sick in our businesslike hospitals; a concern for working conditions in offices and factories has been carried past creating an optimum physical environment and into the area of creating an optimum emotional one. The list of examples could be expanded, but only to the point that we are trying to establish, as we move through time, a civilization that will permit every man an equal opportunity to become himself, possessed of life and liberty, free to pursue happiness (with a decent regard for the opinion of mankind) within a world he can truly call his home.

None of this work is easy. At every point arguments, bickerings and objections are raised by people with special interests. I am sure that my generation can understand that some progress toward a concern for the human condition has been made, because we have a clear idea of how far we have come with such difficulty through so many dangers in the most chaotic, murderous century of recorded history. Neither the Negroes, however, nor the estranged, privileged, white college youth are notably willing to adopt such an optimistic point of view. The Negro has for so long been the principal victim of our society that talk of progress enrages him.

Whenever his anguish takes the form of violence, he is trying to tell us that he needs everything right now. I should say that we understand the message he tosses along with the bottle of flaming gasoline, but at the same time we know that if violence is, indeed, the only means he has of getting at what most of the rest of us share, such violence must be directed against specific targets in a coherent, responsible way. In this regard, I must say that I welcome the Negro revolution, which I conceive to be long overdue. After all, freedom and equality of opportunity are not gifts which can be wrapped in Christmas paper and sent to someone in the mail. Rather, as Jefferson said, they must be fought for and won. So long as the Negro does not fight for them, then he will never have them.

I should say that my generation has less sympathy for our estranged college youth than for the Negro, however. Whenever I hear students cry out that they need "a human relationship," I think I understand them. I do not believe they are asking us for a license to go to bed with each other. What comes through loud and clear to me is that they are encountering singular difficulty in finding a quality of humanity in the average American's relationship to anyone or anything in our land of show business where the show goes on and on and on.

To be sure, in a world of very slippery values, it is understandable if the immature should decide that some things are real, whereas others are not; but a more adult view is that everything about America is only too real. The gravel in the pan is just as real as the grains of gold. The difference is, the gravel is real gravel, and the gold is real gold. The essential problem is that one must often be able to distinguish one from the other, and this is not so easy to do in a country where the gravel glitters as brightly as the nuggets, and is often considered by a majority to be a perfectly acceptable substitute. But we all eventually find, I think, that the stream and the miners are more important than either gravel or gold.

Once we know this to be true, then we can get about the busi-

242

ness of deciding how best to use the American stream for the benefit of the greatest number of our hopeful, riparian population. And this, I submit, is the business we are currently embarked upon.

At this writing, we are being delayed by another miserable business in Asia. I think that our responses to the Vietnam situation are muddled by our inner tensions. Which America is dealing with Asia? The America of the trash and violence, or the America of the Revolutionary ideals, or, more probably, the inextricably intermingled America of junk and hope? Our protesting youth may be comforted to know that all three current American generations detest our Asian war, but for different reasons. Our parents seem generally to believe that armed Communists led by intransigent dictators are our enemies, but that the place to deal with them is not Asia. My generation generally believes that aggressive dictators must be throttled wherever they are found, because we think that history and our personal experience of dictators advise us that this sad duty is wise. Some of our children seem to believe that our Asian enemies are not aggressive, intransigent, dictatorial, nor even inimical, but are idealistic peasants like the embattled farmers of Concord and Lexington, and that we should love them instead of bombing them.

There are of course many refinements of these points of view, none of which is necessarily the exclusive property of any one of our three current generations. For example, many of my contemporaries believe that Asian Communism is analagous to German Nazism in posing a threat to our own security, while others of us say the situation is by no means analagous, and that if we must fight Asian Communists, we should not do so in ways, places, and at times chosen by the enemy. Others of us say that we have no business being in Asia anyway, and agree with those youngsters who believe that the Viet Cong is right, and the United States wrong.

While I have no intention of debating the correctness of any of these points of view—other than presently to state my own—I

243

must say that matters would be much easier to resolve if our Government were to take us into its confidence. Not only does the young man en route to Vietnam have a perfect right to demand to know why this particular trip seems necessary, but by tradition and legal right, our Government exists at the will of the governed, and is at all times responsible to the public.

The Government has tried to explain. The administrations of Presidents Truman, Eisenhower, Kennedy and Johnson have for these past many years all said that what we are doing in Asia is opposing aggression; that this is not only in the spirit of our Revolution but also in the spirit of the United Nations charter; that it is keeping faith with our dead of Hitler's war in preserving the principles for which they fought. The four administrations have all said that the aggression we are opposing is, furthermore, a clear and present danger to our security, and that if we do not stop it where it is now, we will eventually have to deal with it elsewhere. In short, we fight today in Southeast Asia so that we will not have to fight in California tomorrow.

Unfortunately, we have not found this explanation sufficient. We should like to know what facts have led our policymakers to this conclusion. We should like to debate those facts. It does nothing for us when President Johnson dismisses critics of his military policies as Nervous Nellies, for I am sure all the rest of us know that asking a question is not necessarily a sign of cowardice. Nor does it do anything for us to be told that the facts are military secrets. A good many of us share Eisenhower's fear that too many of America's decisions are being made by a small group of industrialists and military men. Most of us share the belief that war is too serious a business to be entrusted to generals. More particularly, we detest secrecy of any sort, and even more particularly, we dislike not being allowed to know precisely why our sons are being killed. Personally, I feel that it is more important for Americans to know why they are fighting than it is to keep this information a secret from both the Americans and our enemies. Without such knowledge, we cannot well wage war or make peace.

While I admit to being as exasperated by the Asian mess as anyone else, I nevertheless continue—largely on faith—to support the war in Vietnam. I cling to certain apparent facts, to feelings, past experiences and beliefs. For example, I know that Belgium did not invade the Kaiser's Germany, nor Poland Hitler's; that South Korea did not invade North Korea, nor the Philippines Japan. Just so, it seems to me that South Vietnam did not invade North Vietnam. It also seems that hundreds of thousands of refugees have fled from North to South Vietnam, and not the other way around, and I assume there must be a reason for this one-way traffic of Vietnamese refugees. I assume it is the same reason why Germans flee from East to West, and not from West to East.

Like the intellectual who loves mankind in the abstract but detests his neighbors in particular, I care nothing about the South Vietnamese in particular, but a great deal about what they represent in general. To me they represent a people in whose country a terrifying invader has appeared, and I am willing to accept the idea that we have moved into that country too, as we did into France and Korea, to defend the premise that no one in this world should be allowed to shoot his way into someone else's backyard. I wish our Government would put its case more strongly on these terms, and also act consistently upon them in all other parts of the world.

Next, if four successive Presidents, including one openly suspicious of a military-industrial clique, tell me that there is good reason why Americans must kill and be killed in Asian rice paddies and jungles, I am inclined to believe them, although I would be happy to know what, precisely, led them to this unanimous conclusion. Whenever I hear that the essential reasons are geopolitical, that it is essential to our security to protect our position in that part of the world, I believe I understand. Still, I should like to hear a President or a Secretary of State spell these geopolitical concepts out in detail, so that both we and our enemies know where we stand.

I do not like being in the position of a German youth believing in his Nazi Government because it is the only one he has ever

245

known. I do not think I am in just that position, because my experience as a soldier, a newspaperman and a citizen assures me that we are not led by Nazis, and no one of my acquaintance among the military or in industry impresses me as being a warmonger. By definition, warmongers want war, whereas every politician, warrior and businessman I have met regards war with as much distaste as I do. We might all widely differ about how to have done with the Vietnam business, but the impressive fact is that we all want to be done with it and all other wars—which was not the Nazi attitude. Theirs was that war was the health of the state. Ours is that war is a waste of blood, time and money. So, certain that we are not Nazis, I continue to have faith in the good intentions of our Government, even though the wisdom of many of its actions may be debatable.

Finally, I believe that we must see the Vietnam war through to a conclusion we can find morally acceptable. I am not concerned with saving face. I am concerned with the fact that the battle has been joined there and that, behind whatever geopolitical reasons there may be, two ideologies are fighting for existence. Both sides claim to have the human welfare of the Vietnamese at heart and, in a general way, this is true. I share the American belief that the American Way of Life—a term none of us can define—is superior to any other nation's way of life and therefore should be adopted by all other nations for the good of mankind. Nothing about Communists leads me to believe that they are not equally convinced that their system should not be triumphant everywhere, also for the good of mankind. Be they Russian or Vietnamese or Chinese or Yugoslavian Communists, they are all in their tactically different ways precisely as messianic as we are, and quite as determined. Like ourselves, they wish to create a world in which human needs can best be served.

The problem is that we and they have such different views of the human good, and of the means by which it can be achieved. I think the one-way traffic in refugees suggests a choice by those who have had some personal experience in the matter. I often wonder what

246

would it mean to me, and everyone else, to live in a society that sentences writers to seven years' hard labor for criticizing the Government. I should think it would be bad for me as a lump of flesh; bad for me as a writer, and bad for the nation in general to establish the position that writers are free only to glorify the state. I find that we are confronted by enemies who do take such a position with respect to writers, and with respect to many other kinds of people besides, and that we in fact are engaged in a shooting war with such enemies in Vietnam. A question arises as to what sort of attitude I should take toward these enemies, whose way of doing things I find reprehensible. I am no Christian to love them. I am only enough of a Christian to suppose, as John Donne supposed, that he who shoots his neighbor wounds me as well. I do not believe that shooting anybody is a splendid way to demonstrate a human concern, or any great way to achieve a humanistic Golden Age. Yet, my purely American reaction to anyone who goes about shooting at the neighbors and intending to jail the survivors is to grab a gun myself and go kill the son of a bitch.

Granted, I have just expressed a point of view that may strike a good many Americans, and many more foreigners, as being more infantile than mature, but I am certainly not claiming complete maturity for myself or for my generation, or for Americans in general. Believing that I speak for a great number of my contemporaries, I think it fitting to close this book with a warning:

I think that we, and certainly all foreigners, ought to be vividly aware of the two Americas—the good and the bad—that exist in precarious tension in the same space at the same time.

It is a mistake to think of them separately, as Hitler seems to have done. He thought the America of the drift, the junk, the hedonism and the disintegration would prevent the other America from fighting in Europe. What he did not fully understand was that the two Americas together comprise a fearfully powerful and most unstable nation. We resolved a considerable number of inner tensions by venting them on him.

While we may be a bit schizophrenic, I do not think we are

incurably so, and I do not believe we are intransigent paranoiacs. I hope that we would be willing to listen to reason, and modify our outlook, if someone should come along and demonstrate just how we can deal in a bloodless, practical and beneficial way with brutal dictatorships. I think the best evidence of our sanity to date— which I do not conceive to be a weakness—has been the limited nature of our responses to provocations when we could, at any time since Hitler's war, have insensately released our limitless destructive power. But I also think we are getting tired of provocations, and I cannot find much evidence in our history to suggest that we are either the most even-tempered people in the world or the most patient.

We are, however, prone to believe that problems may be simply solved; to believe that there are just two sides to a question—right and wrong; to think that courses of action may be reduced to two choices—either this or that. In seeking to balance our inner tensions, we often swing first far to one side, then to the other. We may dither a bit in making up our minds what to do, but once a decision has been made, we almost never do things by halves. This simplicity of thought has in a great measure helped to bring us to a height of power, but the danger to the world should be obvious. In the Civil War, and in Hitler's war, our terms for peace were *unconditional surrender*. We see no semantic difficulty presented in this phrase, which another people might very well regard to be a contradiction in terms. To Americans, unconditional surrender makes perfectly good sense. I hope that our point of view on surrender is appreciated by the Asians, because I fear that it will become our foreign policy with respect to them if the wretched, lethal affair in Vietnam drags on much longer. I should think the most profitable time for our Asian enemies to offer some compromise would be now, while we Americans are still debating the wisdom of this war. I hope that by the time this book appears, a compromise will have been reached, because I know that every passing week is bringing America closer to a decision, and I have no great confidence that we will not look into the duality of ourselves and decide to say with Wilson, "Force to the uttermost," and say with Grant and Franklin Roosevelt, "Unconditional surrender." I offer neither apology nor defense for this horrid thought. I believe it important to express, however, because it has occurred to me, and since I know myself to be much more like my American contemporaries than different from them, it is fair to suppose this thought is widely shared. Perhaps what the world should completely understand is that in America, as nowhere else, man is most free to be himself—and therefore as likely to wreck a world as to create one. All we need is the proper provocation to move swiftly in either direction, and I should say that he who shoots at us is employing the most improper sort of provocation—one that will set us, and the world, off in the worst possible direction. It is well to recall that one of our earliest flags was one of the most representative we have ever had. It showed a rattlesnake and bore the legend, DON'T TREAD ON ME.